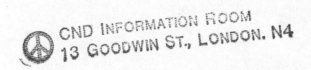
GRANT EVANS was born in an Australian country town in 1948 and studied at La Trobe University, Melbourne. As an editor of *Digger* magazine he travelled to East Timor in 1974 and wrote one of the first detailed analyses of political developments there. His research has also covered Papua New Guinea and the Southwest Pacific. Grant Evans is co-author of *The Red Brotherhood*, an account of Indochina since the US withdrawal in 1975. He teaches sociology at La Trobe university.

Grant Evans

Verso

The Yellow Rainmakers

**Are Chemical Weapons
Being Used in Southeast Asia?**

Verso Editions
15 Greek Street London W1

Filmset in VIP Times by
Preface Ltd, Salisbury, Wiltshire

Printed by
The Thetford Press
Thetford, Norfolk

ISBN 0 86091 068 7
      0 86091 770 3 Pbk

Contents

MAP OF THE NORTHERN PROVINCES OF LAOS SHOWING PLACES MENTIONED IN THE TEXT

China

Vietnam

Burma

Phong Saly

Luang Nam Tha

Ban Houei Xai

Chieng Khong Camp

Oudomsay

Luang Prabang

Sam Nuea

Sam Nuea

Mekong River

Ban Nam Yao Camp

Xieng Khouang

Plain of Jars

Phonesavane

Thailand

Sam Thong

Long Cheng

▲ Phu Bia

Sayaboury

Vang Vieng

Muang Cha

Ban Son

Ban Don

Hin Heup

Sab Tuang Camp

Vientiane

VIENTIANE

Nong Khai Camp

Ban Vinai Camp

Foreword

A decade ago it appeared that the superpowers would reach genuine agreement on the banning of chemical and biological weapons. Today there are ominous signs of a renewed bio-chemical arms race. The change has followed United States allegations that the Soviets are promoting bio-chemical warfare in Southeast Asia and Afghanistan. In early 1982 the US committed itself to upgrading its already formidable chemical weapons stockpile and in June, in the course of a speech to the second United Nations Disarmament Session, Ronald Reagan directly linked a 'verifiable' nuclear arms deal with the USSR to the issue of a 'truly effective and verifiable chemical weapons agreement'. The previously obscure issue of chemical weapons now occupies a central place in the contemporary debate over disarmament, alongside nuclear weapons.

This book focuses on charges that relate to Laos and Kampuchea. I am not qualified to comment on the situation in Afghanistan.

Since late 1978, when I first noticed the reports of 'medicine from the sky' (later popularized as 'yellow rain') from Laos, I have followed the issue closely. In early 1980 I made some enquiries among Hmong refugees in Thailand, and inside Laos, Vietnam and Kampuchea, but as I was preoccupied with other matters I assumed someone else would investigate the reports. When American journalist Sterling Seagrave published *Yellow Rain: A Journey through the Terror of Chemical Warfare* in late 1981,* I

*Published in Britain 1983.

was hoping it would clarify the issue one way or another. However, his book was based on very little detailed investigation in Southeast Asia and was largely speculative and sensationalist. Therefore in early 1982 I returned to Southeast Asia for two months' research, five weeks of which I spent in Laos, to try and solve the mystery of 'the yellow rainmakers'.

I would like to acknowledge the help of the following people in the writing of this book: Elizabeth Astbury, Daniel Bellamy, Bob Cooper, Peter Cox, Bob and Wendy Eaton, Ben Kiernan, Gavan McCormack, Mathew Meselson, Marion Miller, Linda and Titus Peachey, Julian Perry Robinson, Kelvin Rowley and Frances Starner.
Given the contentious subject matter it is more than usually necessary to disassociate all of the above from responsibility for the opinions expressed in the pages below. All errors of fact and interpretation are mine.

September 1982

1
The Allegations

The US Government began its search for evidence of chemical warfare in Southeast Asia in 1979. It was a time of acute regional tensions: in late 1978 the Vietnamese had invaded Kampuchea, the Chinese invaded Vietnam in February 1979, and thousands of refugees were fleeing the Communist Indochinese states. This 'Third Indochina War' quickly erased memories of earlier US involvement in the region and allowed Washington to launch a diplomatic offensive against its former Vietnamese enemy which, it argued, was acting as a proxy for the Soviet Union in Southeast Asia. A highly charged political atmosphere surrounded the search for evidence, from the first.

Internationally a renewed climate of Cold War characterized US-Soviet relations. This was partly a consequence of the cementing of diplomatic ties between the US and China in December 1978 and the de facto anti-Soviet alliance that flowed from it. In this respect there was a close fit between US policy toward Vietnam and Washington's global priorities. The New Right was sounding the alarm about Soviet military strength and its allegedly expansionist plans. These rising voices in American politics swooped on the allegations of chemical warfare in Southeast Asia as new and concrete evidence of the Soviet threat. The wave of conservatism that swept the Reagan administration into office two years later created a political environment even more conducive to charges of Soviet arms control violations.

In a series of editorials on 'Yellow Rain' in November 1981 the *Wall Street Journal* said: 'Except to the willingly obtuse, the evidence is conclusive. The Soviets have long been engaged in the development and production of chemical and biological weapons. They have used these warfare agents in Yemen in the 1960s and now in Cambodia, Laos and Afghanistan.' The editorialist attacked sceptics for giving the Soviets 'the benefit of every conceivable doubt'; he gave no indication of what might constitute reasonable doubt.[1] The editorials, however, implied that normal rules of evidence cannot be applied when dealing with the inherently untrustworthy Soviets. On the eve of the second special session on disarmament of the UN General Assembly in June 1982, the editor of the *Journal*, R. N. Bartley, warned President Reagan that negotiations with communists are 'not an after-office poker game. At this saloon they don't check the six-guns at the door. Someone may blackjack you and run off with the pot, or pull a knife or spike your drink with mycotoxins.'[2] The State Department has since admitted that their investigations were influenced by this onslaught from the *Journal*'s editor.

Other governments and private individuals, however, have remained sceptical.

Strenuous US Government efforts caused the UN to commission an investigation into the chemical warfare charges in December 1980; one year later it returned an inconclusive verdict. Thus the American government was compelled to produce, for the first time, a comprehensive argument bolstering the charges of Soviet use of chemical warfare. In March 1982, Secretary of State Alexander Haig presented a report to Congress titled *Chemical Warfare in Southeast Asia and Afghanistan*, which he said 'contains the most comprehensive compilation of material on this subject available, and presents conclusions which are fully shared by all relevant agencies of the United States Government.' The key judgements on Southeast Asia were:

'*Laos*: The US Government has concluded from all the evidence that selected Lao and Vietnamese forces, under direct Soviet supervision, have employed lethal trichothecene toxins and other combinations against the Hmong resisting government control and their villages at least since 1976. Trichothecene toxins have been positively identified, but medical symptoms indicate that irritants, incapacitants, and nerve agents also have been employed. Thousands have been killed or have been severely injured. Thousands also have been driven from their homeland by the use of these agents.

Kampuchea: Vietnamese forces have used lethal trichothecene toxins on Democratic Kampuchea (DK) troops and Khmer villages since at least 1978. Medical evidence indicates that irritants, incapacitants, and nerve agents also have been used.'[3]

The *Report* argued that until late 1981 'there remained one major unresolved issue – the exact nature of the chemical agents in use.' The discovery of trichothecene mycotoxin on a leaf and stem sample from a village in Kampuchea resolved this problem according to Mr. Haig. The 'smoking gun' had been found. Up to the time of the mycotoxin allegation the US had not a shred of physical evidence of biochemical warfare in Southeast Asia; it only had the testimony of refugees, and intelligence derived from 'national technical means' to support its case. But as will become clear later the mycotoxin charge is not impressive evidence. There has been considerable scientific controversy around its significance – not the least of which is the fact that Soviet production of mycotoxin weapons is unproven.

In November 1982 the new Secretary of State, George Shultz, released an *Update* on the Haig *Report* timed specifically for a forthcoming UN debate on the question of Soviet use of chemical weapons. The Shultz *Update* was largely an amplification of the earlier US charges. However, the report by the UN Group of Experts in early December 1982 was generally regarded as tougher than their 1981 report because although it said the chemical warfare charges against the USSR and Vietnam 'cannot be proven', it added that the experts 'could not disregard the circumstantial evidence suggestive of the possible use of some sort of toxic chemical substances in some circumstances.' A UN General Assembly draft resolution that followed on December 8 noted this conclusion and stated that chemical weapons 'may have been used' in Southeast Asia.

This was still a long way short of the American demand for UN condemnation of the Soviets and Vietnamese. Washington's inability to sway the General Assembly on this matter is surprising. Normally it has no trouble with resolutions condemning the Vietnamese presence in Kampuchea, and the Soviet occupation of

Afghanistan. But it cannot persuade any of its major allies to fully support its position, allies with whom it has shared, presumably, all of its information on the matter. If the evidence was as 'conclusive' as the US claims, this situation would not prevail. Yet it is undoubtedly the case that the absence of strong countervailing opinion to that of the US over the 'yellow rain' issue has forced the UN Group of Experts to toughen their conclusions.

The Soviets, and their Vietnamese and Lao allies, have denied the allegations of chemical warfare and the production of mycotoxins for such purposes, saying that 'until [the US claims] the generals and the diplomats have not taken any interest in them.'[4] We shall review the physical evidence in detail in Chapter Four, but the important point we must register for now is that the mycotoxin hypothesis was developed on the basis of *refugee testimony*. According to the *Wall Street Journal*, in 1980 'a CIA officer new to the refugee reports asked the simple question: "What possibly could produce such symptoms?"' These were 'death, often with victims choking on their own blood, . . . within 45 minutes to an hour after exposure.'[5] The answer, he asserted, was the *fusarium* strain of mycotoxins. Since Alexander Haig's announcement of the mycotoxin find in September 1981 the US effort to prove its case has gone into documenting the mycotoxin charge. The Americans have taken the refugee evidence as given, and a great deal of scientific ingenuity has gone into moulding scientific hypotheses to match the multiple symptoms described by refugees. No one has seriously analysed the refugee evidence even though it remains the bedrock of the chemical warfare charges emanating from Southeast Asia. At one level this is perfectly understandable. The problem of biochemical warfare is above all one for the physical sciences, whose job is to make tests to discover whether chemical warfare agents are being used.

The facts are that the physical scientists have found no evidence for the use of *known chemical warfare agents*. Claims that either nerve agents or irritants have been used are based purely on extrapolation from the *symptoms described* by refugees, just as the mycotoxin hypothesis – mycotoxins are not a known biochemical warfare agent – was also developed on the basis of refugee testimony. Therefore, in this situation the refugee testimony cries out for scrutiny by a social scientist.

As we shall see, the refugee evidence upon which so much speculation has been based does not in fact provide a solid base for assuming chemical warfare has been occurring in Southeast Asia. But having demonstrated the weakness of the refugee evidence the nagging question remains, why all the stories? In the second half of the book I argue that the stories from Laos are largely a product of uncontrolled rumours among a tribal people, the Hmong, whose recent history and world view predispose them to believe and recount gassing stories that have no basis in fact. The stories from Pol Pot's Democratic Kampuchea are more obviously propaganda.

The book concentrates on Laos and the Hmong tribespeople because here we find the origin of the chemical warfare allegations in the region. Laos, let alone the Hmong, is a subject as obscure to most people as mycotoxins. Laos has the smallest and poorest population in Southeast Asia. When the Pathet Lao took power in 1975 its annual per capita income was a mere $70.00. The country's tiny population of three and a half million is spread over a largely mountainous terrain two-thirds the size of its fifteen-times more populous neighbour Vietnam. The people themselves are so ethnically diverse that one expert was prompted to comment that the 'colourful ethnolinguistic map of [Laos] published by the Human Relations Area Files resembles a Jackson Pollock painting.'[6] Between one-third and one-half of the total population is ethnic *Lao* (chiefly in the lowlands); 10–20% are tribal *Tai* (living in the upland river valleys and plateaux); 20–30% *Lao-Theung* (Mon-Khmer-speaking people living on mountain slopes); 10–20% *Lao Sung* (Hmong and Yao living above 3500 feet in order to cultivate opium). There are an estimated *sixty-five* ethnic groups in Laos. The Hmong population is approximately 200,000, though no one knows the exact figure. The largest concentration of Hmong is still in southern China, from whence the others migrated south in the nineteenth century and spread across the peaks of northern Vietnam, Laos, and Thailand.*

*Only recently have the Hmong been commonly referred to by that name. In most literature they have been referred to by the Thai and Chinese terms *Meo* or *Miao*. Many Hmong object to the use of this term, which could have pejorative origins although it is not necessarily used pejoratively by non-Hmong. In Laos today they are referred to officially as Hmong. In China they are called Miao, and in Thailand Meo.

The Hmong in Laos have, in the past twenty years, gone through a very turbulent period. We need to examine this tragic time in order to put the refugee stories about chemical warfare in a clearer perspective.

The Rise and Fall of the 'Secret Army'

Many US journalists and politicians have spoken of the 'extermination' of the Hmong by the communists, and Alexander Haig's *Report* writes of 'genocidal campaigns against defenceless peoples'. Yet the grim irony is that the Hmong had been dying in large numbers during the civil war in Laos before 1975, and fears that they were disappearing had circulated through the mountains for years.

The Hmong people, particularly those in Xieng Khouang province, were swept into the vortex of the civil war in Laos in 1961, when neutralist soldiers were forced to retreat to the Plain of Jars following an American-supported right-wing counter-coup in the capital Vientiane. American Special Forces personnel had already been active in the region searching out people whom they could use to form a counter-insurgency army. They discovered a young Hmong lieutenant-colonel, Vang Pao, who had joined the French *bérets rouges* counter-insurgency force in 1947. Now he would work with the American Green Berets. The initial backbone of Vang Pao's 'Secret Army' were the men who had fought with him in the French *Groupement de Commandos Mixtes Aeroportés*. The formation of the Secret Army was modelled on then current US counter-insurgency strategies being applied in South Vietnam. There, the Americans were already building up Special Forces among the *montagnards*, and had begun the policy of relocating the Vietnamese peasants into 'strategic hamlets' in order to place them out of reach of communist recruiters. A modified version of this strategy was used in Laos.

Before the retreat of the neutralists to the Plain of Jars, Vang

Pao and his US Special Forces advisers had already worked out a plan for the re-location of some 70,000 scattered Hmong hill-tribesmen in the region to a small number of mountain retreats around the Plain.[1] When the plan was finally put into action it became a disaster and the uprooted Hmong were faced with mass starvation.[2] Here is how one writer described the plight of 5,000 of these Hmong refugees:

> 'Small children sat quietly in the ochre mud of the hillside, too enervated to seek dryness or comfort, and too weak even to plead for help as their vacant eyes, many caked with the drying pus of conjunctivitis, stared blankly . . . A woman whose brown teats hung like empty leather pockets from her open tunic tried vainly to pacify her tiny daughter, almost mummified in starvation, . . . an emaciated Meo man emerged from a bamboo lean-to shelter and fired his flintlock musket into the air, . . . Three shots, thus aimed at the sky, . . . were the Meo signal for death. . . . From farther up the hill, as if echoing the shots, came three more reports. Another death.'[3]

This was the first of a long series of forced marches the Hmong people would be forced to endure at the command of their own pro-US leaders.

The US had turned to the hilltribesmen because the main area of Communist strength and activity was in the mountainous two-thirds of the country. The Royal Laotian Government Army, composed mainly of lowland Lao, was notoriously unreliable. But to win the allegiance of the Hmong, the US capitalized on the ever-present ethnic antagonisms that pervade a multi-cultural society such as Laos. They had done this with the *montagnards* of South Vietnam who had believed that the Americans would help free them from the domination of the ethnic Vietnamese. They thought that the backing of a 'great and powerful friend' like the United States would enable them to create an independent state. The Hmong in Laos had similar aspirations which could be exploited by the US to serve broader strategic aims in Indochina.

A vital element of Hmong folklore has been that an ancient king will return and establish a Hmong kingdom: a land of their own for these nomadic people. Indeed, during the unsettled times of the late fifties and early sixties, a Messianic movement swept through the Hmong population of Xieng Khouang prophesying that Christ would soon come to the Hmong in a jeep, wearing American clothes and handing out modern weapons. When Van Pao approached Hmong chieftains for their support, he said the US would help them achieve their aim of independence. Nor was he acting in bad faith at the time. With the arrival of American weapons and support Vang Pao unsuccessfully tried to proclaim an independent Hmong state in 1966.

Some refugees in Thailand have since petitioned the United Nations to find them a separate homeland, and when I talked with Hmong in Xieng Khouang province in early 1982 they said that many people still believe that an independent Hmong state will appear.

The 1962 Geneva Accords virtually partitioned Laos into two separate zones, but the Plain of Jars remained the major contested area that each side claimed to control as the legitimate representative of the neutralist forces. This ensured that the province of Xieng Khouang would experience the most vicious and catastrophic effects of the war. And so would the 75,000 Hmong who lived there.

By the end of the decade the Plain of Jars would become one of the most heavily bombed areas in all Indochina as between 300 and 400 US aircraft flew daily missions over Laos from bases in Thailand and aircraft-carriers off the South Vietnamese coast.

'Since the fighting had begun in late 1960', wrote Don A. Schanche in 1970, 'some 40,000 people, almost 10% of the population of northeast Laos, had been killed or had died of injuries or illnesses related to the war. In any other area of the world, a similar situation would be incredible, but virtually every resident of northeast Laos was at some time a war refugee, either driven from his native village by the action of the two sides, or brought to near starvation by the total disruption of the primitive rural economy of the region.'[4]

According to a US Senate enquiry in 1971, intense bombing was the main reason given by refugees for moving down from the flattened Plain of Jars. All their villages and towns had been razed.

Out of around 350,000 refugees in mid-1971 it was estimated that about 150,000 were hilltribesmen, of which 60% were Hmong. They were settled in a forty-mile strip above the sweltering Vientiane Plain at a place called Ban Son, to the south of the main CIA base at Long Cheng. By late 1973 these 90,000 Hmong had been joined by another 40,000, all of whom were dependent on American aid supplied from the air.

USAID doctors Charles and Patricia McCreedy Weldon described the condition of these Hmong at that time: 'Each time the war forced a move as many as 10% of the people died. The majority were already weakened by diseases, and the exertion killed them. Up in the mountains malaria was almost unknown. Now it infects 60 to 80% of the refugees. None of the 116 Hmong villages where we work is free of it.'[5] This high 10% death rate applied to moves under favourable conditions; if fleeing refugees became lost in the mountain forests it rose to a staggering 30%. For villages which had moved ten or more times over five years, for example, as many had, the effect was catastrophic and among them stories of the Hmong disappearing altogether gained currency.

In its heyday in 1968 Vang Pao's CIA-backed 'Secret Army' numbered close to 40,000, of whom about half were Hmong. The other half was made up of other hilltribe groups, lowland Lao, Thai, and some Filipino, Cambodian and Burmese mercenaries. A major series of offensives by the Communist forces between 1969 and 1971 brought them within striking distance of Long Cheng. Thousands of Hmong were killed or wounded in these campaigns. Desertions became more frequent and recruiting fell off, leading to cruel attempts to press-gang the villagers into the service of the Secret Army. 'Vang Pao's officers came to the village and warned that if we did not join him he would regard us as Pathet Lao and his soldiers would attack our village', said one Hmong leader in 1971.[6]

The disruption to production caused by the removal of men for the tasks of war was offset by USAID-supplied rice and other staples to the families whose men were away. This was then quickly transformed into a further source of leverage on the Hmong villagers as two journalists explained at the time:

'Long Pot was never a willing participant in the alliance with the Americans, and by 1971 its people had had their fill of Vang Pao and the CIA. Gair Su Yang stood firm and said no to an order from Long Cheng for more men for the army. In retaliation the Americans suspended rice drops and the people became hungry as food stores ran out. By then the war was at Long Pot's doorstep . . . The Pathet Lao overran the district and chased out the single Royal Lao and Vang Pao garrison. The villagers began to move their valuables into the forest; they knew what was about to happen. In a matter of days Royal Lao T-28 bombers and American jets from Thailand systematically razed Long Pot and the ten other villages in the district, using bombs, napalm and anti-personnel bomblets. . . . Long Pot was now behind Pathet Lao lines and had become a free-fire zone. Thus two-thirds of Long Pot's citizens fled into government-held territory . . .'[7]

It was at this time as well that a neutralist-inclined high-ranking Hmong official in the RLG, Ly Tek, established a Hmong resettlement village at kilometre 52 north of Vientiane as a conscious attempt to break the stranglehold that Vang Pao had over the Hmong in the RLG zone. 'We know what fighting means', he said; 'that the Hmong are the ones to die'.[8]

By 1972 the strength of Vang Pao's army had fallen below 30,000 men, with the Hmong accounting for only 20% of his forces, increasingly augmented by 'volunteers' from Thailand.[9] By 1973 there were 20,000 US-paid and trained Thai mercenaries fighting in Laos. Hmong were not flocking to Vang Pao to become his 'freedom fighters' and in fact many had come to regard him as a corrupt warlord who had grown rich on their misery.

Few Western observers dwell on these sad facts today as they write about the 'extermination' of the Hmong under the Communists. In fact Hmong fears about 'genocide' began well before the Communist victory. 'Meo chieftains are beginning to see that the men and boys going off to war don't come back', wrote Australian journalist John Everingham in the early 1970s. 'They are frightened by the growing lack of husbands for younger women *and believe the tribe is disappearing*'.[10]

The Collapse of the Army

A United States Senate investigation into the extent of CIA activities in Laos, released in August 1971, said that 'the Royal Lao Government continues to be totally dependent on the United States, perhaps more dependent on us than any other government in the world'. For the fiscal year 1970–71, it stated, a 'partial total' of US expenditure in Laos amounted to $284 million, including $162 million for military aid, $52 million for economic aid, and $70 million for CIA activities. This did not include the cost of the thousands of Thai mercenaries in Laos nor the cost of the massive US bombing operations there. By the beginning of 1973 the total was closer to $400 million. The Royal Lao Government budget was $14 million.[11]

Following the ceasefire agreement between the RLG and the Pathet Lao in February 1973, the US was obliged to scale down its operations in Laos. When the provisional coalition government took over in April 1974 it faced massive economic difficulties caused by wartime disruption and devastation. There were 350,000 refugees in the country requiring rehabilitation and resettlement. Between 70,000 and 100,000 tons of rice needed to be imported annually to feed the 'urbanized' population, along with other foodstuffs, clothing, medical supplies and raw materials. Exports were few and the country's adverse balance of trade and payments became critical as US aid, which had previously covered the shortfall, was cut back. Inflation, which had averaged 7% a year between 1965 and 1971, rose to 70% in 1974 and then doubled again over the following year.

In these conditions, it was not only the urban economy of Vientiane and the Mekong cities that began to collapse, but also the economy surrounding the Long Cheng base area that USAID had hoped would become the commercial centre of the northeast. This was a product of dwindling mercenary pay and skyrocketing prices and also of problems of supply. Air America, the CIA airline which had provided the goods for this mountain-based commercial network, came under pressure from the Lao government to cease operations. In 1973 Air America dismissed 42 of around 100 pilots, abandoned some 350 landing strips and turned over a dozen

C-123 military transports to the Lao Air Force. In 1974 the coalition government asked the company to comply with a 4 June deadline for the departure of all foreign military forces. As far as we know, Air America broadly complied.[12]

But it was not only the economy that collapsed with the withdrawal of American aid; the entire army disintegrated as well. One of the first groups to mutiny were two companies of tribal Special Forces – mainly composed of Yao and Lahu tribesmen, and some Hmong – based at Ban Houei Sai in Nam Tha province in the far north west. With the support of the local population they demanded the strict application of the ceasefire agreement, the neutralization of Houei Sai, and interestingly enough, the repeal of a 1971 law forbidding the growing of opium poppies.[13]

A *New York Times* correspondent gave a graphic description of the crisis following the complete collapse of the RLG forces by mid-1975:

'The United States placed its faith in the irregular army which it created and directed, and relegated the Royal Vientiane Army to insignificance . . . When the Central Intelligence Agency stopped paying and supplying General Vang Pao's irregulars they were integrated into the Royal Vientiane Army; there was no effective army left on the Vientiane side, both parts of the amalgam descending to the same level of low pay, low morale and, consequently high corruptibility . . . The Royal Army was paid and supplied, also by the United States, but through its own command, whose corruption, inefficiency and feudal rivalries increased throughout the war . . . The entire Vientiane army was beset throughout the two years of truce with growing morale problems . . . Corruption among the command and poverty among the troops was exacerbated by the falling value of the currency. The paper strength of the Army, about 55,000 troops, always conceded to be a gross over-estimate, fell to what a neutral expert put at no more than 10,000 at any given moment. At least a third of every unit's troops was always away, trying to raise enough food or money to keep their families alive.'[14]

However, even though the Secret Army was subject to the same disintegrating pressures as the RLG Army it was never more than nominally integrated into the latter as required by the peace agreement. Even after the departure of the 17,000 Thai mercenaries in mid-1974, and the melting away of lowland Lao, and many Lao Theung, Vang Pao was able to maintain an army of between 6,000 and 10,000 through the tremendous power he exercised over the Hmong in his immediate region. Vang Pao was a true warlord and ran his army and his Military Region II accordingly.

During 1974 the Social Welfare Department of the new coalition government attempted to carry out a survey among the thousands of people displaced by the war, and they discovered that 80% of those they were able to question wished to return to their villages in the Pathet Lao zone. Major General Vang Pao, however, refused to allow the mixed census teams into his region to ascertain how many Hmong wished to return home. Therefore only a small proportion of the estimated 130,000 displaced Hmong were able to take advantage of the rehabilitation programme.[15] As Vang Pao knew from his very first major operation on the Plain of Jars in 1961, military control of the Hmong population was the key to his success and to his survival. And once again he would cause many thousands of Hmong to suffer as a result of his ambitions.

The last major military action by the Special Forces took place in mid-April 1975 when they attempted to stop left-wing neutralist and Pathet Lao forces from taking over the strategic junction of Highway 13, the main road between Vientiane and Luang Prabang, and Highway 7, which feeds onto the Plain of Jars and through to Vietnam. They were routed by 6 May, and Vang Pao fled to Thailand in the following week. During this week he used his own private airline, Xieng Khouang Air Transport, composed of three C-47s supplied by CIA and USAID finance in 1967,[16] to ferry out some of his leading officers and their families to Nam Phong and Udorn airbases in Thailand. Close to 3,000 were evacuated in this way.

Those left behind were instructed by Vang Pao and his officers to hide the modern weapons they had acquired over the years and only to surrender older weapons to the communists when they came. Soldiers were instructed to retreat into the mountain forests to prepare for guerrilla warfare against the new government.

However, the initial reaction of many of the Hmong to Vang Pao's flight was panic and confusion. Several thousand of them from around Ban Son and Pha Khao began to stream down Route 13 toward Vientiane and Thailand – a distressing crowd of army stragglers, and refugees of many years, carrying their few possessions. The government responded by sending out Ly Tek to try to calm the crowd, but, bitterly resented by many of Vang Pao's men who formed the spontaneous leadership of the Hmong crowd, he was ignored.

The crowd rolled on, gathering up more Hmong as it moved down the highway, the level of panic and despair intensifying with each passing day. 'On 21 May the family of Vang Neng left Phou Kang', writes Larteguy of one family involved in this exodus. 'In the days before there had been an increasing number of suicides among the old people who were too old to accompany their children or their grand-children on their exodus, or who decided they had had enough. They hanged themselves, took *nivaquine*, opium or certain vegetable poisons which the Hmong knew the secrets of. They killed their pigs, cattle and buffaloes, but those they invited to come to these grand feasts and who at other times would have stuffed themselves full, touched neither the meal nor the alcohol. They were too distressed.'[17]

The Hmong Cabinet Minister, Touby Lyfong was then despatched to talk with the people, also on 21 May. 'Vang Pao has gone', he said, 'because he was too involved in the war. But you have committed no crimes, so why are you leaving the country?'[18] But, according to Larteguy, they would only accept Prime Minister Prince Souvanna Phouma's guarantee of their safety. Touby returned the following day to say that the leader of the Hmong who had supported the Pathet Lao, Faydang Lobliayao, would soon come to give them the guarantees that they wanted.

The crowd was not satisfied with this either and surged on to a place called Hin Heup where, on 29 May, their way was barred at a bridge by Pathet Lao and neutralist troops. Apparently by this time its size had swelled to twenty or thirty thousand people; some of them were Vang Pao soldiers and their families determined to get to Thailand, others simply frightened people being swept up by the events. The soldiers told them to return to their villages, but the crowd rushed the bridge whereupon the troops opened fire and five people were killed and around thirty wounded. A Thai photographer, Anant Chomcheun, who was on the scene the following day, reported seeing Pathet Lao troops herding groups of Hmong back to the hills at gunpoint, while others melted into the countryside off the highway to continue their trek toward Thailand. 'I want to stay with my father Vang Pao', one Hmong told the photographer.[19]

As the first reported violence since the Pathet Lao had begun moving into former Royalist preserves, this relatively minor incident had enormous repercussions among the Hmong. Today the incident has entered Hmong refugee mythology as a gigantic confrontation involving many deaths. Clearly the government in Vientiane could not allow such a large mob of people to descend on the already chaotic capital without risking even greater chaos and bloodshed. Moreover they were not going to allow Vang Pao's army simply to relocate itself across the Mekong from where it could conduct raids on Laos. In its use of emissaries, and of minimal violence when a showdown came, the government did what it could to avoid bloodshed. However, the Hmong had been told for many years by Vang Pao that they would be killed when the Pathet Lao came. In the atmosphere of panic and desperation that dominated the refugee crowd, the violence at Hin Heup appeared to confirm these predictions. When they got back to their villages many people dug up the weapons they had been told to bury and began to take revenge. Meanwhile the story of the 'massacre' at Hin Heup began to spread through the mountains to other Hmong communities.

The Governor of Xieng Khouang province today, Yong Yia, flew to the CIA base at Long Cheng not long after Vang Pao had left for Thailand. He told the Hmong there that they had nothing to be afraid of and that as he too was Hmong he had no reason to want to kill them. But, he told me, many of the people there still respected Vang Pao and had decided to go to Thailand no matter what. There were also many who wished to return to their villages. I asked some of these ex-CIA Hmong who are now re-settled back in their old village areas in the hills above the Plain of Jars, why so many of their comrades left for Thailand. Almost invariably they replied, 'because of relatives', while some added that Vang Pao had 'bribed' them to go.

We also have a description of the communist arrival at Long Cheng from a major in the Secret Army, Mouah Houa, who left Laos in late 1975. He said that, although there was no shooting, 100 men were chosen to attend a nearby 'school' for two weeks. When the 100 failed to reappear after this period, the villagers asked the Pathet Lao when their people would return. They were told it would be another two months. But they still failed to return. According to Mouah six of the 100 escaped and walked four days to get to their village. They described how they had been forced to attend meetings or had been put to work. He believed that those who did not return were eventually killed and he was convinced that the same fate awaited all Vang Pao soldiers.[20]

While we have no way of knowing the exact fate of these people, Mouah's general story has a familiar ring. In South Vietnam as well as in Vientiane people being sent off to 're-education' camps were told that they would only be away for a month. Many were kept for five years. Naturally their families panicked when they did not return, and the Communists' duplicity cost them a great deal of public trust. Such feelings were very acute amongst the Hmong, for whom familial ties are so much more important than for the lowland Lao. The idea of their families being split up by the Communists terrified them more than anything else. When stories circulated of men being taken away by the Communists 'never to return', many people went to hide in the forest and resisted Pathet Lao encroachments or fled to Thailand. The fact that there appears to have been only a small number of Hmong taken for 're-education' does not matter. The fact that it had happened was enough to set the rumour network crackling. The idea that the Pathet Lao would split up their family if they returned to Laos is probably the strongest fear among the Hmong refugees in Thailand today, not chemical warfare. Hmong returnees I spoke with in Laos said this had been their main apprehension before returning.

The Lao revolution has often been referred to as the 'gentle revolution' because of the general absence of violence and reprisals associated with it. Clearly most writers who have used this phrase have had in mind the revolution as it happened in the capital of Vientiane and in the cities of the lowlands, rather than the revolution as it occurred in the mountains where most of the reporters had never been. However, there seems to be little reason to revise this appraisal when we do focus on what happened among the hilltribes. The violence at Hin Heup was not of the Communists' making but a product of the collapse of the 'refugee economy' in the mountains and the flight of the top leadership of the Secret Army, which led to panic among the Hmong who had been dependent on that structure. Even so, reliable reports of this incident indicate that the casualties were low. There is also no strong evidence of systematic persecution of ex-CIA soldiers, though it is certain that their officers were taken off for re-education in the same manner as lowland Lao officers of the RLG.

Many of the better-off Hmong could afford transport to the Thai border and by early June another 5000 people had been added to the 3000 who had flown out with Vang Pao. The flood of thousands of refugees into Thailand with the promise of thousands more to follow was not welcomed in Bangkok. In the unsettled political environment the Thai government did not wish to complicate its relations with Vientiane and they therefore ordered Vang Pao to leave the country – which he did on 18 June 1975 after recording a message for the Thais urging the Hmong not to leave Laos. A December request by Vang Pao to return to Thailand was also rejected.

However, like the old Vientiane regime (though not nearly so much), regional military commanders in Thailand exercise independent military and political power that can often cut across policies formulated in Bangkok. For the whole of the civil war in Laos the activities of the Secret Army had been coordinated by the CIA from Udorn, from where they sent supplies and airstrikes deep into Laos as well as to North Vietnam. Indeed, for many years the Thai northeast military region was run semi-autonomously by the Thai army and the CIA. As we have already seen thousands of Thai 'volunteers' were involved in the fighting in Laos. It was not surprising therefore that the same Thai liaison officers from Long Cheng were put in charge of the Hmong refugee camp established at Nam Phong. Indeed, the attitude of many of these military men toward the Hmong was that by 'fighting communist forces in Laos with Thai soldiers, they were indirectly fighting in the defence of our country'.[21] The Thai military allowed Vang Pao to move around freely in the north of the country before June, leading some people to speculate that he was helping the Thai military to organize the refugees into a new intelligence and defence line along the Lao-Thai border and also into a force which could possibly be used against Thai Communist Party insurgents in the north, who are mainly hilltribes people. A Thai MP from Nan province claimed at the time that the US had supplied 3,000 million baht in aid from the Hmong at the request of the Thai military.[22]

The Lao government was very worried by these developments and they accused the Thai authorities of sending these refugees back across the border to spread false rumours and cause trouble. One Thai newspaper, *Prachatipatai*, claimed that the way the Hmong refugees were being treated 'reveals that administrative power is not now totally in the hands of the cabinet and that another influential group has more power than the cabinet'.[23] In early September *Le Monde* reported that right-wing Lao officers were operating out of 'Command 333, a clandestine operations centre at present directed by the Thai General, Paitoon Inkaranuwat' at Udorn. A month later a *Washington Post* correspondent reported from Vientiane that about 5,000 members of Vang Pao's forces were still fighting around Long Cheng. 'Meo sources hint they are receiving food and medical supplies from neighbouring Thailand. The sources suggest that Thai Air Force pilots, possibly acting without the knowledge of their commanders in Bangkok, are making airdrops to the embattled Meos . . .'[24]

It was at this time that the Thai Interior Ministry decided to establish a camp for the Hmong in the Pak Chom District of Loei Province, just twelve kilometres from the Lao-Thai border. This was Ban Vinai camp. Just why this site was chosen has never been quite clear. However, the fact that the Deputy Police Superintendent of Loei, Lt. Colonel Srit Suthikiri, had warned as early as 5 June that the Pathet Lao were supposedly sending 300 communist insurgents into the Pak Chom district to attack government outposts, gives weight to the contention that part of the reason for establishing Ban Vinai was to use it as a base for counter-insurgency.[25] The refugees used to establish Ban Vinai were 12,700 Hmong from Nam Phong airbase – that is, the supporters of Vang Pao. In its first three years the camp was very isolated and only accessible by a seventy kilometre dirt road. Moreover it was largely off limits to journalists during this time. Very few people knew about the camp and the Hmong were able to establish a community and begin farming the surrounding land. Sometimes they farmed as far away as twenty kilometres, staying out in the fields a week at a time. The housing built for them by the US consisted of permanent, barrack-type structures more suggestive of a special military base than a refugee camp. Indeed, in many ways Ban Vinai was the former CIA base of Long Cheng transplanted into Thailand.

By the end of 1975 the total Hmong refugee population in Thailand was estimated at 33,765.[26]

The Question of Hmong Armed Resistance

Because much of the discussion around the allegations of poison gas and chemical warfare suggests that there is large-scale Hmong resistance to the Pathet Lao regime, and that this is the government's rationale for resorting to extreme methods of warfare, the actual size and capabilities of any Hmong force in Laos is an important question.

One estimate of Vang Pao's forces has already been given; that they stood at between 6,000–10,000 at the end of 1974. The upper range of this estimate was confirmed in an interview with Mr. Vue May, now second-in-command at Ban Vinai and a former major in the Secret Army. He flew out to Nam Phong airbase with the other officers and their families on 14 May 1975. He said that there were around 10,000 soldiers at Long Cheng before his departure and that about 50% of them made their way to Thailand in the following six months, often travelling by truck or taxi to Vientiane and then crossing to Thailand. This estimate by Vue May complements the one given by the *Washington Post* that around 5,000 soldiers were still fighting around Long Cheng in

October 1975. Vue May also confirmed that soldiers and a number of officers had been left behind to organize a resistance. Reports in late November and early December claimed that there was still fighting going on there.

It is important to get the scale of these battles into proper perspective. As far back as 1968 one journalist described the Secret Army's operations in this way: 'Waging a classic Maoist-style guerrilla war since they learned not to stand and fight when outnumbered, the Meo cut communist lines of communication, mine roads, shoot up convoys and retreat to their peaks. The fighting is on a small scale. Operations rarely reach company size in the hills.'[27] This was the scale of operations when the Hmong soldiers could rely on US fighter-bomber support, and military and food supplies as well as medical aid, all flown into their remote mountain-peak redoubts. And even with all this they had been taking a beating from the Communist forces from the late 1960s onwards. In the absence of such comprehensive support it is obvious that the Hmong resistance could not sustain anything like the same scale of operations after May 1975, unless they fought far better without Vang Pao than with him.

The comparison with Mao is not strictly correct either. As the veteran French writer on Indochina, Bernard Fall, commented on the efficacy of the French GCMA and the US Special Army guerrillas, good military training is no substitute for a strong ideological motive for fighting.[28] This the Hmong never really had and their tribal composition ultimately restricted their ability to grow into a political threat to the government.

Even so by early January 1976 the *Bangkok Post* was claiming that 'over 20,000 Meo soldiers' were operating around the Phu Bia range.[29] Where the extra 15,000 soldiers came from the *Post* was unable to explain. There were reports of Hmong forces having retaken Long Cheng, but they remained unsubstantiated. In late January the Lao Information Minister, Sisana Sisane, said that there had been clashes with Hmong forces. Ambushes of road convoys had occurred near Van Vieng sixty miles north of the capital, but he maintained that the problem had not reached 'serious proportions'.[30] A report from Vientiane two days later said a Hmong 'mountain stronghold' had been overrun. A 'huge quantity of ammunition, M-16 rifles and M-79 grenade launchers' were found in a cave.[31]

But just how much arms and ammunition the Hmong had been able to store before the fall of Long Cheng was seriously questioned by John Everingham in February: 'The quantity of ammunition stored in Long Cheng following the ceasefire (in 1973) was kept low enough to discourage Vang Pao from any personal military adventures that might embarrass the US. The force it left behind presented no long-term threat to the Pathet Lao.' Everingham estimated that Hmong members of the Secret Army numbered only 4,000 in May 1975 and that most of these had since left for Thailand. He also quoted the appraisal of an American official in Vientiane who said that 'probably a couple of hundred Meo are running around the mountains in small groups holding out while they can. I don't think they can last long. Certainly they aren't getting any aid from us'.[32]

In June a former Hmong colonel told the *Bangkok Post* that guerrillas 'are fighting against the Pathet Lao and because no one is supporting them have to use ammunition sparingly. They are also badly in need of weapons'.[33] This was hardly an inspiring picture of the state of the 'resistance' in Laos. Speaking from Ban Vinai he went on to say: 'If the US supports us again we will certainly go back and fight. We could seize certain areas in Laos for use as strongholds to launch combat troops against the Pathet Lao.' The US, however, was not to be drawn into another adventure in Laos.

In July came the first refugee reports of the use of napalm against the resistance. They were not eyewitness reports, however, and the Hmong leader who told the story said the resistance forces were now operating under the name 'Army of the Sons of Heaven' or 'Chao Fa' and were preparing the way for the return of the Hmong king.[34]

The resurfacing of barely submerged millenarian impulses as the US-supported military and economic structure disintegrated was not surprising. Not only had this structure channelled these beliefs, it had also become a kind of surrogate for this king. USAID man Edgar 'Pop' Buell was known widely as *Tan Pop* by the Hmong. *Tan* is a Lao honorific word, and *Pop* a Hmong deific that means 'sent from above'. *Pop* Buell held a semi-divine status among the Hmong as he descended into their villages by airplane or helicopter and 'magically' called into his portable radio causing huge airplanes to appear spilling pallets and parachuting loads of rice, utensils and medical supplies from the heavens. Refugees told to relocate themselves would miraculously find supplies waiting for them at a remote spot and therefore believed heaven was on their side. To anyone familiar with the upsurge of Cargo Cult activity in Papua New Guinea following World War Two there is an uncanny familiarity about these events. There, millenarian cults, often led by tribesmen who had worked with the allies and become sergeants, built airfields in the highlands to await the coming of 'cargo' by plane, or built jetties to receive the ships loaded with cargo if their villages were on the coast. The striking difference between the millenarian upsurge in Papua and the situation of the Hmong before 1975 was that in the highlands of Laos the 'cargo' actually arrived. And the very fact that it did arrive, that there was a 'saviour' for the Hmong at work, inhibited the development of cult ritualism to conjure up the legendary king. Nevertheless in the turmoil of the late 1960s a full-blown millenarian movement did begin among the despondent Hmong refugees. It gave rise to an esoteric script for the Hmong language composed of letters from the French, Lao, Chinese and Russian alphabets, and it was proselytized by a Hmong farmer and supposed herald of the coming king. Vang Pao's organization felt its authority directly threatened by this movement to the point where it was deemed necessary to assassinate the 'great teacher' in 1973. Nevertheless the movement was kept alive by a small group of adherents who continued teaching the new script.[35]

The emergence of the Chao Fa movement out of this earlier one dramatized the fragmentation of the old Secret Army into uncoordinated groups, some of whom joined the millenarian sect. The key individual leader of this group was Txong Zuu Heu, a former army sergeant, who had already begun to reject Vang Pao before the latter's flight in 1975, and who was now committed to setting up an ideal Hmong society. There are no reliable estimates of the size of the movement, though it clearly had a wider spontaneous appeal than did the defeated Vang Pao. The 'sky soldiers' of the sect submerged themselves in ritual that drew on supernatural forces to provide them with invulnerability to guns. One student who had lived in Luang Prabang in 1976 told me that people there were told over the local radio that a number of Chao Fa soldiers had been killed while attacking a Pathet Lao army post on the outskirts of the city; he went out to look at the dead men who he said were wearing arm- and headbands to protect them from bullets. A Lao helicopter pilot told me he had seen, when flying through the mountains, long thin towers built straight up into the sky by the people who wanted to 'be closer to their god Chao Fa'. A Hmong provincial official in Laos was careful, when discussing this issue with me, to make a distinction between forces who had remained loyal to Vang Pao and the Chao Fa movement. He said that because Phu Bia was the highest mountain in Laos, many Hmong believed that this was where Chao Fa himself resided and this was why the movement was based there. Part of this official's explanation for the Hmong migration to Thailand was that the story had been spread among the Hmong that Chao Fa had now gone to Thailand and that the Hmong people should follow him there.

Because the sect has always represented a challenge to the authority of Vang Pao's men, the leadership in Ban Vinai camp denounce the very notion of Chao Fa's existence as a communist invention, and are very touchy about any discussion of the subject. This was particularly apparent when in March 1982 a number of ordinary Hmong mentioned the Chao Fa in front of these ex-CIA people. They positively flinched when I asked a young tribeman who Chao Fa was and he replied enthusiastically 'God of the World!'

The New 'Genocide' Stories

Reports of serious clashes – indeed any clashes – were rare in early 1976, but in October came the first of what was to become a long series of articles on the 'genocide' of the Hmong who were now being 'systematically liquidated'. This report spoke of the 'pounding of hill-tribe villages with napalm and gas bombs', and the strafing of everything moving in the villages. The people suffered 'from third-degree burns, nausea, paralysis, bleeding from the mouth, and eventually death due to the napalm and gas bombs'.[36]

There were almost no reports of clashes over the following year and relatively few hill-tribespeople left Laos in that period: 3,873 to be exact. It was over a year later, in November 1977, that reports of major clashes around the Phu Bia massif began to appear – and all sides generally concur that this was when the major showdown occurred between the government and the Hmong resistance forces.

A senior foreign affairs official in Vientiane explained the evolution of the conflict to me. After liberation the government had sent people, often unarmed, to persuade the Hmong mountain villages to cooperate with the government. Many of these people were killed and tortured and the army called for stronger measures. However, these were resisted because it was felt that strong reprisals would not only frighten Hmong peasants not involved in the resistance at all, but other mountain tribe groups as well. But by the end of 1977 the Party leadership agreed that a sharp and hard military action would be necessary to break the back of the resistance.

Former Secret Army Major Vue May concurs that this was when the last major action took place, saying that their ammunition was by then exhausted.

Most important, however, is that the reports from this period contain the most authentic-sounding stories of the use of gas.

In a campaign lasting two months the Pathet Lao launched heavy attacks around Phu Bia. Estimates of the number of troops involved ranged between 10,000 and 30,000, while Hmong casualties were listed as between 1,000 and 7,000. A *Bangkok Post* article claimed to document these casualties with extraordinary precision: 1,300 killed, 800 wounded, and 5,400 captured – all according to Thai intelligence sources . . .[37] The number of Hmong people allegedly involved ranged from 20,000 to 60,000, while some reports added that another 40,000 non-Hmong tribesmen were involved.

A major operation was under way – that was certain – but obviously the details of it were obscure and the press reported random estimates given by fleeing soldiers and intelligence sources. A sign of the changing mood in the region was that John Everingham, who had previously given one of the lowest estimates of Hmong fighting strength but had been brusquely ejected from Vientiane in 1977, was now prepared to quote a former CIA army captain's estimate that there were 20,000 men under arms. Yet he did say 'the rebels have clearly run out of ammunition, food and medicines. Tired and defeated, thousands of the weary tribesmen struggled south through mountains to cross the Mekong river into Thailand.'[38]

A Hmong major told another journalist: 'My group of 30 fighters got separated from the others a month ago. We had only fifty rounds (of ammunition) per man, no food and no medicine.'[39] Another survivor said: 'They have succeeded in breaking down all defences.'[40] The Government forces had obviously shattered the resistance and the Hmong guerrillas and their families had broken up into small bands starving in caves and in the forests.

Scattered amongst the refugee reports of the fighting were a couple that mentioned the use of gas. A lieutenant-colonel, Yong Kwang, had told Thai police that after aerial bombardment of their position troops moved in and 'used some special weapons fired into caves' where they suspected the Hmong were hiding. The refugees described the weapons as 'gas' according to the Thais.[41]

In another report a soldier called Tang Wang claimed that gas-masked 'Vietnamese troops' were using 'poison gas' among Hmong in difficult-to-attack mountain caves.[42]

Yet another said the Pathet Lao attacks involved the use of 'bombs, napalm and chemical products', including a 'white powder which makes you cough'.[43]

These reports of the use of gas are plausible: first, because of the combat situation – a context lacking in many later reports; secondly, because the gas is said to have been used in a very specific way, to flush out soldiers from caves. We know that the Americans used riot control gas extensively for precisely this purpose during the Vietnam war, and there is no a priori reason to believe that either the Pathet Lao forces or the Vietnamese forces assisting them would not use these weapons too if they felt they were effective. It is well known that massive American stockpiles of these weapons had been left behind in Indochina.

During 1978 political tension throughout Indochina rose dramatically. In May the first wave of 'boat people' pushed off from Vietnam, relations with China plummeted, and fighting on the border between Vietnam and Kampuchea escalated into a full-scale war – all of which was over-shadowed by the growing publicity given to the very real cruelties of the genocidal Pol Pot regime. For most of this time there were few reports of fighting in Laos and little attention given to the gassing stories. However, as regional tensions reached a new and dangerous pitch, a sudden spate of reports about the 'genocide' of the Hmong hit the pages of the world press.

Cast against a vague background of fighting in Laos the Pathet Lao were alleged to be using napalm, phosphorous bombs, defoliants and poison gas. 'This campaign has become so brutal, so systematic, that it can only be characterized as genocidal,' said Dr. Levi M. Roque of the Nong Khai camp. 'It is punitive, for the Meos fought with the Americans. Its aim is forced assimilation, driving people from their homes, making them abandon their traditional way of life, and it is barbaric.'[44]

The most important sources of the gassing story at this time, however, were two unnamed French doctors who were widely reported as claiming to have treated several survivors of gas attacks and to have collected 'more than 150 detailed eyewitness accounts'. They claimed 'the gas is similar to hyperite', a toxic gas used in Flanders during the First World War. The two French doctors were Marie-Noëlle and Didier Sicard, both of whom had been ejected from Laos, along with the whole French mission, in mid-1978.[46] The Sicards have since written a book on their experiences called *Au Nom de Marx et de Bouddha. Révolution au Laos: un peuple, une culture disparaissent*. It provides no factual details to support their case. The supposed '150 detailed eyewitness accounts' never surface and they make no mention of them in their book, though they do repeat the gassing charge in asserting that 50,000 Hmong had been massacred by the Communist government.[47] Yet the Sicards' ability to lend their professional standing to the gassing allegations in 1978, combined with the mounting hysteria in Southeast Asia, launched these stories into the world press. Another key source quoted at the time was an 'American researcher', Thomas Stearns, who claimed his interviews revealed the use of poison gas, but the results of his labours have never been made available for scrutiny.[48]

On inspection the sources for the stories at this time seem to lack a grounding in solid evidence, but when they appeared in print they were extraordinarily effective.

The Pol Pot government and China were quick to recognize the efficacy of these allegations for their own propaganda purposes. In early November Phnom Penh radio said the Vietnamese were firing 'poison gas' shells into O Yadao and Ratanikiri province. The report was immediately repeated in the *People's Daily* in China. Phnom Penh radio added to these charges on 12 November, and denounced the 'genocidal nature of the Vietnamese'. The Vietnamese immediately rejected all of these allegations.[49]

The Pol Pot government knew a Vietnamese invasion was imminent and was trying to rally world support for their regime. The charge laid by the Khmers Rouges that the Vietnamese were practising 'genocide' was the first major attempt to exploit the issue of chemical warfare – while providing no evidence that it was occurring.

From this point on, allegations about gassing and chemical warfare generally become more politically ambiguous and unreliable, and more numerous. In this atmosphere the US Government began to collect its evidence.

3
The Refugee Evidence

In May 1979 two American political officers – Tim Carney of the Bangkok Embassy and Ed McWilliams then based at the State Department in Washington – set off on a tour of all the refugee camps in Thailand containing Hmong to collect information on chemical warfare. They gathered reports from the Ban Vinai and Nong Khai camps, but their investigations produced none from the northern camps. Soon after, the US Army Surgeon's Office sent a team of three to Thailand, from 28 September to 13 October, to investigate claims that chemical warfare agents had been used.

The evidence gathered by Carney and McWilliams and by the medical team in 1979 is the most substantial body of refugee evidence collected and published by the US Government. The details of both were released in a *Compendium* of reports on chemical warfare in August 1980, to which an *Update* was added in March 1981. These interviews are the main source for the subsequent allegations – as well as countless journalistic articles – and therefore deserve close scrutiny.*

---

* The main sources of evidence are: 1) *Use of Chemical Agents in Southeast Asia Since the Vietnam War*. Hearing before the Subcommittee on Asian and Pacific Affairs of the Committee of Foreign Affairs, House of Representatives, 96th Congress. 12 December 1979. US Government Printing Office, Washington 1980. Hereafter cited as *Hearing*. 2) *Reports on the Use of Chemical Weapons in Afghanistan, Laos and Kampuchea*, August 1980. A compilation put together by the US Government, hereafter cited as *Compendium*. 3) *Update to the Compendium on the Reports of the Use of Chemical Weapons*, March 1981. Also produced by the US Government and hereafter cited as *Update*. 4) '*Yellow Rain*'. Hearing Before the Subcommittee on Arms Control of the Committee on Foreign Relations, United States Senate, Ninety-Seventh Congress, First Session. 10 November 1981. 5) *Chemical Warfare in Southeast Asia and Afghanistan*, Report to the Congress

Dr. Sharon Watson, a senior expert on mycotoxins at the US Armed Forces Medical Centre, claimed in March 1982 that the US possessed 'thousands' of interview reports. This is a striking claim because by March the previous year the US had published everything it had in both the *Compendium* and *Update*, and these interviews totalled no more than 200. Presumably the 'thousands' were all collected over the following year. However, they have not yet been released to the public and all the specific accounts referred to by the US in its major submissions up to March 1982 can be found in the above documents.

The Problem of Evidence

The gassing stories told by the Hmong acquired credibility, indirectly, as a result of the Kampuchean refugees providing much valuable evidence of life under Pol Pot. When I expressed the need for caution with respect to the Hmong stories, to a leading journalist from the influential *Bangkok Post* in early 1982, he replied: 'Ah, but people doubted the Khmer refugees at first too.' This claim is not entirely honest. From the fall of Phnom Penh newspapers published accounts of atrocities. Presumably what this journalist meant was that *some* people dismissed the Khmer refugee stories of atrocities, and others were very cautious about them. His retrospective criticism of the sceptics overlooks the fact that it was their initial scepticism that ensured the subsequent very high standard of evidence from researchers working among Khmer refugees. Indeed, it has been the sceptics who have subsequently produced the best work on the Pol Pot years. To date, however, none of the research into the gassing allegations remotely compares with the research done into the Pol Pot regime.

François Ponchaud argued in his *Cambodia: Year Zero* that one had to be very careful with refugee testimony: 'They tend to

from Secretary of State Alexander M. Haig, Jr., 22 March 1982. United States Department of State, Special Report No. 98. Hereafter *Report*. 6) *Chemical Warfare in South East Asia and Afghanistan: an Update*. Report to Congress from George P. Shultz, November 1982. Hereafter *Shultz Update*.

blacken the regime they have fled in order to justify their exile and make people feel sorry for them. Home-sickness, the passage of time and collective fabulation lead them to exaggerate what they have seen, generalize from isolated events and invent things that never happened'.[1]

Taking these serious constraints as a benchmark, the Khmer specialists began a process of painful and meticulous crosschecking of stories. They would try to get two different people to give the same account of an incident before they would give it credence. By building up a stock of accounts which could be crosschecked, the researchers then felt confident about giving credibility to similar stories which could not be crosschecked. Slowly, they were able to reconstruct a relatively clear picture of the Pol Pot years. This work has of course been greatly facilitated by the Vietnamese invasion, after which researchers and journalists had extensive access to the country.

The inaccessibility and secrecy of Kampuchea under Pol Pot made researchers particularly dependent on refugees for information about what was occurring inside the country. This has never been the case in Laos. Whereas the Khmers Rouges expelled all foreigners from Kampuchea, diplomatic missions, aid organizations and missionaries have had a continuous presence in Laos since the Communist takeover. This includes the US embassy in Vientiane, the only American diplomatic mission in Indochina. Journalists and aid workers have travelled the length and breadth of the country; to my knowledge the only province which has never been visited is the most northern one, Phong Saly, which has not figured in the gassing stories.

Our ability to crosscheck refugee accounts with those of travellers inside Laos makes the situation radically different from pre-1979 Kampuchea. We are not nearly so dependent on refugee stories and we can double-check their veracity with that of independent first-hand observers.

The Khmer researchers also warned that the context of the refugee stories had to be established and how war and revolution had directly affected their lives. In this respect a person's social background was an important variable when judging any particular story. Ponchaud said of his own methodology:

'In weighing up the value of each refugee's testimony, his personality has to be taken into account; I was instinctively suspicious of people who had 'revelations' to make and came bearing sensational things. I also mistrusted those who spoke French, and those who came from the wealthier classes and had too much to lose under the new regime. I was mainly interested in the ordinary people, the army privates, the peasants and labourers who could neither read nor write nor analyse what they had seen but whose illiterate memories could supply exact details.'[2]

Only when researchers had gathered evidence from the whole social spectrum and then controlled it for social background, were they able to recognize that many of the details of what people were saying were essentially similar, their overall interpretation varying according to their social class.

By and large, researchers have followed the opposite procedure in the matter of the chemical warfare allegations. For example, one journalist wrote: 'Few who have interviewed Hmong refugees have any doubt that, if details of individual accounts appear to be muddled, the substance of what they are reporting is accurate: that they have been the targets of persistent air attack involving the use of biological or chemical agents.'[3] Others have also noted how the *details* of the gassing stories have varied widely but have also accepted that chemicals 'must be' the culprit.* Yet such interpretations are the most treacherous, and this is particularly so in the case of chemical warfare where details of allegations are paramount.

Theoretically we also have to take into account the possibility that since gas attacks by their very nature leave few survivors, crosschecking among refugees could be very difficult. However, the evidence suggests that there have been many survivors from alleged attacks whose accounts could be crosschecked. In this

---

*Most notably, a Canadian report adopts this dubious methodology when after noting the 'many inconsistencies' in the refugee testimony says that what it calls the 'principal facts' should not be overlooked 'i.e. attack by either artillery shelling or airplanes, distribution of some sort of material that causes some degree of suffering and/or death of a variety of forms of life (man, animal, plant) are always represented.' *Study of the Possible Use of Chemical Warfare Agents in Southeast Asia*. A Report to the Department of External Affairs, Canada, by H. B. Schiefer, Toxicology Group, University of Saskatchewan 1982, p. 24.

respect the volume of reports has little bearing on the issue – except perhaps if we find that few of them can be crosschecked, which would be surprising if gassing was occurring.

Finally, allegations could be crosschecked with intelligence information. None of this sort of information has been available to me, nor made public. Therefore any American claims made on this basis cannot be judged, and in the absence of details it cannot be admitted as evidence unless all the other evidence conspires to make such claims look credible.

In summary, refugee evidence is only reliable when handled carefully, can be internally crosschecked, can be crossreferenced with evidence gained from inside the country, and against what is known of government policy. If we cannot make the stories tally, at least in a significant number of cases, then we have no solid reason for believing them, let alone making definite charges on the basis of them.

The Refugees

The Hmong refugee camps are found in the far north of Thailand, all of them in remote areas except the Nong Khai camp which housed some nine and a half thousand Hmong until they were relocated to Ban Vinai in 1979. Ban Vinai has always been an exclusively Hmong camp; Ban Nam Yao and Sob Tuang have more Hmong than other hilltribe groupings, and in Chiang Kham and Chiang Khong the Hmong are a significant minority. (See map on page 6.)

We have already observed that Ban Vinai was established by the remnants of the Secret Army. The Nong Khai camp was situated just downstream from Vientiane and was a natural landing place for Hmong travelling directly south from Phy Bia, or for those who travelled down the highway to Vientiane and then crossed the river. Nong Khai was also the main camp for the defeated lowland anti-communist elite. The former CIA forces re-grouped at Nong Khai and Ban Vinai; in the latter camp they held complete sway while in the former they had to share camp power with the lowland right wing. These two camps were the centre of the elusive 'Lao resistance' in the aftermath of the communist victory.

Lowland ethnic Lao resistance to the new regime has never been significant. Internally divided and ideologically unmotivated, most ethnic Lao simply wished to travel onto the prosperous west as quickly as possible. In contrast the Hmong elite had been ideologically hardened by their Green Beret trainers, and throughout the civil war were much more committed than their lowland counterparts. This commitment was buttressed by a strong sense of ethnic and cultural separateness from the lowlanders. These people were less interested, as a group, in migrating to the west, and the ordinary Hmong tribesmen under their control were even less interested. As rather depressing tales of life in the west have filtered back to the people in the camps, enthusiasm has waned further. Thus, in 1981 only 63% of Hmong accepted for resettlement overseas from Ban Vinai showed up on the appointed day to accept the offer. Among the lowland Lao, on the other hand, the emigration rate was 88%.

The remote northern refugee camps are much less politicized than Ban Vinai or Nong Khai. No single political or ethnic faction dominates these camps, and the different ethnic groups live on their own separate hills or sections within the camp and generally do not get along well. In Ban Nam Yao what 'politics' there is has a millenarian bent. As one man said wistfully: 'we will wait to see if the king – the white king – will fix up Laos so we can go back'.[4] Significantly there are no reports of gassing or other forms of chemical warfare from these camps, although the US Government, journalists, doctors and others have inquired among the inmates about these reports.

It is significant that the chemical warfare allegations come exclusively from camps dominated by the old right-wing leadership who have every interest in propagating stories that discredit the new regime. Investigators into the charges of chemical warfare have worked through this leadership. Colonel Charles W. Lewis, Medical Corps, US Army, who led the medical team to Thailand in late 1979, told the December 1979 *Hearing*: 'As the great majority of the Hmong refugees are at the Ban Vinai camp as well as the Hmong leadership, this is where we concentrated our efforts and obtained the majority of our interviews.'[5] And as I discovered on my visits there, the leadership of the camp clears all interviewees. I gathered my first list from aid personnel in the camp and then suggested to my Hmong translator that we go to interview these people. He said it was impossible without first clearing the list with the camp leadership. Fortunately perhaps, the man in charge of this, a former Lieutenant Choumoulee, was feeling ill with a relapse of what he described as malaria and syphilis. He did not know the people I was seeking (they were from among the most recent arrivals), but presumably was off his guard both because of illness and because people who come to investigate the gas story are generally uncritical. Choumoulee explained to me: 'All the people who have got the gas have to report to me, and I report them to the American embassy in Bangkok. And all the people who want to speak to the people who have got the gas have to come to me first.'

The leader of Ban Vinai camp is former Lieutenant-Colonel Vang Neng, first cousin of Vang Pao. Surrounding him are various former officers of the old CIA army such as this second-in-command Vue Mai. However, the social control exercised in Ban Vinai camp is more complex than a simple hierarchical military command structure. The social cohesion, indeed coercion, found there also arises out of a collective desire for cultural unity through which the Hmong hope to assure their social survival.

This was well illustrated when in October 1980 Vang Neng's name came up on a list of refugees accepted for resettlement in the US. His parents were already in Alabama; his second wife and their four children had been settled in Georgia. His fervour for a military campaign to regain the lost position Laos had subsided, and he wished to go. Other members of the Hmong leadership, however, had not given up hope and they soon mounted opposition to his departure because, as they saw it, Vang Neng was their living link with Vang Pao and therefore with the US, who they still hoped would help achieve their aim. A meeting of the Hmong leaders in the camp on 7 October rejected Vang Neng's plea to go by seventy votes to three. At the meeting Vang Neng argued that Vue Mai could easily take his place, but Vue Mai, seen as one of the camp's hardliners, shrewdly refused to accept the position of leader. A few days later Vang Neng was persuaded to remain when an anonymous death note was posted on his house and at the camp hospital.[6] The seriousness with which he treated this threat was shown by the fact that he was still 'leading' the camp when I visited in March 1982.

Outsiders are not privy to the internal workings of the Hmong leadership at Ban Vinai, but it is clearly capable of strictly enforcing its will on any member of the camp. Except for Sa Kaeo camp, which for a year or so was under the strict control of the Khmers Rouges, there is nothing equivalent to Ban Vinai on the Kampuchean border. Yet even Sa Kaeo was, like the Pol Pot regime itself, a more or less unmediated form of military control whereas the social fabric of the Hmong camps is much more intricate. In this respect family structure and ethnic identity has played a key role. The more nucleated family structure of the Khmer or lowland Lao compared with the Hmong has meant that social control beyond the immediate family is lacking and that there is less sense of solidarity. Hmong culture, in contrast, revolves around ethnic solidarity institutionalized through the family and clan system. In their common situation as refugees in Thailand this sense of solidarity among the Hmong has become very marked.

Ban Vinai camp is like a large western-funded Hmong cultural revival centre, and its leadership is self-consciously concerned to promote a sense of Hmong identity and Hmong culture. Hmong history, traditions and values are inculcated in a rigorous education system. There is an element of fanaticism in the way they are going about it that imparts a feeling of paranoia, but it is understandable after twenty years of constant migration, war and death, which, many Hmong feel, were destroying their people. Nor is their current status as displaced persons calculated to give them a sense of security. Indeed, it is a perfect environment for the overdramatization of their recent history. In the hothouse atmosphere of the camp the pressures towards conformity, particularly on general political issues, are very strong.

In Chapter Two we saw that Ban Vinai was established as a special camp in late 1975 for the remnants of Vang Pao's army. There appeared to be a number of motivations for establishing it in Loei province. One was to use elements of these forces against communist-influenced hiltribesmen in Thailand itself. Many of the CIA Hmong had received training in that part of the Petchabun mountains south of Ban Vinai prior to 1975. Since then a number of young Hmong men, tired of kicking up their heels in the confines of the camp, have been recruited for duties protecting various road-building projects from the Communist Party of Thailand forces who operate in the Petchabun ranges. The second reason for establishing this camp was defensive. In the unsettled atmosphere following the Communist victories in Indochina the remnants of the Secret Army were one of the few armed right-wing groups from Laos still interested in fighting. They could act as a bulwark against what the Thai military saw as a threat of armed infiltration from Laos. Third, they could be used to conduct intelligence operations inside Laos, and, presumably, sabotage. It was not an ordinary refugee camp.

The attitudes of Vang Lue, a preacher with the Christian and Missionary Alliance at Ban Vinai, give an interesting insight into the state of mind of the non-military Hmong leadership. Vang Lue had spent most of his life as a refugee – shifting from camp to camp as a young boy in Xieng Khouang province until he ended up at Long Cheng because his three brothers were fighting for Vang Pao. From Long Cheng he was sent first to school in Vientiane, then to a seminary in Thailand. In 1971 he spent some time in a seminary in South Korea, but had been at Ban Vinai since it was founded in late 1975.

Like the rest of the tiny Hmong intelligentsia Vang Lue largely owes his education to the Americans and in return he gives the US and its policies his unreserved support, spicing his rhetoric throughout with bible-belt anti-communism. Courteous but dogmatic, Vang Lue's discourse is not subject to ordinary rules of rationality. When I tried to discuss the gassing issue with him, we made no headway because if he was told something by a Hmong then he would believe it, no matter what evidence a Thai, an Australian or an American might marshal against it. In short it was a question of ethnicity not rationality. Indeed, at this point he burst out that he would not care if all the people in Australia or America were killed. All he cared about was the Hmong, which is, perhaps, an understandable outburst.

Vang Lue was not a member of the Secret Army – though it must be said that he was about as close to it as one can get without actually joining – and he occupies an important leadership position within the Hmong community at Ban Vinai. He is an opinion-former within that community. Yet the opinions he holds, like those of the rest of the Hmong leadership, are in many ways trapped in a circular logic. In an environment where anything that a Hmong says is to be believed no matter what outsiders say, one can see how even the most unlikely stories would be given credence. Indeed, such an intellectual universe would tend to blind the camp leadership to the need to present coherent chemical warfare stories to researchers, if they are to stand up as evidence.

It is hard to tell how much outright fabrication has gone on at Ban Vinai. While I was there a Hmong-speaking American told me that she had seen one lot of Hmong new arrivals brought in, accompanied by one of the camp leaders. On arrival one of the men pulled up his sleeve to display scabies scars and said they were caused by gas. Then she heard him a little later asking for something to deal with his scabies. The next day this man was paraded through the camp as the latest victim of a gas attack. There are, of course, other explanations for this kind of behaviour which we will return to in the later part of this book. For the moment it signals the need for extra caution when considering the stories told at this camp.

A problem with all the evidence gathered by the US, as presented in the *Compendium* and the *Update*, is that no attempt has been made to establish the social background of the interviewees, and such information only emerges accidentally. For example, one informant reeled off at the end of his interview: 'For reference: I am a former Vang Pao's soldier attached to BRIG-11, REGT-22, BN-204/2, Rank Lieutenant, Serial No. 290632.'[7] Out of an approximate total of 110 cases contained in the *Compendium* – approximate because there is not only some doubling-up in the document of the State Department's and the medical team's evidence, but also the reproduction of some newspaper articles based on this US-collected evidence – forty-five people voluntarily indicated that they were soldiers and resistance fighters. In the absence of specific information in the US interviews I attempted to use a rough measure to ascertain who the other informants were. Because former Secret Army soldiers were familiar with aircraft and military equipment, I decided that if refugees could identify the type of aircraft (L-19, T-28) or the calibre of artillery (105 mm, 155 mm) they were probably soldiers. On such a basis the number of soldiers represented in the interviews rises to 85 or 77%, but even this is almost certainly a conservative estimate. For example, in one account a refugee does not identify himself as a soldier directly, nor does he specify the type of weaponry used, yet he speaks of those he was with as 'defenders'; it is thus highly likely that they were soldiers. However, I did not count him as a soldier because, as in the remainder of the accounts there was not enough information included in the text of the interviews. It may be objected that civilians in a war zone could be familiar with aircraft types, but this is not my experience with non-military Hmong.

It is safe to say, I believe, that the vast majority of the refugees interviewed by the US teams were soldiers. This narrow range of informants in itself gives the information gleaned from them a potential political bias. We therefore need to approach it with the utmost care and must apply to it the most stringent criteria for measuring reliability.

US Methodology

We do not know the details of how Carney and McWilliams collected their evidence for the State Department, but Colonel Lewis told the 1979 *Hearing*: 'Our team attempted to be very selective in talking only with those Hmongs who had either been direct witnesses of attacks or those who had been exposed to chemical agents themselves . . . To achieve conformity in our results, we used a prepared questionnaire . . .'[8] The questionnaire used by Colonel Lewis (reproduced in the *Hearing* document) is perfectly reasonable if one has already established that chemical warfare is occurring and the main problem to be solved is simply what type of chemical agent is in use. However, there had been very little investigation of the subject and any inquiry by the US in 1979 really needed to investigate the veracity of the reports and any alternative explanations for them. Colonel Lewis' team did not do this. It assumed that chemical war was going on. (This is corroborated by journalist Sterling Seagrave's account of the team's work.) An obvious weakness in this approach is that because it seeks an affirmative answer it invariably gets one. Indeed, an investigation of this sort would have the effect of buttressing the stories rather than subjecting them to critical scrutiny. There was no serious attempt to crosscheck the stories, nor any attempt to interview Hmong who may have given a different account.

In this light I think we must conclude that the interviews gathered by Dr. Lewis and his team can only be of limited value, and they certainly are not of the standard which would allow hard-and-fast conclusions to be drawn from them. Colonel Lewis was not daunted by 'minor details' of critical procedure and concluded: 'First, chemical agents have been used against the Hmong. Second, the reported effects of these agents suggests the use of a nerve agent, a riot control agent, and that an unidentified combination or compound has been used in these attacks.'[9]

The team was given some 'samples' of the 'gas' for investigation which, however, produced no scientific evidence of the use of gas. Thus Lester Wolff was prompted to ask:

'How come you are able to say that a lethal chemical was used and they [chemical experts] can't prove anything has been used. How did you come to this conclusion, Colonel Lewis?
COLONEL LEWIS: Sir, that conclusion is based on our clinical judgement. It is based on the interviews and the information we obtained from the Hmong refugees.
MR WOLFF: So, in other words, it is actually from the interviews rather than from the samples of the material?
COLONEL LEWIS: Yes, sir.'[10]

The same situation pertains today, and as each claim that physical evidence exists is challenged, the allegations ultimately fall back on the refugee evidence collected by the US.

To his credit Representative Wolff struck the only note of caution about the refugee evidence during the whole hearing when he noted the difficulties the US had had 'in sorting out that material we have had with reference to our MIAs as a result of certain refugees giving out information that may or may not have been misleading, and trying to pin it down in some fashion to some substantial evidence'.

Colonel Lewis countered this by arguing that 'in some cases we were given such exact and absolute detail of things that occurred medically, we could not really doubt the validity of what the individuals were telling us.'[11] He cited only one case of a *description* of a skin condition, from a single refugee whose credibility we throw into question as a whole below. There was no physical evidence on hand.

Indeed, whether the medical details 'in some cases' may have been very accurate and actually corresponded to known tropical diseases and maladies we do not know for sure, because the team was not testing alternative hypotheses. Other explanations for the various symptoms described had been ruled out of court by the assumption that gassing was occurring.

A CIA report was also presented to the Committee which claimed a 'lung irritant such as chlorine or phosgene and a blister agent such as mustard' had been used in Laos. No evidence was given for this conclusion, besides the refugee stories. A former Hmong soldier testified, as did an aid worker from the conservative International Rescue Committee. The State Department made a submission that rather strangely dated the beginning of the gas attacks as 1974. This has subsequently been revised without explanation by the State Department, but not before John Everingham repeated it in a 1980 issue of the *National Geographic*.

The Evidence

The 'gassing story' at its most rudimentary level, or perhaps we should say at its most general and abstract level, is perhaps the only consistent element of the story: a plane flies over, something is dropped, people get sick and some die. Beyond this general description there is little consistency.

Today's press-packaged story of 'yellow rain' is largely an invention. The colour of the 'gas' ranged across the spectrum – black, blue, green, white, grey, yellow, red, colourless – and the description of the substance and its mode of delivery also varied considerably. Indeed the use of the word 'rain' was rare. A common description was smoke, which was *interrupted* as gas, while at other times it was described as a powder or as a spray. The time the 'gas' took to effect its victims varied from seconds to weeks; the distance at which it was lethal varied considerably; sometimes it killed plants and at other times not; sometimes it killed all animals, while at other times it is merciful to dogs, and so on. The variation in the stories is in fact so great that only when reduced to its most general terms is it at all coherent. Yet when considering refugee stories, and in particular when they relate to chemical warfare, *the details are all-important*.

One element of relative consistency is that rockets are often named as the mode of delivery used for the gas. But this is hardly exceptional or compelling evidence. Soldiers were familiar with rockets and many of them had seen smoke rockets fired from L-19 spotter planes (commonly referred to in the refugee accounts) as markers for fighter-bombers prior to 1975. Indeed it may have been precisely this that they have witnessed since 1975 – directed against themselves.

The other serious problem with the US evidence is that very few of the refugee stories can be crosschecked. It is absolutely vital for us to be able to do this with at least some of the stories, for only on this basis will we be able to accept at face value stories that cannot be crosschecked. Conversely, if the stories that can be crosschecked do not tally, then those that cannot may be considered unreliable.

Two reports in the US evidence are easily cross-referenced. They both concern fighting at Tam Se Sam Liem, east of Phu Bia. One is reported to have taken place on 7 February 1978, the other on 12 February.[12] Both informants were soldiers and the date discrepancy could easily be a minor oversight on their part. We can assume for the moment that they are describing the same incident.

One of the soldiers said the attack on them was conducted by two L-19 planes with rockets containing yellow and black gas. The other said it was a helicopter that sprayed something 'like rain'. For the first man the 'yellow gas killed plants in three days', while the second soldier said it 'did not hurt plants'. The symptoms according to the first man were burning eyes, head pains, bloody vomiting and respiratory difficulties. The second man said 'helicopter rain' did not affect people unless they drank contaminated water or ate contaminated food, in which case it caused diarrhoea.

How can we explain the serious discrepancies between the two stories? First, we could simply conclude that one or both are lying. Or, second, we could say that they are in fact describing separate incidents five days apart. If we say this, we have to assume that the first soldier left the village three days after the attack on the 7th – which would explain why he does not mention the second attack but was around long enough to observe the plants dying. We would also have to assume that the second soldier arrived in the village after the 7th. Even so, we would have to explain why the second man did not mention the alleged first attack by referring to the ill and dead people and its effect on foliage around the village; he said he observed the opposite. It would be foolish to assume that the remaining villagers did not mention an attack on the 7th to the 'newcomer'. In short, whichever way we try to crosscheck the stories of these two men they do not add up; indeed they contradict each other, and hence at least one must be discounted as unreliable.

The only other stories in the whole of the US evidence that can be crosschecked in any meaningful way are those reported from Pha Mai, Vientiane Province, for April and May 1979. But we are hampered by the sloppy way the American Government collected and presented its evidence in the 1980 *Compendium* from which these incidents are taken. There is obviously some overlap between the mid-1979 evidence collected by the State Department officers and the evidence collected by Colonel Lewis's team in October, partly under the guidance of the State Department officers who had toured the camps earlier. However, in their presentation of the evidence the US gives no indication whatsoever where this doubling-up occurred. The obvious effect is to inflate the number of cases that the US claims to have documented.

In any other situation we would perhaps be justified in throwing out such 'evidence' and asking the US at least to systematize it. Unfortunately we must persist in trying to make sense of the evidence as it stands.

The attacks on Pha Mai were combat operations against Hmong soldiers. However, out of five accounts of attacks on Pha Mai from March to 1 May 1979, only two can be crosschecked with any confidence and only one is detailed, describing a fairly conventional military attack. This latter account alleges that the attacks took place on 4 and 25 April and on 1 May. The US Foreign Service Officer summarized the story: 'There had been no military pressure on the village other than those attacks, though a ground probe of the area by Vietnamese or Lao soldiers wearing gear to protect them from gas followed the 1 May attack. Source claimed that the gas was dropped from what appeared to be a C-130 and from MIGs. He stated that he saw many small yellow clouds descending on the village area on 1 May, heard air burst and then saw white, then green clouds which fell like rain. Source stated that over thirty of the village population of approximately 600 died as a result of the three attacks . . . said that some victims died as a result of the yellow gas.'[13]

Unravelling this story, what we appear to have is three attacks, two conventional and one with gas on 1 May. Casualties from the 'gas' are specified as 'some', though the three engagements took over thirty lives. One can safely deduce from this that most people were actually killed by conventional means, and it certainly is plausible that in fact all of them were. Unfortunately there is no detailed description of the 'gear' allegedly worn by the Vietnamese or Pathet Lao soldiers. The specifics are important; other Hmong have described this 'gear' as a simple gauze mask or the chewing of a shirt collar, both of which are utterly inadequate as protection from gas.

But the main complication in the evidence of this particular refugee is that he appears to have been interviewed by the State Department in May and then by Colonel Lewis's team in October without any acknowledgement of the fact. That is, we appear to have a problem of doubling-up. The dates of the alleged attacks are exactly the same, with one omission, but what makes it look like doubling-up rather than independent corroboration is that this person had given the State Department officers a sample of 'yellow residue' when they did their rounds of the camps. The Lewis team interview simply remarks, for this man, 'sample collected', that is collected earlier: it did not mean Lewis's team collected the sample because the only specimen they collected was from a refugee from Ban Don which allegedly came from an incident in October 1978. Therefore we can be fairly certain that the person who supplied the yellow residue to the State Department is the same person mentioned in Lewis's team notes, which of course means that we cannot use this informant's account for the purposes of crosschecking what happened at Pha Mai. We can, however, check the story he told in June with that of October; and when we do, we discover that there are significant discrepancies between the two stories, sufficient to cast doubt on them even if they were told by two separate people, let alone the same person telling a different story.

This man told Lewis in October that he had travelled out to Thailand on a six-day trek with seventy-eight other people. Thus there was more than ample opportunity for Lewis to corroborate this man's particular story by interviewing other refugees who had come with him from Pha Mai. No attempt to do so was made, however. There are three other reports in the US evidence from Pha Mai around the same period, but we are not given specific dates in these reports ranging over a three-month period, and they all vary enough in detail to throw all the stories from Pha Mai into question concerning claims about chemical warfare. If they are all from the same group of seventy eight refugees who came out of that area – which is possible – then their accounts are rendered even more unreliable. The planes involved in the alleged attacks differ, the mode of delivery differs, and the colours of the 'gases' differ from one story to the next. The symptoms from each of the accounts also vary except for blurred vision, vomiting and difficult breathing. Only the last strongly correlates with a chemical attack, but could equally have been caused by smoke, cordite fumes, a riot-control gas or indeed be an index of common respiratory problems. Only two of the five accounts indicate bloody coughing or vomiting, none bloody diarrhoea, both of which are supposed to be the key symptoms of the alleged mycotoxin poisoning that lies at the centre of the entire controversy.

There are also two reports from a village called Muong Ao near Phu Bia in March 1978.[14] The dates given are not precise so we shall assume the sources are describing the same attack. One claims the attack was carried out by 'planes' which fired fifty rockets, both high explosive and gas. The other says the attack was launched by a single L-19 'via a "piece" one metre long and as thick as an arm that exploded 100 metres in the air'. One said the gas killed all plants, the other that it produced holes in the leaves but did not kill them. One said the gas was blue, the other white. One said there were thirty people killed, the other sixty. However the symptoms described in this case were similar: diarrhoea, vomiting blood, cough, blurred vision, burning running bloody nose. From general reports it would appear that there was considerable military activity in the area at this time as part of the offensive which had been launched around Phu Bia in November 1977. But once again these two stories from Muong Ao are not consistent enough to stand on their own, nor strong enough to give us confidence in other accounts.

Few other accounts in the US evidence can be crosschecked. There are two 'reports received by the US Government' – from whom we are not told – that chemical warfare attacks took place in Muong Cha, near Phu Bia, around July/August 1979.[15] The person who supposedly witnessed these attacks did not report any effects on anyone or anything.

In the 1981 *Update* there is a report of a group of nineteen soldiers who claimed to have been gassed, but even the person who interviewed this group was compelled to comment that some of their story was 'inaccurate' (though the precise nature of these inaccuracies was not spelled out). They were interviewed as a group and their spokesman was an officer, Vang Seng Vang. It seems they nodded in agreement with his account, a mode of corroboration which is hardly satisfactory.[16] In another account a five-year-old child used to crosscheck his father's account. The child described different coloured gases from his father, and sores that the father had said were caused by 'gas' were not attributed to any specific event by the child, who simply said he had had them 'a long time'.[17]

The accounts we have been surveying are the best produced by the US in that they can be crosschecked to some degree. We have seen that none of the stories tally; in fact they often contradict one another, and they provide us with no firm reason for believing them, or for believing the stories that cannot be crossreferenced. I think we must conclude that even the best of the US refugee evidence is weak by almost any standards.

By way of concluding this attempt to crosscheck the refugee stories we shall turn to an account which Colonel Lewis chose to present in full to the 1979 hearing. It cannot be checked with other US evidence, but this person has been subsequently interviewed by Jane Hamilton-Merrit and by myself, among others.

The name of this refugee is Ger Pao Pha, and the following is his story as it was presented by Colonel Lewis to the US hearing in December 1979:

Date: 28 September 1978.
Location: Pha Na Khun at foot of Phou Bia.
Mode of attack and Material/Agent Used: Two L-19 airplanes – first one sprayed yellow-and-green powder that was not wet like rain – but fell to ground. Second plane few minutes later – fired rocket that exploded twenty metres overhead releasing red smoke/gas.
Number of people in village/unit: 300 (about fifty were out of village at time of attack).
Number of people affected: Only nineteen or twenty survived.
Number of people killed: Approximately 230.
Animals: All animals died.
Miscellaneous: The yellow and green powders made everyone feel dizzy, confused actions, blurred vision, difficult to move, people fell down, jaws were stiff (clamped shut) could not speak and had almost immediate vomiting and diarrhoea before the red smoke came down.
Red smoke caused all to start coughing, have massive nose bleeds within five minutes; blood came from nose and mouth and people fell down and were dead in less than 15 minutes.
At onset of attack, he ran with twelve-year-old son about fifty metres out of village to a small cave where he could see people dying. He and son were made very ill by smoke.
Medical findings: His symptoms – dizzy, headache at temples. Eyes – no pain, no tears, blurred vision – could not see beyond ten metres; son's eyes were very red and the black part of eyes (iris) was smaller and lighter in colour. Throat – very sore, could not talk, voice weak and hoarse, larynx felt tight. Coughed repeatedly and coughed up blood. Burning pain in chest with

coughing. Marked shortness of breath – could only say one or two words. Substantial pain with breathing, very difficult to breathe because he was so weak. No vomiting or diarrhoea. Skin – yellow material got on his legs – caused much itching – scratched skin off – 10 days later had crusted lesions. Sleep – unable to go to sleep for five days. Muscles – so weak he could not move or even pick up a pack of cigarettes. Lasted two days. Several hours after attack a military unit of ethnic Pathet Lao soldiers with AK rifles and B-40 rockets entered the village. Carried all those alive (nineteen or twenty) into centre of village – gave them an injection into upper arm. Next morning they were carried one or two kilometres to Muong Om Village. Kept in a hospital for five days and given injections on second and fifth days. Was very weak but could walk short distance. Sent to a detention centre.

Soldiers wore a 'cloth mask' (like dressing pads) over nose and mouth. Describes five of his group that acted 'crazy' and two died on eighth day and three more died on tenth day after attack (all in their twenties). States the skin peeled off in sheets, very large sacs of skin with fluid in them and very sick. Their bodies (skin) turned black within three hours of death. Sounds like Toxic Epidermal Necrolysis.[18]

Lewis did not make any general comment on Ger's statement when he presented it at the hearing, though it was this testimony which he had referred to earlier as providing 'such exact and absolute detail of things that occurred medically'. It was also Ger's account that gave rise at the hearing to speculation 'that Hmongs had been used as human guinea pigs for chemical warfare experimentation', and the injection given was presumed to be some antidote to the 'gas'. One of the medical team, Colonel Welzel, did remark that 'if there were a testing programme involved, one would expect to see more after-the-fact investigations of attacks than the single instance'.[19]

Jane Hamilton interviewed Ger at the beginning of 1982. It is worth reproducing most of what she writes:

'Hugging his child with tears in his eyes as I photographed them

together, he explained that he and his son were the only survivors of a family of fifteen. Thirteen had died from the gas. "I
saved my boy", he told me, "by putting a rag soaked with opium
over my face and over my son's face who was under my arm."
As he speaks he demonstrates. "We manage to get out of the
village and hide in a cave with sixteen other people. We are all
very sick. After only one day in the cave, the Vietnamese come
to catch us. We cannot resist. When the Vietnamese come into
the cave, they are all chewing the corners of their collars. When
we go about one kilometre from the area, they stop chewing
their collars."

I asked him why the Vietnamese were chewing their collars.
"They have medicine to protect themselves from the gas sewn
into their clothes", he answered without hesitation.

I had spoken with Ger because he had been interviewed by
the UN . . . He was outraged when, apparently not understanding the tortures of the damned that this man had been through
by losing his entire family except his small son by bio-chemical
warfare, a member of the UN team asked him if he had come to
Thailand for political or economic reasons.'[20]

Merrit is aghast that anyone should dare question the story or
motives of this old CIA soldier, whom she says conducted a
heroic struggle against communism in Laos on behalf of America.
To her the truthfulness of Ger's account, like that of others, is
self-evident.

Oddly enough the UN team who visited Thailand in November
1981 said 'it was unable to locate in the camps any of the alleged
victims whose names appeared in the United States submissions'.[21]
This can only mean that Ger concealed his earlier account from
the UN team. Did he do this because he had now changed his
story? In fact, the summary account of Ger's story contained in the
UN Report adds yet another variation; the mode of delivery of the
gas is no longer a rocket but a low-flying airplane that 'sprayed
smoke'.[22] To which we can add the substantial variations contained
in Ger's story as told to Jane Hamilton-Merritt: the opium-soaked
rag as his own ready-made gas mask; the soldiers chewing their
collars; while the description of the injections at the village, of the

hospital, and of the soldiers wearing gauze masks has disappeared; also, the soldiers have mutated into 'Vietnamese'. These variations were repeated to me in March 1982.

Interestingly, during 1980 and 1981 it became more common for press reports to mention that Hmong carried opium-soaked rags as primitive gas masks, which I think hints at the nature of press feedback into the refugee camps in Thailand.[23] Opium is always a hook-line for the western press and Ger had perhaps re-fashioned his story accordingly.

But Ger is a 'star-witness' for the Hmong leaders in Ban Vinai Camp. He was presented to me by the camp leadership after I approached them to provide me with some 'gassing victims', and was introduced as having been interviewed thirteen times before by various organizations and journalists – the US team, the UN team, American TV, and the week before I was in the camp, by an Australian TV crew, as well as other journalists.* Ger was a well-rehearsed witness, a fact that leaves him open to crosschecking over time. For instance, he gave an account to a *Guardian* journalist in September 1981 in which he said that only forty people died from the attack; on this occasion he arrived for the interview with a little 'daughter' who he said was the only other survivor of the attack.[24] It may be presumed that his little son was busy with something else that day.

Even though the object of my investigations was the gassing allegations, I chose in my interview not to discuss this question until I had obtained various biographical details of my interviewee. Sometimes this would take a long time and for a well-rehearsed gassing victim like Ger it was a very frustrating approach. On a couple of occasions in our two-hour-long interview he interjected 'I thought you wanted to talk about the gas', and then would try to initiate a discussion of the gas story, which he would signal by beginning to raise his handkerchief to his mouth as a demonstration of the opium gas mask.

Actually Ger's personal history is an interesting and revealing

---

*Ger's story has been paraphrased out of the US evidence many times by journalists. Seagrave reprints it in full, and a good recent book on the history of biological and chemical warfare this century, *A Higher Form of Killing*, by Robert Harris and Jeremy Paxman, also paraphrases Ger's story.

one; he joined the French GMCA back in 1950, and had been involved in all the major battles in Laos since then. He had gone to Long Cheng as part of the original contingent of Vang Pao's Secret Army and had risen to the rank of lieutenant.

After Vang Pao's flight from Laos in May 1975 Ger returned to a village called Than Lo, near Phu Bia, with forty soldiers and 260 others where they began to 'fight the Pathet Lao'. They stayed in Than Lo village for three years growing food. The soldiers would conduct occasional guerrilla raids, but the scale of the fighting was not large. But by September 1978 Pathet Lao attempts to quell the Hmong guerrillas caught up with Ger, his soldiers and their families at Than Lo. They were forced to flee to Na Teng where fighting once more forced them to flee to Pha Na Khun close to Lima 63, an old CIA airstrip. Here there was fierce fighting and, according to Ger, strafing by a plane killed 242 people out of 260. This was on '18 August 1978'.

Thus by taking Ger through a straight narrative of what had happened to him, it emerged that he and his soldiers and the families with them had been involved in a number of serious engagements involving heavy loss of life, but as told in this form, no gas was used.

I then asked him about the gassing incident. He said a single Raven plane flew over and fired a rocket that burst overhead, letting out a red gas that killed '242' people immediately – at which point it transpired that this was the same incident he had described as strafing a little while before in our interview. I asked how high the plane was and he said he could not see the plane. So how did he know it was a Raven? Then he said he could see it but it was very high. How long did it take the gas to fall? With a whoosh of his hand he said very fast, about three seconds. I asked how he would describe the gas. He said he did not know, but it was like a vapour; he knew it was gas because he was a soldier.

In an attempt to get more precise details of the attack I asked Ger where he was in relation to his wife and other children when the attack took place. He said that he and others went into a cave when the attack began. His wife, he said, was just outside the mouth of the cave, about twenty feet away, cooking. Could he see the gas from the cave? Yes. And did the gas come into the cave?

No, the wind blew it away. Why did he need to put a handkerchief soaked in opium over his mouth if the wind blew the gas away, and how did he know that this is what he should do? At which point he said there had been gas attacks at Than Lo, but could not remember the dates. He was clearly beginning to move outside his established story, at which point the interview began to disintegrate. I asked what they did with the 242 dead people. Did they bury them, for instance? (The importance of funeral rites for the dead amongst the Hmong is well known.)* No they did not, he said, there were too many. Did he bury his wife and children? No, he was too afraid and left for Thailand.

These last questions would have been good opportunities for Ger to describe the aftermath of such an attack, but by this stage he had become very wary of my questions. (Unfortunately, at the time of our interview I did not recognize Ger's importance and did not probe him about his previous accounts and the discrepancies.) I did not hear Ger's story on the entry of troops into the area, though early in the interview when he had tried to channel it towards the gas story he had thrust his collar into his mouth and begun a demonstration of the 'collar antidote'. After many exhausting and fruitless attempts to pin him down on details, he wished to conclude the interview.

For a story we are unable to crosscheck with any other, Ger's account varies too much over time for us to be able to give it credibility. It has been treated at length here because of the prominence this particular account has been given. As a key bearer of the story for the ex-CIA leadership and as an ex-officer himself, Ger's story under any circumstances would have to be treated with circumspection, yet he has most often been presented in the media and elsewhere as an ordinary Hmong hilltribesman too unsophisticated to tell such a tale if it was not the truth. Clearly someone with Ger's background is not above lying for propagandistic purposes.

---

*I was concerned about the trauma that this could create for refugees unable to give the proper rites to dead relatives on the way out. An anthropologist at the Tribal Institute in Thailand suggested that this would leave a great deal of residual guilt in those people who arrived at the camps in Thailand, and give rise to emotional disturbance and tension.

What also interested me about Ger was that he appeared to have two self-contained stories. One, a narrative that leads through a series of conventional engagements until there is a showdown at Pha Na Khun. And a second, gassing story, in which the conventional aspects of the engagement disappear altogether. It is this that makes one suspect that the gassing story has been tacked on subsequently, and not terribly firmly.

The tales told by Ger and other ex-Vang Pao soldiers have, for obvious reasons, a much stronger political bent than those told by ordinary Hmong peasants. This emerges clearly in the following fascinating account given to me by a fifty-five-year-old farmer, Cha Ten Tha. It provides evidence not only for an argument that many Hmong have moved from Laos for purely economic reasons, but also of how 'gas' is being used to explain natural events.

Cha Ten Tha lived in a village close to Ban Don, Vientiane Province, in 1979. There were seventy-seven families in the village and a total of 479 people, with each family owning their own dry rice field. One day he saw a plane fly over the fields and one month later, in August or September (there was some calendar confusion here) of 1979, the rice died.

The villagers were short of food and decided to call in the Pathet Lao *Chao Muang* ('district chief') of Ban Don district. The *Chao Muang*, Pot Chieng, arrived at the village with a Pathet Lao army officer, Gong Jap, and they proceeded to explain to the villagers that there had not been enough rain in that area that year and that was why the rice had not flourished. They said they were sorry about this and would do what they could to help the villagers though their resources were limited. They implored the Hmong villagers not to get upset or panic, and not to move elsewhere. Times are difficult but will get better, they said.

As a result of these pleas the villagers decided to stay and planted the fields with dry rice for the following year. Then, said Tha, in October 1980 a plane flew over the fields again and the rice died fourteen days later. Some time during this fourteen-day period a sixty-seven-year-old woman died while in the fields, and according to Tha's story, 300 chickens and three dogs also died out in the fields with her.

Once again the villagers' crop had failed and they were now very

worried because they had no food at all. *Nai Ban* ('village chief')
Cha Ten Tha once again called in Pot Chieng and Jap to ask them
what they should do now that their fields were dead. Pot Chieng
said he could not make a decision on what they should do and he
therefore sent for an official from Vientiane to talk to the villagers.
A month later the village heads were called to Chieng's office to
see the high officials.

At this point in our interview Cha Teng Tha's voice dropped to a
sinister tone: he said there were two Soviets at the meeting. He
said Chieng and Jap told the Soviets and the high official the
problem and the villagers themselves requested that the Soviets
supply them with rice or at least the money to buy the rice. The
Soviets replied that they were not in a position to help them
directly – but one of them dipped into his pocket and handed out a
very small amount of money. They then ate a lunch of chickens
and Lao alcohol together. At the end of the lunch the Russians
took some photos of the Hmong, said Cha Teng Tha, his voice
once again taking on a sinister tone.

After returning to their village empty-handed to discuss what to
do next, the villagers once again called in Chieng and Jap to whom
they explained that it was impossible to stay in their village any
longer. Pot Chieng said he understood their problem and would
provide papers for anyone who wished to travel to another area
to stay with relatives who could help them.

Cha Teng Tha and his family left to go to stay with relatives at a
village called Na Naou. Chieng had explained that Tha would have
to show his papers to a PLA officer called Hong Tai at a place
called Na Ho. Tha's voice once more became dramatic as he
explained their arrival at Na Ho and I was expecting to hear that
Hong Tai was really a PLA tyrant who tried to jail or shoot them or
worse. But no; Tai said everything was okay and that they should
just keep straight on down the road to Na Naou. But ten miles
further down the road they went across country to Thailand, a
forest trek that took them four days. They arrived at the beginning
of 1981.

Cha Teng Tha's story is fascinating for a number of reasons,
which we should consider at this point.

First, his account is a good example of the economic predicament of many Hmong in 1979, and their response to it. Second, however much Tha distrusted the Pathet Lao, it is obvious that they did all they could to help the Hmong, though their ability to do so was extremely limited. Moreover, when the authorities could no longer assist them they facilitated the Hmong's movement to villages where relatives could help them. There was no sign here of any aggressive harassment of the villagers by the Pathet Lao authorities, or by any one else. Cha Teng Tha's adoption of sinister tones at different points in his story suggests that he has learned in the camp that any talk about Soviets and Pathet Lao, whatever they are doing, requires such tones; it may also reflect a certain parochial suspicion of strangers and outsiders, especially if they happen to be officials.

The 'gassing' by the plane of the crop, the old woman, the 300 chickens and the three dogs, seems to have developed since Tha arrived in Ban Vinai and heard other gas stories there. As he did not describe the gas to me, it is clear that he had since connected the presence of a plane with the death of the rice crop and the death of the old woman. The figure of 300 chickens would appear to have been added for dramatic effect; and the three dogs . . . ?

There is nothing in this account to suggest that the Pathet Lao had any motive for dropping gas or defoliants on this village. What we seem to be dealing with is a rather garbled version of the gas report, picked up in the camp by a Hmong tribesman to explain two successive years of crop failure.

As we can see in the case of Cha Teng Tha ordinary peasant accounts of gassing are much less coherent (certainly at one level) than that of a veteran like Ger. This contrast can also be seen in the following accounts given by Hmong who had arrived in Ban Vinai only a few weeks before my arrival there. I had obtained their names from aid-workers and, as I said before, presented them to Choumoulee who did not know these people because they were such new arrivals in the camp. He took the list and told me to return the next morning.

When I arrived I found Choumoulee speaking with a young man, twenty-seven-year-old Chong Her Chung, who claimed his little boy had been gassed. I had seen this man and his son at the hospital the day before. The doctor who looked at the child said there was no physical evidence of gassing. But he was on my list and I wanted to talk to him anyway.

Chong Her Chung had moved from his village, Tu Lak, Luang Prabang Province, in 1975 to stay with relatives at Muang Cha, just south of Phu Bia. His relatives were farmers, and he stayed at Muang Cha for the next six years. In the US evidence Muang Cha is often cited as a place where gas attacks occurred. If they did, Chong Her Chung, oddly enough, did not witness them.

In early 1981 he and his wife and child and six other families left Muang Cha to go to Ban Don, an area containing many Hmong resettlement villages. It appears that they had decided to go to Thailand but were unsure about how to get there, and they were hoping to get advice and directions once they reached Ban Don. It took them two months to walk there because they had to forage for food as they went, and by the time they reached Ban Don they were extremely hungry and his baby had diarrhoea. However, they had not been harassed in any way on their trek. At Ban Don they tried to get some food from a village, but this led to their discovery by Pathet Lao soldiers who took them into Ban Don. They fed them and made them attend a seminar for a month where they told the Hmong that they should 'forget about Chao Fa', settle in the villages of their native homeland Laos, act peaceably and all would be well. However, Chong said, their relatives had already gone to Thailand and so they decided to continue on their way. The journey took them another fifteen days, in which time they saw no soldiers and had no trouble.

When did the gassing occur? He said at Ban Don, when he was working in the fields with relatives. 'Everybody' in Ban Don became sick, including the Pathet Lao, and that is how they knew they were gassed. I asked about the colour of the gas which he said fell like a 'rainshower'; red and yellow, but when it landed on your skin it was brown like red and yellow mixed. He, it seems, was unaffected by it while his little boy had diarrhoea (which as we have seen he already had before they arrived at Ban Don). I enquired about deaths; two men and three babies. And, were they buried? Yes, after a full week-long traditional ceremony.

What is clear from this account is that Chong Her Chung and his family had been subject to no violence or harassment by the Pathet

Lao at any time. Neither during his six years at Muang Cha, nor when he was taken to the 'seminar' at Ban Don, nor at any time on the trek óut. As we shall see, stories of gas are current on the Vientiane Plain, and appear to be operating as a general explanation for illness. Just when Chong decided that gas had affected his son is not clear but there is really very little in his story which suggests that this was the case. It must be asked what sense it makes for the Pathet Lao to spend one month asking the Hmong to settle down in Laos, then to rain gas on them, and also, apparently, on themselves?

I received a similar account from a sixty-year-old woman, Xia Moua, who had arrived very recently in Ban Vinai accompanied by her twenty-three-year-old son, Xor Yang. Choumoulee was unable to locate her and after some coaxing I persuaded my interpreter to help me track her down. In fact she was such a recent arrival that even her neighbours in the camp did not know where she lived; we were sent on a wild goose chase across the camp before we eventually found her.

Xia Moua was born at Nong Het, a large Hmong settlement near the Vietnamese border. The fighting on the Plain of Jars in the 1960s had forced her to flee to Xieng Khouang township and then to Long Cheng. Her husband, never a soldier, had died in 1977 from fever and pneumonia. Xor Yang cut in to say that they never became soldiers because they were used to working in the fields and were afraid. They stayed in their village near Long Cheng after it fell to the Pathet Lao but fighting nearby in late 1976 made them decide to move. They moved frequently over the next two years and had a very difficult time due to malnutrition and sicknesses, such as bad colds, boils, stomach aches, diarrhoea and malaria. It was during this period that her husband died. They then settled for three years in a village at the foot of Phu Bia. At the end of this time they said the ground was exhausted and they had no food to eat. Some of their relatives had left for Thailand in 1975, so they decided they would now try to go there.

They first travelled to Muang Om where they stayed for five months, and then travelled on to Ban Don where they were caught by the Pathet Lao. Xor Yang was taken to a seminar for twenty days while Xia Moua, considered too old, stayed with relatives.

Xor Yang said he did not understand very much of what the Pathet Lao told him, but they did say that he should not stay in the forest, and should settle down in a village in Laos. They told the Pathet Lao that they agreed, but had privately decided to travel on to Thailand anyway to join their relatives. It took them only fifteen days to walk there, and as on their trek to Ban Don they had no trouble from soldiers.

But just outside of Ban Don she got diarrhoea, a bad cold, fever, and began vomiting. She said this was caused by gas. How did she know it was gas? She did not know, and it was only because others said her illness was caused by gas that she knew what it was. Moreover, she was the only one in the group of travellers who was affected. How did the gas get there? She did not know, but there were no planes. Xor Yang cut in to say that he knew there was gas around because he hung his shirt outside one day and when he put it on again he noticed yellow spots on it. Somebody had told him this was gas, he said.

Xia Moua was obviously puzzled by all this concern with detail and when I asked her how she knew her condition was not caused by bad food or water, she said she really did not know what caused her sickness; all she knew was that she was sick. I concluded the interview by thanking her for being so patient, whereupon she volunteered the information that when she had been placed in a holding centre on her arrival in Thailand two American journalists had visited her and asked if she had been gassed. She had replied, 'yes'. She said she had been afraid to do otherwise.

This story brings out very clearly the simple and direct correlation in an ordinary Hmong's perception between 'gas' and illness. If told that gas is what has caused their diarrhoea, or anything else, then it is accepted. Presumably because she had not been in the camp very long, nor obviously had much contact with her camp neighbours, she had not noticed that planes were an important ingredient in a gas story. Indeed there is nothing in her account that could realistically be said to resemble an attack by lethal chemical weapons. Her own and her son's tale in fact document the Pathet Lao's relatively careful handling of migrating Hmong.

I also chose to speak to some recent arrivals who did *not* claim that they had been gassed. The most interesting was Thao Pao

Yang, a man in his late twenties who had arrived from Xieng Khouang only a month earlier. He was an educated Hmong who had gone to college in Vientiane until 1976; he was very articulate about his reasons for leaving Laos. He said the industrialized west was rich, Laos was poor and so he wanted to go to France. We soon discovered that we had both recently been to one of the villages where ex-Vang Pao troopers had settled in the hills around the Plain of Jars, Bank Nok. He had been there during the Hmong New Year in November 1981. I was there in February 1982. He confirmed the basic picture I had gleaned of these villages, and having discovered that I knew the area he spoke very frankly and openly to me.

After leaving college in Vientiane in 1976 he returned to Muong Om where he said Chao Fa soldiers came to the village and forced the people there to join them. For a little over two years he was compelled to fight with them in the area around Pha Mou, to the north of Muong Om. During some fighting in early 1979 he and his family managed to escape down onto the Plain to 'stay with the Vietnamese' at Muong Su. Yong Yia, the provincial governor, came down to them and took Thao Pao Yang and his family and other Hmong families back to Phonesavan. I asked him what he thought of Yong Yia. He said he liked him very much 'because he is the chief Hmong in the Lao Patriotic Front and because he works for the people'. What about Faydang and Niavu Lobliayoa, two of the most prominent Hmong in the communist government? He said he liked them too; they were Hmong.

From Phonesavane he was sent to Nong Het where he was put to work constructing storehouses and domestic buildings. He stayed for some months, returning to an area north of Phonesavan for nine months' agricultural work, then returning to Nong Het to begin normal rice cultivation. In all, this man travelled extensively through the Xieng Khouang area, both in the Chao Fa and afterwards. I asked if he had heard about gas or been attacked with it. He had never been attacked with it and had only heard about it once, in Phonesavan in 1980, before coming to Thailand. He emphasized that he had only heard about it and did not know if it existed or if the story was true.

Thao Pao Yang, like most other Hmong in Ban Vinai, spoke

always of 'the Vietnamese'. This usually denoted Pathet Lao soldiers. Thao Pao Yang said that this was because 'for the Hmong',
all Communists are Vietnamese. Does that mean Yong Yia is a
Vietnamese, I asked. He laughed good-naturedly at the illogical-
ity, and replied no, Yong Yia was Hmong. In this respect the
Hmong are probably only marginally more dogmatic than other
ethnic groups in Asia, with nationality overriding ideology. However, the blanket term 'Vietnamese' has always performed an
important function for the old CIA Hmong because it has helped to
obscure the fact that their Hmong were fighting against other Lao
and in particular other Hmong.

I also spoke with another young Hmong who had studied in
Vientiane in 1972–74. He returned to the Phu Bia area in late
1974 to be with his wife, parents and relatives. Because his father
worked for the Americans the family fled into the 'forest' in 1975;
they were afraid that 'the Vietnamese' would take away his father,
or kill him. They spent three years living in a remote forest hamlet
near Phu Bia, by which time he said they ran out of food. They had
to shift and decided to leave for Thailand in 1979. While this
young man did not want to leave Laos his father was still afraid of
being caught, so he left because 'relatives should all go together'.
Now this man spoke seriously about the possibility of returning to
Laos with the UNHCR.

Like Xia Moua and her son, and Chong Her Chung, he and his
relatives travelled down through the areas which according to
some reports are being devastated by chemical warfare. From
Muong Cha to Muong Om, they then got lost around Phu Kao just
north of Vientiane, and finally crossed the Mekong east of Nong
Khai. It was not until he reached Thailand in late 1979 that he first
heard that people had had trouble with gas and fighting in the Phu
Bia and Muong Om areas. His family group's only problems had
been food shortages and malaria on the way out.

Thus we can see that there is a dramatic difference between the
tales told by Hmong closely connected with the ex-CIA leadership
and those told by ordinary Hmong. These people left Laos because
of poverty and illness, and to join relatives already in Thailand.
There is no sign of Pathet Lao mistreatment of them, and the way
they tell their gassing stories indicates that many Hmong are

ascribing natural calamities and health problems to an ill-defined idea of gas.

A Lao Pilot Tells All

The 'Key Judgements' contained in the 1982 Haig *Report to Congress* were supposedly also based on the 'testimony of those who were engaged in chemical warfare or were in a position to observe those who did'. While in Xieng Khouang Province, Laos, I tried to investigate the story of an American-trained Lao pilot, Touy Mannikham, whose account Haig's *Report* called 'one of the most complete descriptions of chemical warfare activities in the 1976–78 period' in Laos. I was particularly interested in Touy's story because it had been featured in a mid-January issue of the *Far Eastern Economic Review*, just before I went to Laos, and therefore it was a good opportunity to try to double-check it.

The *FEER* article said that 'American officials who spent the most time with him were impressed with the consistency of detailed technical specifications, descriptions, names, places and his personal observations'.[25] One is less impressed, however, with the various printed versions of Touy's story. The first is found in the 1980 *Compendium*.[26] This version was reprinted in full, as Annex A of Haig's *Report to Congress*, with one significant alteration. This alteration gave Touy's missions in Laos a formal status by saying they were carried out as part of an operation 'called Extinct Destruction Operations'. No explanation is given for this alteration, which obviously adds weight to allegations about 'genocide'.

The account carried in the Haig *Report* says that Touy flew rocket strikes from late 1976 onwards from airfields at both Long Cheng and Phonesavane, the provincial capital of Xieng Khouang. In late 1976, he claims, they began using rockets which were different from US-manufactured rockets. 'As part of his routine flight activities, the pilot (Touy) would check his aircraft and, in doing so, examine the tip portion of new smoke rockets that had been transported from Phonesavane. He said that most appeared "loose" in the portion where the tip and canister joined, whereas the tip and canister of the ordinary explosive-type rockets at Long Tieng (Long Cheng) were noticeably more tightly connected.'[27] He claimed he was supervised on 'gassing' missions by either a 'Lao staff officer' or 'Vietnamese army staff officers'.

The other versions of Touy's story are the one contained in the March 1981 *Update*[28] and the *FEER* article already referred to. It is puzzling why the elements contained in the *Update* were not incorporated into Haig's *Annex*. After all the Secretary of State reassured readers that all the information in his *Report* 'was reviewed, recorded and tabulated . . . [and] screened for possible duplication'.[29] We have already noted the sloppiness of the US research procedure, and the absence of the *Update* material can only increase our scepticism about Haig's reassurances.

The first thing that must be noted about Touy's testimony is that he does not know if he fired rockets containing 'poison gas'. In the first version the rockets are consistently referred to as 'smoke rockets', and in the later *Update* as ' "coloured smoke" which he *now believes may have been* poison gas.' [My emphasis.] In other words his knowledge is retrospective. Touy contradicts this, however, in the *FEER* article where the author of the article claims that Touy could not at first admit to having consciously dropped chemical weapons because he would have been condemning himself out of his own mouth, thereby jeopardizing his chances of re-settlement in the United States. As it turned out he was rejected by the US for re-settlement because of 'collaboration' with the Communists, and therefore he told all to the *FEER* before leaving for New Zealand in late 1981. He said, 'Yes, by the end of my flying I knew it was gas. There was no other answer to the strange things I saw and heard. But as soon as I found out for sure, I stopped flying for them and refused to teach others.' That was in late 1978. Unfortunately the *Review* failed to ask him how he found out 'for sure', and we are left with basically the same evidence as he had offered on earlier occasions. The major puzzle about this important addition to his story is why the Pathet Lao did not shoot or imprison him when he refused to carry out his duties. If Touy's story is true, he had stumbled upon top secret information, and furthermore he had indicated to the Pathet Lao that he was not a reliable guardian of it. In any army this would be a cause for imprisonment. In an army supposedly carrying out violations of international treaties and committing mass murder a death sentence for such a breach of security and discipline would be axiomatic. Yet Touy was allowed to go about his normal life and finally cross to Thailand one year later. Such a scenario seems quite incredible.

Alongside the abence from Touy's account – as presented in the Haig *Report* – of his August 1980 *Update*, it is also perplexing why Haig's paper did not incorporate the later alteration in Touy's story as well as a number of minor additions contained in the *Review* article. Does it mean the State Department does not give them any credence? Perhaps. But I would suggest that the US had to make a calculated trade-off as to which story by Touy they would use. One of the complications with Touy's later stories is that they do not mention rocket attacks on a Hmong position at Bouamlong in 1976. The earlier story which mentions Bouamlong allows the US to claim that they can crossreference Touy's stories with an account by a village chief interviewed by the US who had described attacks over seven days at Bouamlong in June 1976. However, the only published US-collected story from Bouamlong is a report from August 1978. Touy's later stories say that he 'now believes' he could have been involved in attacks using gas rockets from 1977 onwards.

Presumably Haig did not incorporate Touy's *Update* in August 1980 because it contradicts the US claim that chemical warfare in Laos is being conducted under 'Soviet supervision'. In the *Update* Touy said: 'he knew of no direct Soviet involvement in handling of the "coloured smoke" rockets. He did observe that there were approximately fifty Soviets at Phonesavane at all times. They wore civilian dress. He did not know what function they performed.'

But in this respect another disquieting fact is that the 1980 *Compendium* contains a report from an 'LPDR pilot' who said: 'The LPLA unit is responsible for the chemical warfare rockets in a special LPDR Air Force unit to which is attached a Soviet expert. In Vientiane there are three persons, led by a Socialist Republic of Vietnam expert, who are responsible for putting the chemicals into the heads of the US-manufactured 2.75 rockets. At Phonesavane, Xieng Khouang Province, there are two persons responsible for this activity along with four Soviet experts.'[30] Haig's *Report* contains no reference to this story, which if true certainly incriminates both Soviets and Vietnamese for involvement in chemical warfare. Why was it ignored? I suggest that if this piece of information had been used by Haig he would have had to drop Touy's statement, or explain why Touy, presumably a member of this LPDR airforce unit, knew nothing of its existence. Thus it was a trade-off between using an account by a person 'directly involved in chemical warfare', and that by an unidentified 'LPDR pilot'.

The really pertinent point is, however, that each story separately casts doubt on the other account, cancelling out the vital criteria for crosschecking.

The Haig *Report* says: 'A review of information back to 1975 shows L-19 and T-28 aircraft were operating from airfields in northern Laos – including one at Phonesavane, where AN2s were seen in 1978. Failure to observe chemical decontamination equipment at airfields does not rule out the presence or handling of chemical munitions. The Soviets supervise the chemical warfare activities in Laos . . .'[31] We have already seen that Touy's statements contradict this latter claim about the Soviets. The reference to the old Soviet AN-2 biplane is supposed to be significant because these are apparently used as cropdusters in the USSR – the implication being that they could be used to disseminate gas. In Laos they are used as passenger planes, and I flew to Phonesavane in one. Their presence at the airfield, or any other airfield, is hardly proof that chemical warfare is being waged. Despite what the Haig *Report* says, the absence of decontamination equipment is a serious weakness in the US case. Touy does speak of some medical checkups after combat missions, which he says were more frequent in 1978. But these checks, as he described them, were very casual and quite inadequate for measuring the effects of gas. However, a much more plausible and simple explanation for these check-ups is perhaps that Touy was hoping to be upgraded to flying the new MIG-21 jets given to Laos by the Soviets in 1977. He said to the *Review* that he stopped flying in September 1978; if compared with his earlier account that 'in October 1978, the Lao Army stopped using L-19 aircraft on combat missions and started using Soviet MIG-21s', this suggests that he was passed over for promo-

tion into the Lao airforce elite – presumably because of his past –
and that he left for Thailand in a fit of pique.

Touy spent a remarkably short time in political re-education,
compared with other RLG pilots, before he was allowed to go back
to his old job. He was apparently able to convince his Pathet Lao
instructors that he had made a complete conversion to the cause of
the revolution. It is perhaps pardonable if we speculate that he
would have told Americans what they wanted to hear once he was
in Thailand. There is no doubt that he was in a particularly invidi-
ous position once he had defected from Laos, for with that move
he had effectively double-crossed everyone as he zig-zagged from
one lot of patrons to another. It is certainly plausible that he saw a
gassing story as the capital he needed to absolve himself from his
'collaboration', and once committed to it found himself unable to
retract. In these respects there is a remarkable parallel between
Touy's account of 'gas warfare' in Laos and those given by US
airmen about 'germ warfare' in Korea in 1952. This may seem
remote from our present concerns but it is instructive to look at
least at one example of the testimonies given by the US airmen in
Korea. US pilot John Quinn was captured by the North Koreans in
January 1952 and gave a long statement about his involvement
with 'germ warfare' for the US. After speaking at length about the
training he had been given for this sort of warfare he went on:

'Rogers, Sayer and myself met in group operations at five
minutes after one and I went into the little room where the alert
operations officer stayed at night. Capt. Reynolds was on duty. I
gave him our names and he told me that I had a special mission.
He said that before I did anything else I was to drop my wing
bombs as close to Pyongyang as I dared to get . . . He said that I
should drop the bombs from 200 feet or lower if possible and for
me not to worry about them exploding that they would be duds.
I asked him what it was all about, remembering the lecture we
had been given on germ bombs, but he said he did not know and
it would be best just to do as instructed and not worry about why
or what. I thought it was germ bombs.

When we went out to the airplane we were met by a guard and
then I was sure they were germ bombs. He said not to worry

about the wing bombs, they had already been taken care of. But I looked up at them when I was inspecting the airplane and noted that what the navigators said, 'the wing bombs do not have any fuses', was correct. We both looked at each other and I said orders are orders and we left it at that. I told him where we were to drop them and he marked it on his map . . . I dropped the four wing bombs, one at a time in rapid succession. They were duds. We both knew then for sure they were germ bombs.'[32]

Many left-wing writers have been impressed by the 'wealth of detail' given by these US flyers and have been prepared to make a circumstantial case that the Americans were indeed conducting germ warfare in Korea. In the recent allegations, many commentators have also been impressed by the 'detail' in Touy's account and see it as part of a circumstantial case against the Lao, Vietnamese and the Soviets. We shall return to more general parallels with the Korean accusations in the concluding section of this book, but we should note for the moment that no firm evidence was produced to substantiate the germ warfare charges against the US. However, the specific parallels between Touy's and Quinn's testimonies are quite striking. In both cases their knowledge of what they were supposedly doing is retrospective. In other words, at the time neither of them was really sure if they had been involved in chemical warfare or not. Both were prepared to provide sinister reinterpretations of the activities of superior officers who did not fully brief them on what they were doing. And just as Touy in his testimony tried to give it credibility by making observations about differently shaped and loose rocket-heads, Quinn made similar dubious points of detail about bombs without fuses.

The US airmen did not give this testimony under threat of physical torture, though there was considerable psychological pressure on them at the time. As prisoners-of-war their position does not exactly parallel that of Touy, but the latter was stateless, and having double-crossed everyone he would have had the fear of repatriation to an unpleasant future in Laos hanging over his head.

Finally, we must emphasize that Touy's story is not supported by clear evidence. His various accounts are inconsistent, and at vital points incredible.

Kampuchean Claims

We have already noted in Chapter Two that the first reports of the use of chemical warfare in Kampuchea by the Vietnamese came from the propaganda department of the Pol Pot regime, as border fighting between Vietnam and Kampuchea escalated into a full-scale war. Coincidentally, perhaps, these charges were preceded by widespread publicity in the Thai and international press about alleged use of gas against the Hmong in Laos. Obviously the Phnom Penh leaders saw advantages in the story for their discredited and doomed regime. The weakest aspect of the Democratic Kampuchea claims was the fact that throughout the second half of 1977 there had been fierce fighting between themselves and the Vietnamese along the border, and a major Vietnamese thrust into Kampuchea in December. Yet there were no reports of the use of gas, which is especially puzzling when one remembers that the Vietnamese had supposedly been making extensive use of gas in Laos since 1976. Why weren't the Vietnamese using gas in their far more serious war against Pol Pot forces at the time, or even in the first ten months of 1978 after negotiations had completely broken down between the two countries?

Besides the general untrustworthiness of the statements by the Pol Pot regime, its failure to report chemical warfare until it had been able to hear or read about it in the international press makes its claims extremely suspect, and the charges from Kampuchea do not deserve the same attention as those of the Hmong refugees.

The Haig *Report* is sensitive to international scepticism about claims made by the Khmers Rouges. It says: 'There were early indications that Pol Pot's Democratic Kampuchean resistance did engage in an organized propaganda campaign on chemical-agent use. These indications made the US Government analysts cautious about accepting Democratic Kampuchea allegations, which increased markedly after the chemical attacks in Laos were publicized. For Kampuchea, therefore, special efforts were taken to confirm such allegations by analysing sources of information that in no way could be considered part of a propaganda or deception campaign.'[33] Just how Khmers Rouges propaganda transformed itself into reliable information is not specified, nor is it specified when it so transformed itself, nor are we given the details of the alleged 'special efforts' that were taken to check the veracity of the Pol Pot propaganda. The wording of the Haig *Report* is in fact deceptive. The Pol Pot 'gassing' propaganda did not 'increase markedly' after the reports from Laos received publicity; the historical record shows that it *began* after the Lao reports were widely publicized.

No medical personnel working in the refugee camps along the Thai-Kampuchean border, some of whom work in camps situated inside Kampuchea, have picked up any hard evidence of chemical warfare. Like their counterparts on the Lao border, some believe it is happening. In other words the chemical warfare stories from Kampuchea also rely heavily on eye-witnesses. These accounts, however, are even more suspect than those from Lao-Hmong refugees, coming as they do from the rigidly centralized and ruthless Khmers Rouges military apparatus which is able to lay down and enforce a line on 'gassing'. By and large they are not in refugee camps run by another government or supervised by an international organization. The stories come from the Pol Pot military structure, which has a clear-cut motive for lying. In the absence of any concrete evidence there is no reason to place any faith in such stories told by such an organization, and Mr. Haig has not supplied us with one.

In an obvious effort to show that the support for the 'gassing' stories is broader, the Haig report claims that the largest non-communist Khmer resistance group (between 3,000 and 5,000 strong), the Khmer People's National Liberation Front (KPNLF), had said their forces had been attacked by a form of tear gas in November 1979. However, General Dien Del, the most important KPNLF commander, told reporters in September 1981 that his forces 'had never been attacked with chemical weapons'.[34]

The 'resistance' groups gathered on the Thai-Kampuchean border are recognized by all serious researchers, and by most aid workers, as a mixture of potential warlords and bandits who have spent almost as much time fighting each other for control of the black market and aid supplies as they have fighting the Vietnamese army. It is an environment full of treachery and dishonesty, in which the Thai army participates enthusiastically. It was only after the Vietnamese offensive in the 1981–82 dry season that these groups attempted to bury their differences and form a united front. The unification achieved in June, however, remains only a paper creation for the purposes of winning international diplomatic and military support. The 20,000–30,000-strong Khmers Rouges military apparatus is still fully intact and under the control of Pol Pot himself. The coalition-in-exile may provide a wider base for the chemical warfare allegations, but this will not make them any more convincing than when they originated from the Khmers Rouges apparatus, especially if those who previously denied being subjected to gas attacks now claim in unison with the Khmers Rouges that they were.

Vietnamese Defectors

The Haig *Report* contains the testimony of a Vietnamese army private who defected to Thailand, and says he witnessed Russians actively engaged in chemical warfare operations in Kampuchea. This assertion is particularly striking because the US also had the testimony of Captain Nguyen Quan, another deserter, who said that his unit had been involved in firing gas shells. The testimony of Quan is as impressive as the private's, yet Haig chose to pass over it in silence. In the 1980 *Compendium* Quan had said 'he did not know . . . if any of the types of gas used by the Vietnamese army were fatal.'[35] Quan had also told reporters that the Soviets only gave military and political advice, 'but did not participate in the fighting'.[36] Haig presumably ignored Quan because what he said tended to contradict Do Hung Son's claims about Soviet involvement and the lethal nature of the gas. Quan seems to have been describing the use of smoke shells or tear gas; without corroborating evidence we cannot be certain.

In July 1982 Quan presented an account of Vietnamese chemical warfare to Lt. Col. Denny Lane of the US Embassy in Bangkok and to Dr. Amos Townsend, a former US airforce colonel who had seen active service in Vietnam. Townsend has been working in Thailand for the International Rescue Committee since 1980 and has since become one of the principal compilers of 'yellow rain' evidence for the US.* Quan's July 1982 account shows much greater superficial familiarity with alleged Vietnamese use of chemical weapons than was demonstrated in his 1980 testimony, but it is also studded with bizarre claims such as the following one concerning Vietnamese chemical warfare training: 'there is a film titled "Truth Concerning the Soviet–Chinese Border". The film says that the Chinese military used more than twenty divisions to attack thirty km. into Russian territory around 1963–64. The Soviets used chemical weapons to poison the Chinese forces. While they were unconscious, they took all their weapons and gave each person a piece of bread and one sausage.'[37]

Despite such fantastic tales, Townsend responded to Quan's account in the most extraordinarily naive and uncritical fashion. Rather than being alerted to the possibility that Quan may have been spinning him a line, Townsend produced a series of technical questions for Quan, which he dutifully answered in a subsequent communication. The content of this exchange is too lengthy to reproduce here, but it is instructive because it demonstrates once again the methodology used by proponents of the 'yellow rain' story when gathering information. They assume chemical warfare is happening and produce questionnaires that not only reinforce this belief but, in the case of Townsend's, actually provide the raw material for the subsequent answer. We have already noted the unsatisfactory nature of this approach.

Had Quan's 1982 testimony been the only one he provided it would, perhaps, look plausible despite various bizarre stories within it. Quan ranges over the supposed history of chemical weapons use by the Vietnamese and Soviets, the production of chemical weapons, training in their use, their employment in Laos, and so on. Indeed, for an ordinary artillery officer, Quan appears to be remarkably well-informed on all matters relating to chemical weapons. On inspection, however, little in the testimony can be verified.

*There is considerable suspicion concerning Townsend's exact allegiances (some of which stems from the fact that he formerly worked with the US chemical warfare establishment at Fort Detrick in the USA). According to journalist Frances Starner, Townsend admitted to a meeting of refugee workers in Bangkok in September 1982 that he was working for the US embassy on loan from the IRC. This was subsequently denied by the embassy, however.

His 1980 account shows no such erudition. Indeed, the *Compendium* reports that Quan 'was unable to give precise details of the deployment by the Vietnamese Army of fatal gases'. In contrast, his 1982 accounts are replete with such detail. What, we may ask, has happened in the interim?

Quan himself provides a part of the answer in a remarkable and pathetic personal plea addressed to Townsend on 11 September 1982. In it Quan describes what happened following his defection in January 1980:

'Thai officers took my wife and me to Aranyaprathet, to meet another Thai officer, an American and an interpreter . . . After two months of work and providing information, they took me to Bangkok for twenty-two days, to re-check and confirm my story five times. After trusting me, according to the interpreter and the American, they said they would like me to work for them for a while. I then said that my hope in coming here was to be able to emigrate to a third country. Consequently they promised that my family and I would be allowed to go to the US if I worked with them . . . On 31 October 1981, I was called to the US INS to complete the necessary forms for my prospective emigration . . . On 28 October 1981, I received a rejection notice . . . I still don't understand why the US has not kept its promise with regard to my emigration . . . Later, on 23 February 1982, my petition for Canada was approved . . . Unfortunately, on 10 May 1982 I again received a refusal notice from the Canadian Embassy. Confused and sad, I asked the Canadian Embassy once concerning my case and was told their refusal was based on the advice of the US . . . Dear Dr. Townsend, I still wonder, why did the Americans I worked with promise something they couldn't deliver? . . . Although my contribution to the Free World in my work since coming to Thailand was to have been in exchange for freedom and re-settlement, I have received nothing in return. Therefore, from now on I prefer not to talk about the Chemical Warfare subject any longer.'[38]

Reading this one cannot help feeling a certain sympathy for Quan. He had delivered the goods on chemical warfare to the US and then was double-crossed. It is also evident that during this period he had absorbed much of the information circulating in Thailand about 'yellow rain' and thus progressively elaborated on his earlier account in the hope that this would further ingratiate him with his new masters and ensure a quick exit to the US for him and his family. Much like the Lao pilot Touy Mannikham, it appears Quan did not realize until too late that the more he said about chemical warfare in Kampuchea, the more it jeopardized his chances of going to the US because it would look too much like what poor Quan expected it to be, a pay-off. This probably applies to Canada as well because the latter, since 1981, has participated in the 'yellow rain' debate in support of the US.

In his letter Quan tries to present his defection in political terms, but the real reason emerges as personal. In his 1980 account Quan had spoken of his family in Hanoi. However, his letter reveals that his current wife is Khmer, which leads one to the conclusion that Quan did what is forbidden to Vietnamese troops in Kampuchea: he fell in love with a local woman and therefore had to flee to Thailand with her. Quan candidly reveals that some of his Vietnamese colleagues 'thought I left for love', and despite his protestations, it is likely to be true because it would have been impossible for him to stay. (What is unusual is that he even discussed his plans to leave with fellow officers.)

I mention these personal matters only to highlight the motivations behind Quan's actions. From the personal perspective of a man desperately wanting to emigrate with his family, his motives for telling a chemical warfare story are perfectly understandable, perhaps even honourable. However, from our point of view, Quan's evidence for lethal gas warfare in Kampuchea has shown itself to be unreliable and probably a total fabrication. Indeed, in October 1982 Dr. Townsend was forced to disclaim some of Quan's testimony:

'It is with no little chagrin that I must now specifically warn those of you who have received the subject material that I have been informed through intermediaries that Nguyen Quan has recently admitted to them that at least some of the material that he provided us was "fabricated". I regret to admit even more than the above statement that I do not yet know which information by Quan is truth and which is fiction . . . It remains my current impression, shared with others, that Quan has provided some useful information . . . As have most physicians I would expect, I have found a degree of historical fabrication by omission or commission to be one of the most common characteristics of patients worldwide. [Interestingly, Quan is now treated as a 'patient'.] Where the stress, real or imagined, is greater, the tendency to fabricate is greater, particularly among the more sophisticated. Few humans are more stressed than refugees. Therefore it would seem most inappropriate for the medically-socially concerned to be either surprised, or overtly indignant, when confronted with a fabrication, particularly one born of fear, frustration and confusion.'[39]

What is surprising about Townsend's admission is that it has taken him so long to discover the extremely problematic nature of refugee stories. Furthermore, this reluctant acknowledgement of the problem by one of the key figures in the 'yellow rain' debate casts further doubt over the refugee testimony gathered by the US and others, particularly accounts given by defectors. How Townsend aims to resolve the problem remains unclear.

There have been other reports from Vietnamese army defectors since the Haig *Report*. In May the *International Herald Tribune* carried the following accounts:

'One of the defectors, Nguyen Van Kich, a twenty-five-year-old radio operator from a village north of Hanoi, said he had often relayed orders to reconnaissance battalions to use "poison powder" against Khmer Rouge guerrillas. He said . . . Vietnamese troops dumped the white powder into streams and ponds from which the Khmer Rouge guerrillas obtained drinking water. . . . "A lot of people said the poison powder is made in the Soviet Union," he said. He said packages containing it were marked in a foreign language. Another defector . . . said that the words on the 500-gram packages were Russian but that he did not know what they meant. . . . Nguyen Van Kich said that Vietnamese troops were sometimes given small vials of a liquid to drink in the event of chemical exposure if they were going to be "in a dangerous place". Tran Van Dung, twenty-one, from Ho Chi

Minh City, said soldiers were given a capsule about two centi-
metres long with Chinese letters on it. If the soldiers smelled
poison gas, he said, they were to break the capsule, sniff the
contents and run away from the area.'[40]

Some defectors claimed that artillery rounds had been used to
deliver gas but none said they were directly involved.

One of the first things we should note about these defectors'
stories is the accounts of the supposed 'antidotes'. The most obvious anomaly, especially given that the Vietnamese are supposed to
be deploying Soviet chemical weapons, is that one of the 'antidotes' is Chinese. Second, the descriptions of the 'antidotes' do not
correspond to medical kits issued by the Soviets to counteract the
effects of chemical weapons. Third, the sniffing or drinking of vials
is an improbable defence against the effects of nerve gas. What
about the white sacks of powder? The KPNLF also reportedly
sighted Vietnamese trucks in November 1981 carrying 'liquid and
powdered chemicals' towards combat zones near the border with
Thailand. This is in some ways a separate issue from the main
allegations, for no one has claimed that this powder is being loaded
into munitions or sprayed from planes. However, both the defectors and the Thai military are claiming that the Vietnamese are
poisoning water sources. This may be true, but there is quite simply not enough information in the Thai claims to assess them. This
issue should not be conflated with the charge that new and lethal
agents of chemical warfare are in use. The mere sighting of bags of
what are assumed to be chemicals is not nearly enough, in any
case, to prove chemical warfare, nor is the spraying of ponds. We
do know that malaria is a serious problem for Vietnamese troops
in Kampuchea and we can just as easily speculate that these bags
of powder are DDT for anti-malarial purposes.

The more solid accounts provided by defectors may point
toward Vietnamese use of tear gas. However, even these would
require independent corroboration and some physical evidence.
Finally, I think we must stress that the testimony of defectors is not
strong evidence. The life of a Vietnamese soldier is worth very

little on the Thai-Kampuchean border, and it is likely that deserters will tell a suitable story in an attempt to ensure their survival.

After this survey of refugee evidence a coda is in order. Psychological studies related to practices in the legal system have shown that people display a disproportionate faith in the testimony of eyewitnesses. Faced with strong countervailing evidence in the form of alibis or even the discrediting of the eyewitness, they are still likely to support the view of the supposed eyewitness. This propensity no doubt accounts for the largely uncritical reception of the stories by alleged victims of 'yellow rain'. It also suggests that much of the argument in this chapter will encounter considerable psychological resistance from readers.

The UN reports by the Group of Experts have done little to dispel this spontaneous tendency to believe eyewitnesses. The 1981 report wrote: 'The Group did not find any reason to doubt the integrity of those who reported on the chemical attacks,' adding rather weakly that 'on the other hand, it could not overlook the fact that it was difficult to determine the objectivity of alleged victims or witnesses.'[42] The 1982 UN report re-iterated this statement, though this time the Group did note the problems associated with hearsay accounts and testimony given by defectors. As physical scientists, perhaps they felt uneasy about investigating this issue, but all the same one would expect them to note that studies have shown eyewitness reporting to be notoriously unreliable. Such studies have indicated that even honest, unmotivated witnesses will readily introduce into their testimony things that never happened, and in the full belief that they did. Once this belief is established it is almost impossible to dislodge. Analysis has revealed that people will make up composite stories, rearrange details in response to questioning, and are dramatically influenced by news media interpretations of incidents they themselves are supposed to have witnessed. As psychologist Elizabeth Loftus observes in *Eyewitness Testimony*: 'People's memories are fragile things.'[43] These observations have been made in the relatively sophisticated West and in the relatively controlled conditions of the Western legal system. Such conditions do not exist in the refugee camps in Thailand. On the contrary, the general atmosphere is conducive to the uncontrolled propagation of 'yellow rain' stories. In contrast to the UN reports this chapter has demonstrated that there are many reasons for doubting the reliability of the refugee stories as well as the integrity of many of the refugees.

The refugee evidence produced to support charges of chemical warfare in Southeast Asia is weak on all counts. It cannot be verified in any meaningful way, and where the stories can be checked they appear – on the essential question of lethal chemical warfare – to be fabrications. Only solid physical evidence of chemical warfare would force us to reconsider this conclusion.

4
Mycotoxins and Missing Evidence

Since September 1981 the chemical warfare debate has tended to revolve around the significance of discoveries of trichothecene mycotoxins in samples from Kampuchea and Laos. Frederick Celec, the airforce officer in charge of the State Department's collection of data on 'yellow rain', says that the scientific critics of the US government evidence have been focusing too much on details in the debate.* By doing this, he says, they are missing the general pattern of chemical warfare provided by the 'victims' and by defectors.[1] The argument is a familiar one, for as we have seen, people looking at the refugee evidence also mistakenly emphasize general patterns and discourage attention to inconsistent details. We refuse to concede this methodological and procedural point to Celec, either in the refugee evidence or in the scientific evidence. Moreover, we cannot be expected to believe scientific data that is weak on crucial details on the basis of refugee evidence that is also weak on critical details. Indeed, such distorted logic points to a grave weakness in the US case.

We have already seen that at the 1979 US *Hearing* Col. Lewis concluded that riot control or irritant gases, nerve agents, and an unspecified compound, were being used in Laos. We should recall that no physical evidence was produced to support these conclusions, deduced from the refugee descriptions. More than four years later the US is still unable to produce physical evidence to prove that riot control or nerve agents have been used. In both of these cases the Americans cannot plead, as they have with respect

*Celec was replaced in June 1982.

to the more serious allegations about the use of mycotoxins, that they are not properly equipped to uncover traces of these agents. Even so, in the body of his report to Congress, Alexander Haig kept all his irons in the fire when he said that besides the deployment of mycotoxins 'medical symptoms indicate that irritants, incapacitants, and nerve agents have also been employed'[2] in Laos. Yet he also says: 'Samples have been collected from Southeast Asia since mid-1979 and from Afghanistan since mid-1980. To date, about fifty individual samples – of greatly varying types and usefulness for analytic purposes – have been collected and analysed for the presence of known chemical warfare agents, none of which has been detected.'[3] In other words the US allegations in respect of nerve agents, mustard gas and riot control agents still rest on American Government interpretations of the refugee testimony we have already examined. The only physical evidence is negative.

By late 1981 the US claimed that it could specify the initially 'unidentified combination or compound' that Colonel Lewis and his team had assumed was being used. On 13 September 1981, during a trip to West Germany for arms talks, Alexander Haig announced that US scientists had identified toxins on a leaf sample from Kampuchea: 'We now have physical evidence from Southeast Asia, which has been analysed and found to contain abnormally high levels of three potent mycotoxins – poisonous substances not indigenous to the region.' American government officials were quick to point out that the evidence was only 'preliminary' and not conclusive.[4] However the 'Key Judgements' contained in Haig's March 1982 Report to Congress were quite definite: 'lethal trichothecene toxins', it said, have been used against the Hmong in Laos and against Democratic Kampuchea troops. He said that the big mystery the US had been attempting to solve since it had begun its attempts to prove that chemical warfare agents were being used in Southeast Asia was the 'exact nature of the chemical agents in use.'[5] No conventional agents could be positively identified but, he claimed, mycotoxins could be. Therefore, he said, they were the mystery agent.

The world press was horrified by the discovery of mycotoxins.

Outside a small scientific community few people had ever heard of their existence and this made the use of such agents sound even more horrendous and dastardly. *Berita Buana* in Jakarta said 'Asian peoples have been made guinea pigs . . . by the Soviet Union.' The *Nation Review* in Bangkok said that 'there was no question where the poison gas comes from . . . the Soviet Union.' And the London *Financial Times* said the use of mycotoxins was a 'disturbing new facet of the arms race'. Few of them stopped to ask some basic scientific questions about these toxins.

Mycotoxins are poisons that some species of mould fungus are capable of generating as they grow. They exist in nature in great profusion, the full extent of which has come to be recognized only recently. The varieties that scientists have studied in greatest detail are those generated by fungi that grow on food plants before or after harvesting. Mass outbreaks of acute mycotoxin poisoning among human populations are now much rarer than they once were, though the threat of mycotoxicosis remains a special problem in high-intensity livestock farming. Most of what we know today about mycotoxins of the particular type that have been implicated in the 'yellow rain' stories, the tricothecenes, comes from agricultural research in the corn belt of North America and the rice-growing regions of Japan. During the 1960s the now well-established theory was put forward that it was these same mycotoxins, or closely related ones, that had been responsible for the last really major outbreak of human mycotoxicosis: in the Soviet Union during the 1940s, when many hundreds of thousands of people had fallen victim to a Russian disease (ATA – alimentary toxic aluekia) whose causation was eventually found to lie in toxigenic fungi. Their growth on cereals had been accelerated by unusual weather conditions and the exposure of the human population to them had been increased by war-degraded agricultural practices. Some of the signs and symptoms of Soviet ATA cases reported in the medical literature resembled some of those described by the Hmong.

A central feature of the initial American claim about mycotoxins made by both Alexander Haig in September and by a State Department *Fact Sheet* around the same time was that 'these mycotoxins do not occur naturally in Southeast Asia . . . [they] are not native to warm climates.' In other words any trichothecene mycotoxins found in Southeast Asia could only have found their way into the environment by artificial means, as a chemical weapon. In their haste to accuse the Soviets, however, the Americans had not done adequate research and various experts soon pointed out to them that such sweeping statements could not be sustained and that there was no obvious reason why, if anybody actually looked for the mycotoxins there previously, they would not have found them. In climatically similar places where they have been sought, they have been found. But without missing a beat the US simply modified its claim to a formula repeated in Haig's report to Congress which says 'the particular toxins that have previously been identified are not known to occur naturally in the combinations found and at the levels detected in Southeast Asia.'[6] The argument about mycotoxins was now focused on the combinations of chemicals and levels measured in parts per million, rather than revolving around the presence or absence of naturally occurring mycotoxins in Southeast Asia. The early statement that trichothecene mycotoxins were not native to warm or tropical climates had no doubt been motivated primarily by a desire to implicate the USSR by pointing to its cold climate, because T2 is produced most efficiently at low temperatures, around 10–12 degrees C.*

Alexander Haig's statement to Congress revealed that the US had become aware of the fact that mycotoxins could occur naturally in the region, and that the discovery of small quantities of them either on leaves or in human blood (and this in a relatively small number of cases) may simply be the result of natural poisoning. Against this Haig argued: 'Surveys of the toxigenic fungi and mycotoxins naturally present in Southeast Asia conducted by the Mahidol University in Bangkok and the Massachussets Institute of Technology have not revealed the presence of T2, nivalenol, deox-

---

*Many participants in the debate appear to be ignorant of the geography of Southeast Asia. The climate is not uniformly tropical. For example, on the Plain of Jars the mean temperature for six months of the year is below 10 degrees C., and at higher altitudes, such as Phy Bia, colder still. Presumably these would be ideal temperatures for trichothecene production.

ynivalenol, or diacetoxyscirpenol, although other mycotoxins, such as aflotoxin were identified.'[7] The US is saying that the combined presence of T2 and the other chemicals at allegedly unnatural levels and unusual combinations, proves the use of trichothecenes as chemical warfare agents in Southeast Asia. Sceptical scientists, however, have argued on the basis of research done in India and elsewhere that the combinations and levels of chemicals cited by the US are neither uncommon nor unnatural.[8]

While these objections have been an important corrective to the selective presentation of the evidence by the US Government, the most important point is the fact that the published research on naturally occurring mycotoxins in Southeast Asia is minimal – and in the cases of Laos and Kampuchea almost non-existent. For the US to be able to make scientifically credible technical claims about combinations of chemicals, their levels and concentration, they must be able to indicate the body of scientific research that they are using as their benchmark. As they have never published a list of such material, I wrote to the State Department in March 1982 requesting a list of scientific articles that would indicate what their background research on this matter was. In that list there was one article on mycotoxins in Thailand, one on Southeast Asia, and well over a hundred others dealing with research in the US, Australia, Japan and the Soviet Union. (Following the initial claim in September 1981 Frederick Celec had said that a search of 3,000 literature references to mycotoxins revealed that none had been reported from Southeast Asia. From this was drawn the negative inference that mycotoxins did not occur naturally in Southeast Asia.)[9] It is, therefore, very clear that the US allegations are based on no specific research into the relevant toxins, a fact disingenuously side-stepped by Haig's references to the work done at Mahidol University and MIT, which make it look as though such research had already been done.

A much more thorough review of the Asian research has been carried out by the Canadian toxicologist H. B. Schiefer who says: 'There are no indications that Thai regulatory agencies or scientists in the universities have been looking for trichothecenes in particular, therefore one cannot say with certainty that these mycotoxins do not occur in Thailand. The same holds true with respect to the occurrence of fungi capable of producing trichothecenes, although Thai mycologists have repeatedly stated that *Fusarium spp.* are very rarely, if ever, isolated.'[10]

Schiefer himself appears personally convinced that 'something is going on' with respect to biochemical warfare in Southeast Asia, although his scientific integrity ensures that he never states this directly. Schiefer's overview of the natural occurrence of T2 mycotoxin omits papers from India dealing with the occurrence of T2 at high temperatures. He thereby perpetuates the view that the trichothecenes reported by the US flourish at low temperatures. It is only T2, not the other toxins, for which this seems true. And even T2 has been found at fairly high levels in the field and in the laboratory at higher temperatures.

Mycotoxins as a Weapon

The Americans have claimed that trichothecene mycotoxins are the main agents being used in both Laos and Kampuchea. What is puzzling, however, is why the Lao, the Vietnamese or the Soviets would be using mycotoxins rather than the lethal nerve agents that the Soviets assuredly do have in their stockpile. According to chemist Julian Perry Robinson: 'As poisons go, the trichothecenes are relatively weak. One may reckon from reported animal experiments that the median lethal dose of nivalenol or T2 (which are the most toxic of the forty-odd currently known natural trichothecenes) in man is likely to be in the range of 50–500 milligrams: similar, in other words, to that of the principal poison gases of World War I (such as phosgene, hydrogen cyanide and mustard gas) and some two orders of magnitude larger than the nerve gases. Why, with all these more readily accessible poisons available, would anyone opt for trichothecenes? What sense was there in having to use a thousand mycotoxin weapons against a target when a dozen nerve gas ones could probably kill no fewer of its inhabitants?'[11]

An American expert on mycotoxins made similar comments before the Subcommittee on Asian and Pacific Affairs in March 1982. Dr. Daniel Cullen said of the evidence presented by the US Government up to that time:

'Physical evidence presented thus far is based upon laboratory analyses of five extremely small 'yellow rain' samples and nine blood samples from survivors of chemical attacks. Significantly, microscopic and micro-biological examinations of samples were not performed, and the analyses lacked adequate control samples. In addition, the precise identity of the sample collectors remains obscure.

Results of these laboratory analyses have been widely variable with respect to the specific toxins detected and their concentrations. Zearalenone, a weakly estrogenic mycotoxin, was identified by Professor J. Rosen of Rutgers University as the predominant "toxin" in one such sample of "yellow rain". Zearalenone, which is not a trichothecene, possesses acute toxicity properties comparable to table salt. Why would a technologically advanced country, such as the Soviet Union, resort to an apparently ineffective weapon?

This heterogeneous composition of "yellow rain" samples, and the toxicity of trichothecenes seriously challenge the feasability of mycotoxins as weapons. Even if pure trichothecenes were used and appropriate formulations for their dispersal were developed, hundreds of pounds would be required to produce lethal effects within an area with a hundred-yard radius. And yet, approximately 70% of chemical attacks occurring in Laos in 1979 involved small rockets with payload capacities of one to several pounds.'[12]

It is worth noting that if hundreds of pounds were necessary, then the US should have been able to collect many more significant samples than they have in fact. Indeed 'victims' should be able to collect it by the cupful.

Extraordinarily, the Haig report admits that 'there is no clearcut explanation of why trichothecene toxins have been used. . . .' All it offers is unsubstantiated reflection: 'Speculation suggests that they are probably cheaper to make and are readily available from Soviet stocks [bearing in mind that the existence of these "stocks" is speculation as well – G.E.]; they are probably safer and more stable to store, transport, and handle in the Southeast Asian environment, and they may require less protective equipment when prepared for munitions.'[13] In other words, Haig's guess is as good as yours or mine.

Probably even more extraordinary is the US admission that it has no knowledge of how mycotoxins could be made into an effective gas form for delivery as a weapon: 'Unfortunately', the Haig document says, 'there are no reports concerning the effects of inhalation of mixtures of the compounds. Therefore, it is difficult to speculate concerning the effects that would be expected in humans exposed to an aerosol of mixtures of these potent toxins.'[14] Having displayed similar ignorance to mine on this matter, Ed McWilliams of the US Embassy in Bangkok drew the conclusion that it simply demonstrated how far in front of the US the USSR was in its development of toxin weaponry and showed the need for the US to 'catch up'. This is the logic of the arms race, not scientific logic.

Ed McWilliams claimed that the reason mycotoxins were being used in preference to nerve gases was that they were an effective 'terror weapon' to drive the Hmong out of Laos. This is echoed in the Haig report which says that they have 'the added advantage of being an effective terror weapon that causes bizarre and horrifying symptoms.'[15] The idea that they are more bizarre and horrifying than the effects of nerve gases or mustard gas, or napalm or phosphorus bombs, is itself a bizarre exercise in subjectivity. One wonders whether Alexander Haig has ever read any accounts of gassing from the First World War. Even so, there are also plenty of easily available 'non-lethal' chemical agents in the world's arsenals which would be equally effective as weapons of terror. The harassing agent diphenylcyanoarsine drove some soldiers to shoot themselves in the First World War to escape the pain it caused. A US officer described the effect of the use of tear gases against the National Liberation Front in Vietnam: 'above all the gas produces an unsurmountable desire to run.'

The United States used 'non-lethal' gases extensively in Vietnam: 'as bulk powder, as CS1, a very fine powder, and as CS2, a silicone-treated moisture-resistant powder . . . The total used for the period 1964–1969 is 13,736,000,000 lb, or over 6,000 tons. The figures for CN and DM are not published. By no stretch of the imagination can this be called riot control. The figures indicate that the gas is used on a large scale in the second and third forms. By any definition, this is chemical warfare.'[16] These agents and compounds derived from them can cause crying, nausea, vomiting, diarrhoea, severe skin blistering, and respiratory problems, all of which may persist for weeks. Their supposed non-lethal effects were shown to be illusory time and again during the Vietnam war. A Canadian doctor's detailed description of its effects bears repeating:

'Patients are feverish, semi-comatose, severely short of breath, vomit, are restless and irritable. Most of their physical signs are in the respiratory and the circulatory systems. Both lungs exhibit rales throughout, severe bronchial spasm; heart rate is usually very high, and all the patients had pulmonary edema. In most cases active treatment for pulmonary edema and complicating pneumonia was helpful and they survived. Those that survived developed a chronic bronchitic type of picture complicated by infections. The mortality rate in adults is about 10%, while the mortality rate in children is about 90%.'[17]

These are the reported effects of supposedly non-lethal gases. Yet we have no reports of comparable quality from either Laos or Kampuchea where lethal gases are allegedly being used.

The Americans laid down carpets of these gases by helicopter to flush communist troops from their bunkers and tunnels prior to a B-52 attack. In Chapter Two of this book I pointed to a number of occasions on which it was plausible that non-lethal gases had been used against the Hmong Secret Army soldiers. However, the US has been unable to find any trace of these either, and one suspects that they have not pursued this line of enquiry too rigorously for fear of calling attention to their own earlier activities, and because the Laotians could be using left-over US stocks.

The Soviet Response

Only after the US had set out its allegations at length were the Soviets in a position to respond in detail to the charges of chemical warfare. Following the delivery of Haig's *Report* in March 1982 the Soviet Government produced a *Critique* which it circulated to the UN General Assembly in May.

Interestingly the *Critique* does not deny the presence of trichothecene mycotoxins in Southeast Asia, or that the US has found them there. However, they attribute these findings to the natural occurrence of these toxins in the environment, and cite a range of western research to support their case.

The Soviet *Critique* of the US evidence makes a number of detailed criticisms of the mycotoxin findings:

'The results of analyses of samples of plant leaves and stems stated in the report raise many questions. First of all, why do different parts (fragments) of the leaf contain different quantities of mycotoxins? When contamination occurs artificially, there cannot be such great variation (by a factor of more than ten) in the contamination levels. Unequal contamination levels for different parts of the leaves are encountered only when contamination occurs naturally because the fungus population is unevenly distributed over the leaf surface.

Furthermore, the results do not indicate contamination levels in the stems. Everything seems to suggest that no mycotoxins were found there. When contamination occurs artificially, as when mycotoxins are actually sprayed by aerosol, the stem cannot remain uncontaminated if the surface of the leaves is contaminated. With certain levels of aerosol dispersal, the stem may be contaminated to an even greater degree than the leaves.

The report does not indicate the number of leaves analysed. It therefore remains unclear whether the figures given are contamination levels averaged over all the leaves or whether they relate only to the single most contaminated leaf. It may be assumed that on certain leaves no mycotoxins were found, but that fact is not mentioned, since it would contradict the assertions that the leaves were artificially contaminated.'[18]

A similar criticism is made of a water sample collected from the site of an alleged attack in Kampuchea. The *Critique* argues that if a group of people have been attacked with toxic substances it should show up in the blood of all of them. 'Therefore the fact that a metabolite of T2 toxin was discovered in the blood of only two of the nine "victims", as stated in the report, should be attributed primarily to natural intoxication.' The fact that traces of these toxins could be found in the blood long after the alleged attack, a fact that contradicts available scientific evidence, they argue, also points in the direction of natural intoxication.

The *Critique* also argues that mycotoxin would be an ineffective weapon because of its low toxicity compared with other weapons. Furthermore, it claims that it is virtually impossible to disperse them serially in dangerous concentrations. Obviously this point is contentious, but given the Soviet argument the onus is on the US to disprove it.

The *Critique* does not consider the refugee evidence in detail, and simply notes: 'if they contradict known scientific facts' then they 'cannot be taken seriously'. In other words, descriptions that do not correspond to the effects of known chemical warfare agents are ruled out. A corollary of this is that descriptions that do correspond require physical evidence to support them before they can be seriously believed. And the *Critique* notes that the US has no proof in this regard. With respect to the descriptions that the State Department *Report* proposes as symptoms of mycotoxin poisoning the *Critique* cites the opinion of Dr. D. Paterson, of the Central Veterinary Laboratory, Weybridge, England, who has done research into the effect of mycotoxins on animals: 'All of the symptoms observed by eyewitnesses were not so specific that they can be considered objective evidence. The symptoms of intoxication caused by mycotoxins vary widely, depending on the type, . . . and for that reason it is not obvious that the symptoms described could have been caused by mycotoxin poisoning.'

The Soviet response to the US charges seems generally sound and scientifically well-informed. Some critics have concentrated on the last three pages of the nineteen-page *Critique*, in which the Soviets allege that the cases of mycotoxicosis found in Southeast Asia are a result of the ecological change brought about by America's herbicide programme in Indochina prior to 1975.[19] This wild scientific speculation by the Soviets, obviously produced for propaganda purposes, mars an otherwise intelligent response to the US accusations.

The Missing Evidence

There are a number of other worrying aspects to the US allegations. Why, for instance, has the US never been able to produce an
autopsy of a dead body or substantial physical evidence if chemical
or biological warfare is proceeding on such a scale?

It is extraordinary that after four years of investigations and
allegedly thousands of deaths that the US has not been able to lay
its hands on a single cadaver. In reference to Laos the US says that
the gassing incidents have occurred too far inside Laos, and that it
has taken the victims too long to get to Thailand (six weeks to two
months is commonly mentioned) for tests to be made on living
victims to be meaningful, or for a cadaver to 'travel well'. It is true
that many Hmong have taken this long to travel out because they
either got lost or were foraging for food. But there are cases cited
in the US testimony, as well as people I interviewed, who took only
two weeks or less to reach Thailand. Theoretically these people
could have been tested. In fact some of the people I spoke with
had been and the results were negative. There is no question that
the time factor is important, and it is true that many known agents
do not persist in the environment for a long time – something the
Haig report makes much of. The physical effects on victims, however, are more long term, especially if they are malnourished, and
one would have expected at least some progress by now from
examinations of people who had allegedly been subject to sub-
lethal doses of chemical or biological agents. But the question
persists: why no dead body or at least tissue from a dead body? We
know for a fact that Hmong guerillas and intelligence teams criss-
cross the Mekong almost at will, and that mercenary teams have
made long-range expeditions into Laos in search of American
soldiers missing in action allegedly held there. Why can't these
Hmong teams bring out a body or at least parts of a body, prefer-
ably the lungs, for autopsy? Of course there would be problems of
transportation and of putrefaction, but it would at least offer
something for forensic experts to work on. I put this question to
Ed McWilliams at the US embassy in Bangkok and he objected
that this was impossible because of the Hmong religious abhorr-
ence of autopsies. This however is contradicted by Vang Neng, the

Hmong chief of Ban Vinai who told Jane Hamilton Merritt in 1980: 'Yes, I have bodies for post-mortems. I learnt yesterday that the communists gassed a village on 14 May, killing ten immediately. This is many days' walk from the Mekong. By the time we carry one body out, it will be spoiled.'[20] This last assessment should surely be left to the forensic scientists – they deserve at least one opportunity to examine an allegedly gassed body.*

If the Hmong object, I asked McWilliams, why not send in a team of mercenaries to get a body or parts of it. He expressed shock at the suggestion that the US would do anything illegal. But, whatever the official position, it is obviously within the capabilities of the CIA to arrange such an expedition which would 'hand over' the cadaver to the US once back in Thailand. Yet as far as we know, there has been no attempt to do this.

The same excuses about the problems of distance or of autopsies on victims do not apply to the allegations coming from the Thai-Kampuchean border area, where it is also claimed by the US that hundreds have been killed by chemical agents. (A Thai paper, *Tawan*, claimed in November 1981 that Kampucheans were being killed by toxic gas at a rate of 1,000 a day!) But once again we are confronted by the fact that there is no physical evidence of the use of known chemical warfare agents and no autopsied dead bodies. This latter fact is particularly striking because a former US Airforce colonel who served in Vietnam, Dr. Amos Townsend, travelled into Kampuchea in late 1981 to gather blood samples from Pol Pot soldiers who were allegedly attacked by chemical weapons. At the Khmers Rouges field hospital he was presented with no dead bodies for autopsies. Moreover, if an autopsy could not have been performed there he could have taken a body back to Thailand with him, or at least arranged for the subsequent dispatch of such a body. Yet not a single body has come to light. This makes the allegation of lethal gas warfare in Kampuchea particularly suspect.

*It is true that there is fear and opposition to autopsies among ordinary Hmong, and this has continued to create problems for Hmong in the US. See Jane Hamilton Merritt's account in the *Bangkok Post*, 28 March 1982. However, according to veteran Asian affairs journalist Frances Starner, many similar problems related to either operations or amputations were overcome prior to 1975, especially among the 'Secret Army' Hmong. If Vang Pao said it was all right they would do it,' she told me. See also *Mister Pop*, op. cit.

Relative ease of access to and from the sites where alleged attacks are taking place in Kampuchea should mean that the US would have significant physical evidence of mycotoxins on foliage rather than a few twigs, and much more than a few 'suggestive' blood samples.

The results of tests on blood and urine samples from Kampuchea, released by the State Department on 14 May 1982, showed what some analysts considered to be 'significant' levels of T2 and its metabolite HT2. According to Amos Townsend: 'Blood samples were drawn by Khmer Rouge medical personnel on two of the victims of that attack [which allegedly took place at Tuoi Chrey on 13 February 1982]. Urine samples were also obtained from these two victims, the blood within twenty-four hours of the exposure, the urine in forty-eight hours. These specimens were later picked up by the author at Nong Pru and subsequently sent to the USA for analysis.'[21] Townsend himself drew blood from six alleged victims on 3 March, and five more on 23 March. He also took blood from four control subjects who were said not to have been involved in the attack. In all, samples were taken from thirteen 'victims' and four controls. Results were released for eight 'victims' and four controls. Four 'victims' had traces of mycotoxins, four did not, and four control samples did not.

According to *Science* magazine these results worried a number of scientists because they wondered how T2 could be found in the blood of some alleged victims several weeks after the attack. Such persistence of these toxins has never been observed in test animals. Also 'several scientists questioned the wisdom of putting so much emphasis on measurements of T2 so close to the edge of the detection limit, in the range of ten parts per billion.'[22] Such tenuous results from an area where it should be easy for the US to gather evidence of chemical warfare makes its allegations look very weak.

The samples of Nong Pru were analysed in the US by Drs. Sharon Watson, Chester Mirocha, and Wallace Hayes, who presented their analytical procedures and results to an International Conference of Mycotoxicologists in Vienna on 1 September 1982. Watson and Mirocha also presented a similar paper to the American Society of Toxicologists on 19 September.[22] These papers form the scientific basis for the November Shultz *Update*. Apart from the findings we have surveyed above, these sources also mention that one of the 'victims' of the 13 February attack on Tuol Chrey died at Nong Pru on 16 March. Apparently an autopsy was performed (by 'Kampuchean physicians' says the Shultz *Update*; presumably Khmers Rouges doctors) and therefore it is very odd that no specific cause of death is given for this man. Tissue sections of the heart, œsophagus/stomach, liver, kidney, lung and large intestine were taken, fixed in formaldehyde, and sent to the US for examination. Traces of trichothecenes were found in all organs except the liver. They were also examined for the presence of another mycotoxin, aflotoxin B1, which is a common cause of food poisoning in many third world countries. According to Watson and Mirocha: 'The levels of aflotoxin detected in the tissues were so high that it seemed prudent to investigate the possibility that the exposure was not due to any natural contamination, but may have been related to chemical attack.' However, their analysis of a previously analysed 'yellow rain' sample for aflotoxin B1 proved negative. Thus Watson and Mirocha observed 'the victims' exposure to aflotoxin was most likely to have been due to contamination of the food source.'

There are, of course, a number of conclusions that can be drawn from this result. A plausible one would be that this man in fact died from food poisoning caused by aflotoxin; and the traces of trichothecenes may also point in the direction of natural contamination. Not surprisingly, this is not the conclusion drawn by Watson, Mirocha and the State Department, all of whom are convinced that mycotoxins are being used as a weapon in Southeast Asia.

Confronted by evidence suggesting death by natural intoxication Watson and Mirocha, followed by the Shultz *Update*, produce a piece of scientific speculation which argues that 'the high incidence of exposure to natural outbreaks of aflotoxin contamination in Southeast Asia may induce a greater susceptibility to trichothecenes in this population.' The combination of these two mycotoxins produces a synergistic effect. The purpose of this speculation would appear to be aimed at surmounting one of the anomalies in the scientific debate about mycotoxins – namely, descriptions by refugees of instantaneous symptoms when all scientific research to date indicates that symptoms of mycotoxicosis brought on by trichothecenes only appear days or weeks after exposure. On the other hand, if the presence of aflotoxin does cause such synergism then one would have expected aflotoxin to have been found in previous 'yellow rain' samples. The Shultz *Update* offers a weak defence, arguing that even though they have not found aflotoxin 'It does not . . . rule out the possibility that aflotoxin is a component of some yellow rain attacks. Preliminary analysis of some more recent yellow samples indicates the presence of aflotoxin contamination not consistent with natural contamination.'[23]

The arguments offered by Drs. Watson, Mirocha and Hayes, and the State Department, concerning the use of mycotoxins as a weapon, and concerning the conditions of natural mycotoxin occurrence in Southeast Asia, are all speculative. This point cannot be made too strongly when these scientists and the US Government claim that they possess 'unequivocal proof' of the use of these toxins as a weapon. They do not. If anything their research is beginning to reveal that mycotoxicosis is an important health hazard in Southeast Asia.[24]

An intriguing and puzzling aspect of the American examination of the soldier who died at Nong Pru is that Canadian Government investigators also analysed anatomical specimens from this man and found no traces of mycotoxins. Indeed, a Canadian report suggests that the Khmers Rouges soldier was suffering from blackwater fever, possibly as a result of complications arising from *falciparum* malaria. However, like the US investigations the Canadian report is also committed to the idea that chemical warfare is occurring and therefore, although they conclude that the soldier died as a result of illness, they argue that some unspecified 'agent' was a 'contributing factor'.[25] However, they offer no scientific evidence for this assertion.

The different scientific results of the US and Canadian investigations are 'reconciled' by their mutual subjective commitment to the belief that chemical warfare is happening – even though objectively their investigations do not prove this. In fact, it can be argued that the scientific evidence they are accumulating increasingly points *away* from chemical warfare.

The possibility of an 'intelligence hoax' must not be overlooked either.* The toxins that have been found are, even on the State Department's own admission, only crude extracts. This strongly suggests a crude production process typical of contaminated surface fermentations on natural substrates (rice, corn, and so on), not the high-technology submerged fermentations that would surely typify Soviet efforts were they to try to produce these toxins as a weapon. The toxins discovered so far can be easily produced by straightforward processes which can be learned from dozens of scientific journals. Any literate person could produce them. This, of course, makes the possibility of samples being faked or spiked very real, especially when they have been supplied by hostile sources – such as the Khmers Rouges medics who drew the samples of blood at Nong Pru.[26]

An investigation carried out by the Australian Department of Defence, concluded in August 1982, proves that 'yellow rain' evidence brought out of Laos is being faked. This investigation, by Dr. H. D. Crone of the Department's Organic Chemistry Division, was not made public and nor was it taken into consideration by the December 1982 UN report. Yet the results of the Australian investigator are explosive because not only do they show deliberate fabrication of evidence but they also demonstrate the natural occurrence of mycotoxins – specifically *Fusarium* and possibly trichothecenes – in Laos.

Dr. Crone investigated three packs of evidence containing leaves with yellow pollen on them, and one pack of pebbles also with yellow pollen on them. The conclusions of this study need to be quoted at length:

*An American, Scott Barnes, claims that he was sent into Laos on missions by the CIA and that others had been sent in to 'seed' false evidence of 'yellow rain' which would later be picked up by Laotian resistance fighters. There is no mention of going after bodies or proof. However, as regards the 'yellow rain' story, Barnes's account does not look reliable primarily because his knowledge of the region appeared so fuzzy. It was published by the Washington based anti-intelligence group *Covert Action Information Bulletin*, 7 April 1982. See also the account of an interview with Barnes in the *Bangkok Post*, 25 April 1982. The possibility that false evidence could be seeded should not be discounted, however. As Peter Pringle has pointed out, T2 toxins are available by mail order for ten pounds and could be obtained by anyone wanting to create false evidence. *The Observer*, 20 September 1981. We have also recently learned that the US was not above falsifying evidence in 1965 during the Vietnam war. *The Age*, 22 March 1982.

'The samples examined are not toxic and in fact are composed of yellow pollen grains, probably with small amounts of binder. The pollen analysis suggests that packs 1, 2 and 3 have a common origin, whereas Pack 4 is different . . . The most likely explanation . . . is that the pollen samples were collected from some rainforest trees. One tree producing pollen from many flowers at one time would furnish enough material. The pollen was contaminated at the collection site or subsequently with pollen from cereal crops and weeds of cleared areas. . . . Since the samples are obvious fakes, they convey no information at all as to the veracity or otherwise of the reports of chemical attacks. The reason for their fabrication can only be guessed at; monetary gain, desire to ingratiate oneself with authority, or as a disinformation campaign. We have discounted the idea that the yellow spots arose from a natural phenomenon. . . . The conclusion is therefore that the yellow spots were deliberately applied, either by brush or by a spraying process. There is no evidence as to which was used. . . . At MRL we do not have the facilities to do mycotoxin assays at low levels. However, such analyses would not be helpful as extensive fungal contamination was present (including *Fusarium*). Therefore, trichothecene mycotoxins at very low concentrations were quite likely present as products of this mould. What is important is whether the concentration could have any military meaning. In this case the answer is definitely no. These are fakes; the presence of mycotoxins in parts per million levels is an irrelevant consideration.'[27]

Dr. Crone's analysis is a serious challenge to American assertions about the occurrence or non-occurrence of certain mycotoxins in Southeast Asia; it also contains an implicit critique of the levels of mycotoxin contamination discovered by the US so far. Furthermore, the December 1982 UN report (by the Group of Experts) now looks as though it has made too many concessions to the US position on this question. In fact the UN report would also appear to have unearthed fabricated evidence from Laos with 'yellow rain' samples apparently being spiked with insecticide and other synthetic substances – but the report refrains from calling them fakes.

The fabrication of evidence raises serious questions about how much of the evidence produced to date has been faked. There is probably no way of really knowing. However, the discovery of fabrications certainly allows for the possibility that the 'yellow rain' story is a misinformation campaign.

So far we have primarily been concerned with evidence collected from organic matter, which is subject to the problem of degeneration of the alleged poisonous substances involved. This does not apply to shell casings, rocket fragments or 'dud rounds' used to deliver the lethal gas. Hmong forces have claimed at various times to have collected these or seen them, but they have never produced them. The same applies to Democratic Kampuchean troops. In mid-April 1982, however, there was a sudden flurry of excitement in Bangkok diplomatic circles when a rocket with 'Soviet markings' was handed over to the Australian Embassy by Lao resistance members. 'We believe that this is "the smoking gun" which will prove once and for all that the Soviet Union is directly involved in the use of chemical warfare in Laos', one source told the *Bangkok Post*. The *Post* report is worth quoting as an example of the speculative hysteria that occasionally grips the Bangkok journalistic and diplomatic community on this subject: 'The rocket itself, said sources who had seen it, is probably American-made and captured by Vietnamese communist forces when they overran South Vietnam. . . . The warhead however has markings in the Russian cyrillic alphabet. . . . From its description the weapon matched the characteristics of a rocket which a defecting Laotian pilot [Touy Mannikham] claimed he had used to spread "yellow rain". . . . The pilot said the warheads on the "smoke rockets" he fired were noticeably looser than similar rockets with explosive tips. This was also noted by resistance team members. . . .'[28] A week later the rocket was proven to be a ten-year-old Soviet B-40 rocket left over from the war before 1975. An Australian television team had paid $10,000 for the rocket. A friend of mine in Thailand who was offered a rocket a week before this incident said he could have picked it up at a bargain $2,000. He commented wryly that it was becoming a Laotian export industry.

The most convincing physical evidence the Khmers Rouges have so far been able to provide is one gas mask which an American 'source' said 'could very well be a Soviet mask', a judgement he made on the basis of a plastic star over the air intake filter.[29] In fact they cannot know. It could just as easily have been purchased in Bangkok by the Khmers Rouges.

The inability of the Americans to produce physical evidence has not been given nearly as much attention as it deserves in the international reporting of the allegations. Very early on, the word went out to the Hmong leaders in Ban Vinai and then to the leaders of the various Khmer rebel groups that they should try to recover physical evidence of fatal gas attacks in the form of gas canisters, artillery shells, rockets or spraying equipment. The gathering of such evidence involves no particular expertise. Hundreds of attacks have been reported and at least some solid evidence of this nature should exist. The State Department has argued that it does not exist because people flee the sites of alleged attacks rather than stay around to collect evidence. This claim, however, is contradicted by refugees who say they did stay in the same place for some time after the alleged attack, and by Hmong who claim to have gathered such evidence but left it in a cave in Laos. Furthermore if the US argument is pressed to its logical conclusion, we should not have any evidence of mycotoxins at all.

Despite the fact that it is relatively easy to move in and out of both Laos and Kampuchea, and despite the fact that the magazine for mercenaries, *Soldier of Fortune*, offered in January 1982 to give any pilot from Laos or Kampuchea willing to fly out his cargo of 'yellow rain' a '$100,000 reward, payable in gold or any other currency', there is still no solid physical evidence to hand.

In February 1982 a scare ran through the Thai press. 'Yellow rain' had been dropped by a twin-propellered plane – assumed to be Vietnamese – on the Thai province of Chantaburi situated on the Kampuchean–Thai border on 19 February. Squadron leader Prasong Soonsiri, Secretary General of the National Security Council, quickly warned people against jumping to conclusions, saying that it could be a 'Vietnamese trick'.[30] However, whether a plane really flew over or not is not certain. When the Thais analysed samples of the substance allegedly dropped, it turned out to be a mixture of crushed flowers and fungus. An analysis was also conducted by the British Government's chemical warfare research establishment at Porton Down which found a mixture of pollen and flower.[31] The Schultz *Update* claims: 'Thai officials later stated that further analysis showed traces of toxin and that the earlier Health Ministry announcement was based on an incomplete investigation.'[32] This statement, however, cannot be reconciled with that of the 1982 UN report which says that 'the Royal Thai Government had stated that chemical weapons had not been used in Thailand itself.'[33] There have been rumours that the Thais have important evidence about chemical warfare in Laos and Kampuchea, which they refuse to release to anyone, including the US Government. Why they should act in this way is baffling. Claims that they are withholding such information from the US military and intelligence, with whom they have worked so closely over the past thirty years, are highly improbable. In fact the Thais have been prepared to give some select outsiders a look at what they have collected. The Australian journalist who bought the dud rocket told me that the Thais had shown him 'secret' information about chemical warfare in Laos and Kampuchea that he found 'very convincing', but unfortunately he had been sworn to secrecy about what he had been shown. If they are prepared to share their 'secrets' with this journalist they are undoubtedly sharing them with US intelligence. Rumours that the Thais are holding back compelling evidence must be treated as a politically motivated attempt to hint that conclusive evidence really exists *somewhere*. Until the Thais release the information they are supposed to possess, the rumours cannot be taken seriously.

In this chapter we have seen that the scientific evidence presented by the US in support of its allegations of Soviet or Vietnamese involvement in chemical warfare in Southeast Asia is weak. It has no concrete evidence of the use of known chemical weapons, and its mycotoxin hypothesis is too speculatively based to support its charges. Finally, the evidence adduced cannot compel us to reconsider our judgement of the refugee evidence at the end of the previous chapter.

In the absence of convincing evidence of chemical warfare in

Southeast Asia since 1975, how can we explain the genesis of the
stories that originated among the Hmong refugees? The following
chapters offer an explanation.

Disease, Danger and Medicine from the Sky

Much refugee evidence suggests that the Hmong are prepared to attribute common ailments to an ill-defined idea of gas. We have already seen examples of this in Chapter 3 when we looked at the stories told by ordinary Hmong refugees, but our attempt to explain the origin of the gassing stories must consider this connection in more detail.

The Hmong inhabit an animistic culture, in which spirits act as the prime movers of terrestrial events. This applies perhaps especially to health problems. An anthropological study of medical problems among the Hmong noted:

'The Meos have no idea of the genesis of illness: they attribute any illness they suffer from to the intrigues of "evil spirits", these being the result of sorcery practised by enemies. Although they originated from China where their ancestors lived for hundreds of years, the Meos acquired no notion of Chinese medicine. Very trusting (*croyants*) they are equally very superstitious, especially when they fall ill, which they believe is caused by the presence of evil spirits.

'When the Meos fall ill they try to cure it by using leaves or flowers or roots. But if these do not help and the illness gets worse, they call on the services of sorcerers: these make offerings to the spirits (chickens, pigs, or even a buffalo) and then extract from the area affected by the sickness leaves, or a piece of stone or iron. If the illness is cured the sorcerer is credited for it and a banquet is given by the family and the family's friends. But if the cure fails the sorcerer, to exonerate himself, will covertly designate the person who caused the sickness and the hate and vengeance of the sick person's family will be directed at him.'[1]

Such a world view would quickly assimilate the idea of 'gas' to explain illness and natural calamities and attribute their causes to the 'Vietnamese'. That natural occurrences will be spontaneously assimilated to a political logic is not surprising in the light of work done on primitive interpretations of disease. These have observed that because disease, like warfare, threatens the viability of the group, political and medical idioms often mesh in political debates and discussions. If disease is the work of sorcery, for example, then it is automatically a political problem.

During my first enquiries into the condition of the Hmong in Laos and into the chemical warfare allegations, in January 1980, I encountered a colourful example of this political-medical logic. An old hill-tribesman in Chieng Khong refugee camp in northern Thailand told me solemnly: 'In February last year the communists rounded up all the old headmen and gave them an injection. They all died. But,' he went on, 'if you ate cooked chicken you died quickly, within one day, and relatively painlessly. If you didn't eat chicken you died in agony over three days.' With the look of an elder who had said his piece, he took a long drag on his large bamboo pipe while the Hmong seated around him nodded in grim assent at this tale of Pathet Lao perfidy. His manner invited no contradiction.

Had he seen the injections take place? No. He had been told by someone. Where did they take place? Only in his district or his province? *Everywhere*, came the unswerving reply. Is there someone close-by I could talk to who did see these 'executions'? No. But, the furrowed and intense face said, it is the truth.

This tale may be a garbled account of a vaccination programme in Laos, or simply an invention. It illustrates the delicacy of assessing Hmong medical ideas.

Yet there are writers who have accepted similar tales verbatim. One Hmong who claimed to have been sprayed with 'white rain' in March 1979 told Jane Hamilton-Merritt:

'In May, four Pathet Lao medics gave injections in the arm to thirty Hmong, including me. It was the colour of water. I immediately became dizzy and could not breathe. Blood spurted from my nose and I fell to the ground unconscious. A relative blew opium smoke over me for several hours and finally the bleeding stopped. In twelve hours I could see again and by the next day I could walk. The next day four new medics came. This time they had injections and pills for forty gassing victims. Some medics gave my people injections and green pills, others injections and white pills. Nothing happened for twelve hours; then they have trouble seeing, can't speak and black out. Fifteen died – five adults and ten children; the rest are very sick for a long time. The medics wrote reports on the people given medicine. Our chief asked the medics about the medicines, but they say they know nothing, only that the government sent the medicines and that it had come from another country. They wouldn't tell us which country.'[2]

Merritt claims that this account is an example of 'medically supervised experimentation', despite its obvious improbabilities. The insinuation about foreign medicine illustrates the teller's cultural suspicion, while Merritt appears oblivious to the fact that Laos has to import all its medicines.

Given these tales about injections inside Laos I was intrigued to discover on my arrival at Ban Vinai in early March 1982 that just a few weeks earlier there had been a confrontation between the western medical personnel in the camp and the Hmong leadership there over a vaccination programme.

Apparently the Hmong leadership and its followers were opposed to the programme because they saw it as an attempt to sterilize their children, their 'future generation'. A fear of 'genocide' by stealth, one might argue. But why did the Hmong believe that the well-intentioned western aid workers at the camp wanted to wipe them out? Obviously, a very high level of group paranoia combined with mystical attitudes to modern medicine played a key role. But what sparked off this paranoia at this juncture?

In January a rumour had swept through the northeast of Thailand, where Ban Vinai is located, concerning a dreaded new 'disease' called *Rohk Yued* ('genital enlarging disease') and it was said to be causing panic among local people. The disease was alleged to have been caused by *chemical powder* sprinkled on men's and women's underwear by *Vietnamese spies*. It was said that one man's genitals had become ten times larger than normal, as had women's breasts after they wore newly bought brassieres. Those afflicted by these devious Vietnamese tricks were apparently advised by quacks to drink dog's blood as an antidote.[3] Simultaneously there were fears of a genital shrinking disease in Udon Thani, said to be caused by noodles, cigarettes or fruit sold by Vietnamese vendors. The *Bangkok Post* reported: 'Local doctors say the disease does not exist; it's all in the mind they claim. But males in the northeast province remain unconvinced and are carefully watching what they eat and drink for fear that they might become only half the man they used to be. ... Dr. Thaweesak Chaosakul said . . . that it's just a rumour which began in 1976, disappeared after two weeks, and has now been resurrected.'[4]

A cold snap the same month brought a variation of this rumour to life in Ban Vinai when the scrotums of little boys – soon to be innoculated – contracted, sparking off a panic among Hmong parents in the camp. The Hmong leadership soon informed the hospital that they would have nothing to do with the innoculation programme until the testicles of all the young boys in the camp had been tested. However, they would not trust any of the doctors in the camp to do the test. They would only accept the verdict of a doctor who had formerly operated in support of CIA activities in Laos, a Dr. Charles Weldon now based at Nong Khai, some three hours away by car. Weldon was soon on the scene examining 468 sets of juvenile testicles over two days. Only three were discovered to have any signs of abnormalities. The programme was then allowed to proceed.*

This bizarre story is very instructive for a number of reasons: it is indicative of the Hmong's difficult relationship with modern medicine; it demonstrates the power of rumour in such a superstition-ridden society; the Hmong leadership's trust in Dr.

---

*One nurse told me that during this saga children kept calling her 'needle' when she walked around the camp. When I spoke with her she was in the middle of a dental health programme and the kids had now taken to calling her 'toothbrush'. She now felt much more benign and less menacing.

Weldon is indicative of its continuing relationship with US personnel active in Laos during the war against the Communists; and it
highlights Hmong paranoia about their 'extermination' and the
intentions of outsiders. It therefore contains many of the ingredients that sustain the stories of fatal gassing.

Another account of injections administered by the 'Vietnamese'
was related to me by an American researcher among Hmong
refugees in the United States. She said a number of Hmong there
dismiss the gassing story on the grounds that the 'Vietnamese' or
the 'Soviets' would be more cunning than to use gas. They felt it
would be much more likely that they would trick Hmong into
going to hospital and then either inject them with poison or poison
their food.

As we can see the Hmong culture's problematic relation to
modern medicine is not restricted to Laos. Indeed, in Ban Vinai
animist beliefs and bad sanitary habits (many people, for example,
are not convinced of the virtues of boiled water) produce skin
diseases and diarrhoea on a large scale. Only the availability of
constant modern health care prevents anything worse. A Finnish
nurse commented on the Hmong in the camp: 'They have their
bark and root medicines and rites to appease the spirits. Most of it
is worthless and some of it is positively harmful.' She spoke of a
two-year-old boy who had come down with a fever: 'They
repeatedly doused him with cold water to cool him off. But the
treatment only sent the fever higher. Only when the child was
close to death did they bring him to us. He died in the hospital and
then they blamed it on the doctors.'[5]

Such primitive ideas of medical causation have dogged the new
Lao government, and they also hindered the work of USAID before
1975. At one time USAID was called into a village at Phu Pha
Daeng, south of Long Cheng, because there had been a series of
sudden deaths there among babies. The surviving sick babies were
quickly whisked by helicopter to a hospital fifteen miles away
where doctors diagnosed their ailment as dengue fever – an acute
infectious disease transmitted by mosquito. The Hmong shaman at
the village, however, had said that some 200 potted plants which
had been left at the village as part of USAID's attempt to replace
opium poppies as a cash crop had offended the spirits. He claimed

babies would continue to die until the plants were removed, and he performed a ritual to placate the spirits of the area.[6] (There is a certain religious instrumentalism here that served to protect the growing of opium.)

The big difference between the Pathet Lao government and USAID is that they do not have a fleet of planes and helicopters available for emergencies, or to respond quickly to epidemic outbreaks. The relatively densely settled areas south of Phu Bia are vulnerable to epidemics, and no doubt many of the Hmong would now blame the Pathet Lao for them. The appallingly rudimentary health system in Laos would be powerless to ameliorate the political effects of such epidemics.

Problems of Parochialism

In tribal communities the notion of the 'outsider' has often been synonymous with 'enemy'. To travel beyond one's boundaries, except in strength, was to risk being killed. The law and order imposed by a state authority, whether it be colonial or indigenous, facilitated movement without fear of being killed, though it also meant that the state itself could become a menace to life or limb, especially if it was controlled by another tribal or ethnic group.

The writ of the lowland RLG government had rarely extended into the mountains. In fact centralized power hardly existed in Laos before 1975, and power was dispersed among the various military commanders and aristocratic families in the military regions, or warlords like Vang Pao. The inability of the old élite to build a unified national government was a major reason for its downfall. The Communists, on the other hand, built a strong nationwide organization even though for many years they were confined to the mountain regions. Thus, in contrast to the lowland-dominated RLG, it was estimated that up to 60% of the Communist forces were composed of ethnic minorities, including Hmong, though the leadership remained predominantly ethnic Lao. It was the Pathet Lao's ability to elaborate a successful minorities policy that ultimately enabled it to project itself as a *national* force and secure victory.

Even so, Laos's rugged topography and the virtually non-existent internal transport system meant that most of the ethnic groups in the mountains were only peripherally affected by either the RLG or the Pathet Lao before 1975, except of course when fighting thundered through their villages, wreaking havoc and bringing 'liberators' in its wake. Bombing and forced re-location, if anything, reinforced people's beliefs that the outside world was an unpredictable and dangerous place.

The general rural suspicion of outsiders, particularly if they spoke a foreign language and were officials of some distant state apparatus, was reinforced amongst the Hmong by cultural traditions harking back to clashes with the Chinese before their migration southward. In Laos they took to the peaks because of the natural protection they afforded, and because the better lowlying land was already occupied, though in some instances the Hmong forcibly ejected the original inhabitants and took over their land. Social injunctions against marrying other ethnic groups served to reinforce Hmong clannishness.

The total collapse of Vang Pao's fiefdom in 1975 meant the disintegration of a Hmong proto-state and brought with it fears of revenge by another alien state. The initial panic that this caused was unavoidable, as was continued suspicion of the Communists by many Hmong trained for years to fear and loathe them. These fears were only partly allayed by the dispatching of Communist Hmong leaders like Yong Yia to talk with the Hmong, or by the use of Hmong soldiers in patrols of Hmong areas. With the best will in the world the Pathet Lao could not avoid being treated by a number of the Hmong with brooding suspicion for a long time after victory. No doubt there was also smouldering resentment against those clans who had gained some social prestige through the redistribution of power towards those Hmong who had fought with the Communists. This was, after all, a social revolution. Many of the Hmong who left for Thailand were those who lost out in the redistribution.

That the Pathet Lao forces were regarded as outsiders emerges clearly in a number of the accounts gathered by the US. The Hmong spoke of Pathet Lao troops visiting their village and then going 'on vacation'.[7] While they were away the village would be attacked by gas, but when the troops returned, sometimes weeks later, 'there was never any explanation',[8] one informant complained. Such descriptions of the comings and goings of Pathet Lao troops sound uncannily like local reactions to the movements of white patrol officers and their troops in numerous colonial situations, oblivious to how closely their activities were monitored and interpreted by the local populations. Sometimes the occurrence of illness or accidents would be attributed to their visits. However, these officers would never 'explain themselves' either, usually because they had no idea that there was something to explain. Yet the attribution of untoward events to the whites was a refracted acknowledgement of their actual power. To continue the colonial analogy, the Pathet Lao soldiers would presumably be dealing with village leaders sympathetic to them who would therefore not necessarily relay the grievances of those who had lost out in the revolution. It may be also that the village leaders simply tell the soldiers what they think they would like to hear, and the soldiers leave the village ignorant of the grievances that had emerged since their last visit.

On other occasions, however, the Hmong complained directly to the Pathet Lao about the 'gas' – though it is extremely puzzling why they should call in the Pathet Lao to explain a 'gas' attack if they thought the Pathet Lao were responsible. Take the following account: 'The source said he saw one MIG in the sky above the village and then saw a cloud of yellow-brown rain-like substance descending. Source heard no explosions. Source, as assistant village chief, composed a letter signed by the village chief to the Ban Don (Lao) area hospital for emergency medical help following the attack. The hospital responded by messenger that it would send a medical team to check into the matter. Several weeks later a six-man Lao medical team did arrive and diagnosed that villagers were suffering from fever and not from gas attack. The district leader (*tasseng*) Mai Chank (a Lao) reportedly said that if the villagers were attacked again, then they had better shoot the plane down for proof.' According to this refugee fourteen people out of 400 had died from the 'gas'.[9]

Perhaps the calling in of the Pathet Lao is another example of the refracted recognition of the Communists' power, but this statement by a refugee teaches us more about medical problems inside Laos and about how they are being handled by officials than anything to do with alleged gassings. The district leader's quip that they should shoot a plane down for evidence would indicate that he had heard many a tall tale before about the causes of illness. Such a dismissive attitude to the Hmong story however could no doubt spark resentment towards the authorities. Clearly the possibilities for misunderstanding arising between the hill-tribespeople and more educated administrators are great. Medical students I spoke with in Vientiane and a doctor in Xieng Khouang explained to me that they are instructed to take special care when treating minority groupings such as the Hmong because of their greater ignorance of modern medicine. Even so, superstition intervenes again and again to complicate their relations with patients in all ethnic groups.

The Hmong who complained that the Pathet Lao offered no explanation to them on subsequent visits described the effects of the 'gas': 'People who drank stream water in the vicinity also got sick with headaches, stomach aches, chest pains and tears. They did not vomit. Boiling water would purify it. Remedies included opium and other traditional cures.'[10] There are instances in which 'gassed' water or vegetation caused illness while the falling gas itself did not: 'Patients reported they were dizzy, like smoking opium; all were coughing and vomiting blood and died one day later. None of the people was affected directly by the gas, but affected when the gas was consumed by mouth on either vegetation or in the water supply. The four people who consumed the evening meal then got sick and died. The rest of the village did not eat the food after watching the others get sick.'[11]

The report of the UN investigating team also provided some interesting evidnece in this regard: 'two refugees, a girl and a boy, reported on what they claimed to have been different occasions of exposure to chemicals. About a month before the interview, the girl ate some leaves which had some yellow material on them, after having washed them in the stream, and had dizziness, coughing and vomiting: the boy referred to an episode in his childhood, which, in turn, had been recounted to him, and to a second one about a year previously, in which he had dizziness, headache, vomiting and diarrhoea, and had developed some lesions ("weeping wounds") on his skin. . . . The most remarkable findings were a goitre and an enlarged spleen in the girl and several skin conditions. . . .'[12]

The statements by the Hmong demonstrate again and again how they attribute everyday health hazards to 'gas'. The idea that boiled water would neutralize a lethal chemical warfare compound is far-fetched, although it does show an imperfect acquaintance with modern notions of hygiene. That the Hmong are attributing multiple ailments, compounded by malnutrition, to an abstract idea of 'gas' is brought out lucidly in the following account of a refugee who claimed the 'gas' caused him not to eat and drink: 'I became very skinny. Twelve more people in my village die of being skinny. . . . I think those new arrivals in the camp who are so skinny – I think they have been hit by the gas.'[13]

Public Health in Laos

Public health in Laos has always been appalling. The symptoms described by the Hmong – allowing for the mandatory exaggerations – correspond to the *common* ailments of Laos in highland and lowland areas. Life expectancy in the country has been estimated at 35 years, and one doctor in the 1960s wrote: 'No statistics exist on foetal mortality for Laos, but I would estimate them like this: 50% of pregnancies do not go to completion. Of one hundred babies conceived, only fifty will be born alive. Of these fifty, twenty will die during infancy from smallpox, cholera, malnutrition, whooping cough or pneumonia. Of the thirty left, ten will die during childhood from malaria, trauma or dysentery.'[14] By 1975 there were no more than twenty trained Lao doctors in the RLG zone, and certainly no more in the Pathet Lao zone. American and other aid propped up a feeble health system that all but collapsed following the Communist takeover as US aidworkers and aid, and most western-trained Lao doctors, left the country. The *Asia Yearbook* for 1982 wrote: 'Lack of education in hygiene, widespread poverty and shortages of medicine and medical personnel combined to make Laos one of the world's unhealthiest

countries. Infant mortality, according to a study in Vientiane province, was 283 per thousand and the national average was estimated at 200 deaths per thousand. Life expectancy was . . . one of
the world's lowest.'

Malaria has always been the country's most widespread serious
disease. For the Hmong, whose immune system is not as
developed as that of the lowland Lao, malaria is a scourge; the
figures of a 60 to 80% incidence of it among Hmong refugees
reported by the Weldons before 1975 demonstrate this. After
1975 the condition of the population as a whole degenerated
even further, if that is imaginable. 'Malaria is now raging in this
country of mountains and rainforests,' wrote Norman Peagam
from Vientiane in 1977, 'causing more death and sickness than any
other disease. One out of three persons in some rural areas
carries malaria [here he is referring to lowland Lao], according
to a recent survey, and many cases involve the highly dangerous
falciparum strain, which causes cerebral malaria and often
cannot be treated with the more common drugs.' He cites the case
of an eight-year-old brought by car to the hospital in Vientiane
suffering from fever and convulsions; he fell into a coma and lay
gasping for air until he died two days later. 'According to doctors
here, the sudden spread of malaria was partly caused by the end of
aid from the United States in 1975 when the Communists took
power. Until then the United States Government had funded a
malaria prevention campaign that had at least managed to contain
the problem in lowland areas near the towns. But since the aid
cut-off there has been virtually no DDT spraying in the countryside
and the deadly mosquitoes have flourished unchecked.' Officials
then estimated that it would take two or three years to buy sufficient supplies of DDT – which of course they have not been able to
do.[15]

The general symptoms of malaria are severe fever, rapid pulse,
intense headache, frequent vomiting, quick breathing and dry
burning skin, associated with high temperature and dizziness. The
falciparum variety can cause sudden, fatal cerebral attacks.
Moreover, there are choleraic, dysenteric, haemorrhagic,
pneumonic and syncopal forms. These complications correspond
to the other common diseases of Laos – cholera, a mainly water-

borne disease (vomiting and diarrhoea, leading to dangerous dehydration), dysentery (bloody severe diarrhoea), pneumonia and other respiratory tract infections – which are very common among the hill-tribes. Typhoid fever, yaws, hepatitis, tuberculosis and trachoma – all flourish, facilitated by widespread malnutrition. Poor hygiene spreads many of these diseases and is a particular problem among the hill-tribes where it also causes sores and skin diseases not found among the lowland Lao.

The haemorrhaging reported by many refugees, which set the State Department off on the trail that led to mycotoxins, besides being associated with a number of the above diseases, as well as with tuberculosis, can also be explained by the haemorrhagic variety of dengue fever. We have already seen that USAID had problems with dengue amongst the Hmong prior to 1975, and UNDP officials told me that it continues to be endemic and occasionally epidemic in the region around Muong Cha, south of Phu Bia, where they have a project. People there vomit blood and break out in horrible brown skin-patches that ooze blood as a result of the fever. The US testimony contains an intriguing reference to this latter symptom when one refugee said of the 'gas' that he 'did not experience blood coming out through his pores.'[16]

Many of these diseases have long ceased to be problems in the West and many are exclusive to the tropics. They are exotic, and the horrible symptoms they produce are unknown to westerners, largely oblivious of the fact that much of the world suffers from these dangerous diseases. Most aid workers have had no training in tropical medicine and are shocked to see the conditions suffered by these people. Often they are ready to attribute them exclusively to the Communists, rather than underdevelopment and poverty. It is important that we also understand that any initial infection makes people susceptible to other diseases and hence the refugees, and people in Laos itself, often exhibit multiple symptoms.

As a result of the dire economic situation in Laos up to 1979, and the inability of the government to provide resources for widespread disease prevention, the poor nutritional state of the population – including the Hmong – resulted in a dramatic rise in their susceptibility to disease. Often the Hmong were suffering from malnutrition, diarrhoea or dysentery, rampant malaria and skin diseases simultaneously. They were constantly vomiting, collapsing with fatigue, and the mortality rate was high. In these conditions, and in a political environment many of them distrusted, they began to leave for Thailand in large numbers. They tramped through the forest eating roots and leaves and sometimes poisonous mushrooms. Whiplashes from brambles and bushes became infected and turned into festering ulcers. As in the forced marches the Hmong had endured before 1975, the death toll was often heavy, especially among babies and old people. These Hmong stumbled over the Thai border emaciated, delirious and traumatized, and when interviewed some said they had been gassed.

I put it to a doctor at Ban Vinai that all the symptoms described to him by the Hmong as the effects of gas – diarrhoea, respiratory complaints, insomnia and impotence, among many others – could be rationally explained by normal medical diagnosis. He agreed. However, he said he was inclined to believe gassing had occurred because he had been told such compelling stories by some of the Hmong. His opinion on the matter was subjective and not scientific. This subjectivity is all the more apparent when one realizes that doctors who have treated Hmong in the northern camps for *identical* complaints do not believe these conditions are the result of gassings. In these camps (Pua Nam Yao, Sop Tuang Maejarim and Chieng Khong) there are almost no stories of gassing from the refugees, no press activity, and no highly politicized Hmong leadership. There, the psychological atmosphere of hysteria that can be found in Ban Vinai and at Nong Khai is absent, and one obtains rational, scientific conclusions drawn from exactly the same empirical symptoms as those that prevail at Ban Vinai. As one doctor who had worked in these camps from 1975 to 1981 told me: 'During that time I heard no reports of "yellow rain" nor saw any conditions which I attributed to such poison. There were plenty of other skin and respiratory conditions, particularly amongst newcomers after seven to ten days' trek through jungle and over the mountains.'[17]

We can see this medical subjectivity in another example.

Two doctors who worked at Ban Vinai gave evidence at US Congressional Hearings in the first half of 1982 concerning the medical problems they encountered among the Hmong at the camp.[18] Drs. Milton Amayun and Richard Haruff both believe that poison gas is being used against the Hmong and they presented evidence concerning the number of Hmong who consulted them for respiratory difficulties. According to Dr. Amayun, only a small number of these could be diagnosed as having either tuberculosis or paragonomiasis (a lung fluke disease) while 'the great majority of our cases remained undiagnosed.' He claims it was only then that he and his colleagues began to listen closely to tales of poison gas and found: 'In almost every one of our "unexplainable" respiratory cases, the story of killer smoke, dust, cloud, powder or rain was a common denominator. ... We named the disease "poison gas syndrome"....' According to Dr. Haruff they constructed three categories for this 'syndrome': 1. 'the first and most frequent type was chronic bronchitis: this was entirely non-specific' ...; 2. hemoptytic pulmonary symptoms: 'In eighty-five patients presenting with hemoptysis, there were twenty-two who had no evidence of infection but gave definite histories that their problem started with exposure to the yellow agent in Laos. The others had tuberculosis, paragonomiasis or were undiagnosable'; 3. what he called the 'congenital form' because it occurred in babies whose mothers were allegedly affected by chemical agents.

Haruff's exposition of this 'syndrome' would indicate that the great majority of undiagnosed cases adduced by Dr. Amayun were in fact non-specific chronic bronchitis. Of those who presented with chronic hemoptysis it is unclear whether those who had TB and paragonomiasis told yellow-rain stories; while it appears that the only reason there is a residual group of 'undiagnosables' is that these people did not tell a yellow-rain story, otherwise it seems they would have been added to the 25% who did. In other words the story determines the diagnosis as 'poison gas syndrome', and not the symptoms. The third category of this 'syndrome' is difficult to take seriously as it is pure speculation and only provides evidence of these doctors' firm belief in the existence of 'yellow rain'.

When one ceases to assume, a priori, the occurrence of 'yellow rain' attacks, Dr. Amayun's claim that the majority of cases were undiagnosed until they created the category 'poison gas syndrome' is shown to be quite misleading, for in fact most were suffering from non-specific bronchitis, and a relatively small group from undiagnosed hemoptysis. This is the real residual medical problem, though the formulation of the 'poison gas syndrome' hypothesis would seem to have pre-empted a search for its etiology. It is possible to argue that generally high levels of respiratory illness point in the direction of gas use. However, one of the only full-length studies of medical problems among the Hmong shows that these kinds of symptoms are very common:

'Illnesses of the respiratory apparatus are very frequent and produce the majority of cases of illness among the Meos. The principal cause of this pathology is always pneumococcus; the stapholococci and the streptococci, however, never by themselves cause these broncho-pulmonary infections.

Living on the summits at an altitude even higher than 1000 metres, where the weather can be freezing, especially in winter, sheltered in houses in which the gables are not shut and where the partitions which serve as walls are not waterproof, the Meos, in particular the children, are inadequately dressed, and are therefore vulnerable to all the sicknesses of the respiratory apparatus from head colds to capillary bronchitis to bronchopneumonia. . . . The percentage of adult deaths from pulmonary infections in relation to the total number of deaths of adults can be estimated at 70%.'[19]

In this perspective the 'findings' of Drs. Amayun and Haruff do not look so dramatic or medically convincing – in particular Haruff's conclusion concerning those found in group 1 of the 'poison gas syndrome': 'The only unusual feature of the cases in this group was that young people were affected with a disease usually associated with the elderly.' Indeed, the doctors appear to know very little about the normal state of health of the Hmong, with their subjective belief in 'yellow rain' over-riding proper medical enquiry. In fact Haruff is so convinced by it that even when he acknowledges incongruities in some refugee reports, he simply expands his original hypothesis to include 'several agents or mixtures of agents' to encompass the contradictions – but offers no concrete evidence for the existence of these multiple agents. Surely normal scientific procedure would have demanded a thorough re-examination of the basic assumption?

It is clear that the social and political environment at Ban Vinai has effected medical judgement there. The influence of such an environment on the medical evidence is illustrated by the reaction of doctors in the United States to another medical problem that has not been amenable to normal explanation. This is the mysterious 'oriental nightmare syndrome', originally reported in the medical literature by physicians working in the Philippines and Hawaii in the 1940s and 1950s, involving the sudden death of apparently healthy people. 'The medical-journal reports of death during sleep sometimes included descriptions by the victims' families of the victim thrashing and making noises before dying, behaviour the families interpreted as reactions to nightmares.'[20] Similar deaths have been reported in recent years to the Centre for Disease Control in Atlanta, USA for thirty-nine Indochinese refugees: twenty-six were Hmong, eight ethnic Lao, four Vietnamese and one Cambodian.

In early 1982 the former Secret Army leader Vang Pao, who now lives on a farm in Montana, attributed these deaths to chemical weapons.[21] This line of thought was quickly picked up by the Hmong families of the victims to claim that 'yellow rain' was the cause of their death. The Centre for Disease Control interviewed twenty-five or thirty-nine victims of this sudden death syndrome, and the result was, according to Dr. Roy C. Baron who is in charge of the enquiry into the death: 'Our epidemiological studies have failed to implicate chemical agents as a cause of these deaths. In particular, the majority of the Hmong victims left Laos prior to the period when the use of these agents began. Of those individuals who stayed longer, only the family of one sudden death victim recalled having seen an attack with 'yellow rain' but stated that the deceased had not been exposed or affected.'[22]

This medical opinion failed to affect the Hmong or impressionable journalists. William Kucewicz writing from Santa Ana reported: 'The Hmong here complain, however, that they cannot be sure they have never been exposed to "yellow rain". If not "yellow rain", they add, other poisons are also being used in Asia. They tell of cases of persons becoming ill, and even dying from tainted water, salt, meat, noodles and other foodstuffs. The Hmong here also talk of "green eggs". Khang Yong Chea . . . saw aircraft drop bluish-green egg-like objects. . . . Rain and water caused the shells of these eggs to evaporate and to expose a "very black" core which gave off noxious fumes, he says. Some of the villagers who breathed the fumes had stomach aches, diarrhoea, loss of sight and bloody vomit.'[23]

What is most extraordinary about this account is not so much the Hmong attributing sudden deaths to 'yellow rain' or 'green eggs' but the dead-pan seriousness with which journalists report it. If western educated journalists believe in 'green eggs', why not the Hmong?

Unlike some journalists, and unlike many doctors in the camps in Thailand, Dr. Baron refused to be swayed. Challenged by Jane Hamilton-Merritt he replied: 'It is not our policy to do anything because a journalist . . . is beating a drum about something. . . . There are other reports than yours that Hmong have been exposed in Laos but we have not seen residual effects over here.'[24] Elsewhere he has explained: 'Throughout the United States sudden, unexpected deaths are not uncommon. What is uncommon is a death that we cannot explain when all the details are available.'[25] Even so Baron refuses to adopt the 'yellow rain' assumption. Similar scientific hard-headedness was not demonstrated by Amayun and Haruff who, without examining all the details, invented the 'poison gas syndrome'.

Dr. Baron's answer to speculation about the nightmare deaths may well apply to the whole 'yellow rain' saga: 'The real story here is about the psychology of the media, not of nightmares.'[26]

A final comment is in order here. A procedure that relies on conclusions drawn from the multiple symptoms *described* by the Hmong is an extremely dubious one. This is especially so when the people providing the descriptions are no longer suffering from the alleged symptoms, or are simply describing the symptoms of others they claim were gassed around them. Such a situation is ripe for imaginative embellishment and the conflation of every medical symptom these people have ever seen or heard about. There is no scientific check on the extent of the invention, and indeed the political-psychological atmosphere of the refugee camp at Ban Vinai encourages exaggeration.

Among the Hmong, both in the refugee camps, and in Laos,

superstition co-exists uneasily with modern medicine. The fact that western doctors in the refugee camps treat the Hmong for their illnesses does not disturb their belief that they are the product of evil spirits or 'gas'. Indeed, it is perfectly plausible that a Hmong will believe his or her scabies is caused by chemical warfare while at the same time consulting a doctor for scabies.

In this respect Hmong can say they have been the victims of chemical warfare and show their scabies or other skin diseases or complaints without any sense of duplicity whatsoever. Moreover, they no doubt find the 'gassing' explanation a much more compelling one than the strange logic of western medicine. The yellow rain story has the advantage of clearly specifying a causal agent for their problems, the Vietnamese or the Pathet Lao.* In a sense it is shamanism writ large.

We can conclude this chapter by taking a look at the way in which some of the 'samples' of yellow rain are being collected. We are indebted to Jane Hamilton-Merrit for this insight. One day at Ban Vinai she was hustled into a 'remote shelter' by a group of young Hmong who told her earnestly: 'We are a team of ten men and we try to get the evidence of the gassing. Villagers tell us that in a site four kilometres south of Phu Heh, there is a place that if people pass by they become sick. The villagers are sure the area is contaminated with poison. So, on 17 October 1981, we go to the area. Six of us scrape the powder from the rocks and leaves.'[27] After much sickness and difficulty, they said, they returned with a 'sample'; it provided no trace of chemical warfare agents. A monograph on the relation between spirits and health in Laos, written many years before the gassing issue ever arose, notes: 'Most Lao still believe that one may become ill by passing near an area where a malevolent spirit lives.'[28] It is little wonder that the

---

* In her study of a neurological disease called *Kuru*, which became epidemic amongst the Fore of the eastern highlands of New Guinea, Shirley Lindenbaum noted the tribe's critique of western attempts to cure the disease: 'South Fore say that doctors involved in *Kuru* research should go directly to the heart of the problem, the wickedness of their enemies. Failure to cure *Kuru* results from the misdirected efforts of Western medicine, which focuses exclusively on medical therapy. Modern technology should be applied instead to improved intelligence-gathering, to detecting the covert operations of those who endanger the general welfare.' *Kuru Sorcery: Disease and Danger in the New Guinea Highlands*, Mayfield 1979, p. 123.

samples of 'yellow rain' brought from Laos have proven so insubstantial.

Having surveyed the health situation in Laos it is astonishing to read the statement in Haig's *Report* to Congress: 'Contrary to commonly held views, the epidemiology of diseases endemic to the central highlands of Laos and the public health situation of the Hmong do not support the view of malnourished disease-ridden and weak persons. . . .'[29] Haig says this conclusion is based on 'many studies', none of which he cites. Until he does so, this statement must stand as one of the most dubious in the whole *Report*. The health of the Hmong is mentioned by Haig to rebut suggestions that the Hmong, weakened by disease, could be describing deaths caused through attacks by riot-control agents such as teargas. The inference is that something much more lethal must be in question. Our argument not only rebuts Haig on this particular point but suggests that an ill-defined notion of gassing is being used by many Hmong to explain endemic, and often epidemic, diseases from which they suffer. Our survey also suggests that the Hmong world view would easily assimilate and spontaneously propagate these stories.

For obvious reasons the chapter has focused on the Hmong, but as we saw earlier when discussing fears of genital disease in north-eastern Thailand, lowland peasants are just as prone to superstitious and alarmist interpretations of disease. An example of this emerged in early November 1982 when rumours of 'yellow rain' attacks swept along the Thai–Kampuchean border. However, according to AP photographer Mangkorn Khamreonwong, these reports began after a number of Kampuchean guerillas and refugees came down with a virulent form of malaria rife in the jungles of the border region.[30] The alleged 'yellow rain' attacks on Thai border villages in February and March of 1982 – discussed at the end of chapter 4 – also seem to be the result of disease-related rumours. These incidents were investigated soon afterwards by a Canadian team enquiring into allegations of chemical warfare in the region.[31] In this respect their survey was unique because lack of timely access to areas attacked by 'yellow rain' has been one of the arguments used by the US and others to explain the difficulties they have had in furnishing conclusive evidence.

The Canadian team discovered in these villages that a number of people became sick allegedly after the appearance of a 'yellow substance'. This substance was still present when the Canadians visited and they took samples. Their report does not indicate what this substance was, but as we saw at the end of Chapter Four other investigations concluded that it was pollen. Presumably it was from species common to the region, such as those mentioned in the August 1982 Australian Department of Defence investigation. The Canadians found no scientific evidence to substantiate charges of chemical warfare – nevertheless they do attempt to link the illnesses in the villages to supposed 'yellow rain' attacks in Kampuchea. However, an alternative and equally plausible rendering of what occurred would be the following. Given that there was fighting between the Khmers Rouges and Vietnamese forces nearby (some villages said they could hear gunfire occasionally) and that there were reports of Vietnamese use of 'yellow rain', the villagers were understandably feeling insecure and therefore when a number of them became ill in a minor epidemic – a common village occurrence – they linked the pollen to what they had heard about 'yellow rain' and to their illnesses. This reaction is perfectly understandable. The response of the Canadian team on the other hand is only coherent within a political logic: their desire to assert the existence of chemical warfare by the Vietnamese even when the evidence before them suggested a more obvious and mundane interpretation. Such scientific subjectivity has been all too characteristic of the 'yellow rain' investigations.*

*Another Canadian report released in May 1982 (*Report on Possible Use of Chemical Warfare Agents in Southeast Asia: Refugee Interviews at Ban Vinai, 5 May 1982*, Department of External Affairs Canada, 1982) carried photos of Hmong with skin diseases. These photos were splashed across the pages of the US press as evidence of the effects of 'yellow rain'. Subsequently they have been shown to be the result of a fungal infection. This was yet another example of the extraordinary ignorance displayed by foreign service officials in Bangkok concerning the common health problems of people even in Thailand itself. Examples of such skin diseases, and worse, can be found in the annual Thai journal of the Princess Mother's Flying Doctor Foundation, *Phaet Aasaa* ('Voluntary Doctor'). See for example, the 1977 issue.

6
Flight and Fear

It is widely believed that the Hmong are leaving Laos because the Communist regime is trying to destroy their traditional way of life by forcing them down from the mountain tops, and that if the Hmong resist these pressures they are attacked with chemical warfare weapons. Very little evidence, as we have demonstrated, has been produced to substantiate these claims. Nevertheless, the fact that Hmong have left Laos in large numbers since 1975 lends plausibility to the argument. However, we showed in Chapter Two that Hmong society had already been traumatized by the civil war in Laos from the early 1960s onwards, and during this time there were large-scale Hmong migrations. We need to return to this period briefly to look at what was happening to the social structure of the Hmong, in order to construct a yardstick to measure the actions of Hmong since 1975.

Even before the civil war, traditional Hmong society had been under strain from the development of its own internal dynamics. Population growth had begun to outstrip annual harvests and the Hmong peasants had responded by extending the area of 'slash and burn' cultivation, and by speeding up field rotation. This in turn hastened soil erosion. The destruction of forests and soils caused by the traditional farming methods under these new conditions was immense. The first Hmong agricultural engineer, Chao Ly, estimated that by the mid-1960s approximately 50,000 hectares of forest land was being destroyed each year in Xieng Khouang province alone. Vang Pao himself deplored the process: 'In one year a single family will chop down and burn trees worth perhaps $6000 and grow a rice crop worth only $240. Our people must come down from the mountains. We must demand our share of the fertile, irrigated land.'[1]

This traditional form of swidden farming has dictated the migratory Hmong way of life, their need to perpetually move in search of fertile land. 'Hmong families are leaving the mountains of Phathong (Luang Prabang) for the heights of Phou Khoui (Vientiane)', wrote a young Hmong sociologist, Yang Dao, in the early 1970s; 'Others are fleeing the Xieng Khouang region for the still virgin lands around Sayaboury ... unknowingly continuing the destruction of the natural capital resources and then getting ready to move to other lands.'[2] Thus there was already a natural migratory shift of the Hmong toward Thailand: mass re-settlement of the Hmong refugees who had gathered around the CIA base areas to Sayaboury province was often discussed before 1975. As it turned out, they ended up just across the border in Thailand.

Pathet Lao policy is designed to arrest this mass destruction and therefore perpetual migration by settling the Hmong in stable villages closer to the plains. This economically rational policy is pursued by many other Asian governments in analogous situations, including Thailand. It must be admitted that all have had mixed results.

In traditional Hmong society, epidemics were also the cause of mass migrations. According to Yang Dao: 'Often catastrophic epidemics of smallpox and malaria will sweep like "evil spirits" through whole villages, and partially decimate them, in the absence of modern medicine. For the Hmong, who understand nothing about these almost immediate deaths which spread like wildfire to encompass whole regions, the only way to "appease the evil spirits" is to leave, but not before sacrificing chickens, pigs and even buffaloes for having "trespassed on their sacred sanctuary" so they will not pursue them with their curses. This explains why you will encounter whole villages wandering along the mountain trails, driving their pigs and cattle ahead of them, carrying whatever is left of their belongings, in search of a less hostile "country".'[3] Disease ravaged the Hmong population as a result of the civil war, fuelling their desire to move even more rapidly, and further.

A most important element in Hmong migration is the desire to be with relatives. The extended family is the basic unit of Hmong society both economically and socially. The clan bond is so strong that even the most distant relative is considered a member of the same unit and clan comrades of the same generation call one another brothers and sisters. Nor is this a mere social convention as with other Southeast Asian cultures. Exogamy is enforced between people of the same clan name even if there is no known blood connection between them.

The clan plays a vital ceremonial function particularly in relation to ancestor worship and funeral rites. For this reason Hmong of the same clan congregate together; the ideal village is one composed of a single clan. Frequently, however, this would not be possible and a common reason for village disputes is families feeling they are being dominated by another clan. Thus they often leave to join relatives in another village or form a village of their own and invite relatives to join them.

In this rigidly patriarchal system the head of the extended family is the eldest male, who is also the head of the clan in the village. Where one clan occupies a village the headman is particularly powerful because he commands both the clan and the village. This power can be extended even further, according to the observations of one French anthropologist: 'A clan chief can reign over an entire region, thanks to the influence he acquires from his clan connections and his clients.'[4] In other words his status approaches that of a traditional warlord.

The war facilitated these supra-clan and village forms of political organization. In order to compete with the Pathet Lao for the allegiance of the hill-tribes in the Xieng Khouang region, Hmong chiefs were given positions of responsibility in the provincial administrative structure, and were buttressed by Vang Pao's ascent to the command of Military Region Two, thereby establishing a Hmong proto-state within a state. This allowed Vang Pao to give vent to fantasies of an independent Hmong state in 1966. The evolution of Hmong social structure in Xieng Khouang also facilitated Vang Pao's recruitment of Hmong for this standing army. But he also tried to cement broader clan alliances, through, for example, his own marriage to the daughter of Touby Ly Fong, the sole Hmong minister in the RLG and head of the most powerful clan in Xieng Khouang.

Obviously, such a social structure gives the head of the family or clan the decisive say in the matter of migration, over its timing and destination. The significance of this after the Pathet Lao victory in 1975 cannot be underestimated.

The Hmong family and clan system has evolved to suit the conditions of a migrant or nomadic population. It is this system that gives the society its cohesion in the instability that any shift causes, even under the most peaceful conditions. It is not surprising that the Hmong clan structure and leadership structure have remained relatively intact over the last two decades of upheaval. This also applies in the refugee camps where various clans are thrown together.

This clan structure quickly adapted itself to the rigours of life in the camps where, disburdened of the need to make decisions on important economic tasks, it could devote much more time to political tasks or intrigue within the refugee camp as a whole and to the closer supervision of clan members. The modern military organization of the Secret Army appeared to only minimally disturb this traditional structure, operating more or less parallel to it.

The high death rate of young males caused by the war began to create a significant transformation of the Hmong family. There was a dramatic increase in the number of polygamous marriages, augmenting the already large extended family households of between ten and twenty people. The war accelerated this development in other ways too, providing the mercenaries with access to cash – not least through the opium trade in which Vang Pao and the CIA were involved – which enabled them to pay the bride prices. Vang Pao, for example, has six wives.

Yet while the Hmong clan structure remained relatively intact, the Hmong economy was virtually destroyed during the war years. As the war swept back and forth across the Plain of Jars, it created such instability that the Hmong stopped going through the laborious routine of clearing large tracts of forest for fields because they feared that at any moment their village could suddenly become a free-fire zone. For many it became easier to rely on the food drops of USAID, and they became quasi-permanent refugees. As one Air America pilot said in 1968: 'Rice comes from the sky, many Lao kids believe, because that's the only way they've ever received it.'

The war also created a sort of artificial 'urbanization' of the

Hmong. These people, who had previously lived in villages rarely numbering over 200 people, and more often half that number, suddenly found themselves living in large agglomerations, around the CIA base at Long Cheng with 30,000 people, the USAID base at Sam Thong with 15,000 people, or Pha Khao with 7,000. These populations were particularly dependent on US aid. When they were initially settled, the families of the mercenaries and the refugees attempted to do some gardening in the immediate vicinity, but predictably the potential for any large-scale crop-growing was soon exhausted. The main source of income for many families was the mercenaries' wage, and these centres became basically commercial trading posts dependent for their supplies on Air America, the CIA airline.

In many ways what happened in these 'urban' areas in the remote and largely inaccessible mountains of Laos was identical to what had taken place in other parts of Indochina – in Saigon, Phnom Penh and Vientiane – where a process of urban growth had occurred not in response to economic development but as a result of the exodus from the rural areas caused by the fighting, bombing and massive injection of American money.

When the Americans were finally forced to leave Indochina it caused massive economic and social disruption in these lowland towns; the 'towns' of the Lao highlands were no exception.

Post-1975 Movement

Until the beginning of 1979 refugees from Laos were the largest group of Indochinese refugees in Thailand. Obvious reasons for this were that Laos was poor, and that it was impossible for the Lao government to seal off its border. For the Lao, the US was simply a boat ride away across the Mekong River. While many of the people who had worked for the US or the old regime left for political reasons, it is generally acknowledged that most people have left Laos because of the country's poverty.

The following table summarizes the departures from Laos:

Arrivals in Thai Camps

	1975	1976	1977	1978	1979	1980	1981
Lao	10,195	19,499	18,065	48,786	22,045	28,967	16,426
Hilltribe	44,659	7,266	3,873	8,013	23,943	14,801	4,305
Total:	54,954	26,765	21,938	56,799	45,988	43,768	20,733

Source: *Refugees and Displaced Persons from Indochina as of 31 December 1981,* UNHCR—Thailand.

As we can see from the table, mainly hill-tribespeople left Laos in 1975. For the next two years the number dropped dramatically to a low of under 4,000 in 1977, while the outflow of lowland Lao rose by 1978 to a figure exceeding that of all the hill-tribes in 1975. Only in 1979 did the outflow from highlands and lowlands balance each other – with a sudden upswing in hill-tribes departures while those of the lowland Lao halved compared with the previous year. After that the number of hill-tribespeople leaving dropped precipitously once again, while the lowland Lao figure declined more gradually.

There have been no allegations of use of chemical warfare against lowland Lao, and we cannot ascribe their departure to this. Why then have they left?

As we can see from the table, the pattern of lowland Lao refugee movement is more uniform than that of the hill-tribes, and if plotted on a graph would form a rough parabola peaking in 1978. This curve would inversely correlate with a graph of economic conditions inside Laos over the same period. As the urban economy of the lowland cities contracted and inflation spiralled upwards, urban dwellers began to leave the country in greater numbers. The new government's aim of food self-sufficiency was quickly dashed as a mild drought in 1976 became severe in 1977. A joint study by the Lao Agricultural Ministry and the UNDP in September 1977 estimated that the harvest was down 40% compared with the previous year, and an appalling 95% in some provinces in the south. Only large infusions of international food aid staved off famine throughout the country. Then, in 1978, the monsoon that promised a good crop turned into a deluge causing flash floods in the mountain valleys and inundating vast areas of the Mekong Plain. Lao Vice-Foreign Minister Kamphay Boupha said half the population was threatened with famine and once again appealed for international help. In these dire conditions many people decided to leave the country.

In mid-1978 the government tried to improve agricultural productivity and expand its minuscule revenue base by attempting to accelerate the formation of collective farms. Hastily implemented, poorly planned, and conducted by unskilled cadres, this drive soon alienated many lowland peasants, particularly in the south of the country. A year later the government called a halt, but not before its actions had spurred on the outflow of refugees. Slowly improving economic conditions, in combination with a more moderate and rational economic policy from late 1979 onwards, have meant a steady decline in the number of refugees from the peak of 1978.

By contrast the hill-tribes' movement has been in two large, sudden waves. The reason for the 1975 outflow is relatively straightforward. The collapse of the 'urban' refugee economy around Long Cheng and Ban Son and of the Secret Army itself compelled thousands of Hmong to leave. However, by the end of 1975, of the approximately 130,000 Hmong who had become refugees inside Laos and had gathered in the region east and south of Long Cheng, 100,000 remained. And, for the next three years the number of Hmong who left Laos was but a fraction of the lowland Lao departures. Why did so few leave over this period, and why the outpouring in 1979?

Before we answer this, however, it will be useful for us to try to place the Hmong migrations after 1975 in some general and comparative perspective. For, as one anthropologist has written: 'The Meo are conditioned to adventure. . . . They appear to have little attachment to places as such. If they are "sons of the soil", they are not sons of any particular soil. . . . Therefore if a new territory appears before them their migration speeds up according to its potentialities.'[5] As we have seen, there was already a drift towards the highland frontier in Thailand, and by 1979 reports of the well-provisioned refugee camps and the promise of new territory were beckoning.

In his 1976 study of Hmong migratory patterns in northern Thailand, William Geddes noted that out of 9,194 households (approximately 73,500 people), 84% had been in the same location for under five years, 72% for under four years, and 59% for under three years.[6] By contrast, the percentage of Hmong who had left the southern area of Phu Bia in Laos over four years was approximately 43% (and even this figure is too high because it is based on figures for all hill-tribes). Thus, in considerably more unstable conditions, out of a group of Hmong in Laos of approximately the same size as the group in Thailand, only just over half as many moved, compared with the Thai group, over a four-year span. Geddes' figures, however, cover both short and long-term movements, while the Hmong movement from Laos is obviously all long-term. By controlling for short-range movement, the actual migratory shifts of Hmong in Thailand and those in Laos could turn out to be similar. With the information presently available we cannot say. However, in this light the Hmong movement out of Laos does not look as spectacular or unusual as the raw figures suggest.

There has been considerable informal and unrecorded movement of Hmong since 1975, especially in Sayaboury province which shares a land border with Thailand. Hill-tribespeople have never recognized international borders, especially land ones, and many Hmong and other tribal groups have crossed into Thailand in the natural process of migration, or to survey the possibilities for moving. Many of these people return by themselves to Communist Laos. For example, in January 1978 the Sayaboury provincial authorities were faced with the problem of resettling 4,000 displaced persons, most of whom had returned to Laos without any official Thai–Lao Government cooperation. Some were from Ban Nam Yao camp, but the majority of them said that they had stayed with relatives in Thailand. Some of these people explained their movements to western aid workers: 'One elderly-looking man with a khaki shirt said he came back from Thailand where he had lived for about one year. Lack of food was the main reason he left Laos, but scarcity of food was also a problem in Thailand, therefore he returned to Laos.' Another Hmong said he went to Thailand in late 1975 after 'bad people told the villagers to go there because soon there would be problems in the area.' Many people in his village 'left in confusion' but returned after three months wandering the hillsides. 'We couldn't find any place to live. The Thai did not like us coming to their area, so we came back to Laos.' (At that time no substantial refugee camps had been set up in this area of Thailand.) Another explained that all but five families of his village went to Thailand. 'Our old village has very poor land and there is not enough place to plant a lot of rice.'[7] That was why they left. However, land pressure is very great in northern Thailand and many people were either compelled to enter refugee camps or forced back to Laos. A group of Hmong stumbling back into

Sayaboury province in March 1981 claimed that they had been robbed, and thirty of their adult members shot by Thai police. Aid workers in Laos saw this latter claim as plausible because of the disproportionate number of small children in the group. Other tribal groups have also been treated in this way. In June 1982, 321 Yao were pushed back into Ban Houei Sai by the Thais, with reports of casualties. It is clear, however, from the accounts given by Hmong from Sayaboury that they moved for economic reasons and sometimes vague political fears. They were not fleeing actual Communist terror, while in some cases they were being terrorized by Thai police into returning to Laos.

The Hmong refugee concentrations in the mountains south of Phu Bia were obviously a major problem for the government that came to power in December 1975, especially as this population contained elements hostile to the Pathet Lao. Government policy was first to assist those who wanted to return to their home areas, and second to begin the process of re-settling the Hmong at lower altitudes and in permanent villages. In this way they would be able to provide schools and hospitals for the Hmong, and also, just as importantly, exercise administrative control over them.

The government's ability to re-settle people in their home areas was severely limited by inadequate transport and by its inability to supply re-settled people with food while they rebuilt their villages and fields. In 1975 only a few hundred Hmong could be re-settled back in the mountains around the Plain of Jars, including ex-CIA soldiers I spoke with at Ban Kuu, and those at Ban Nok did not return from Long Cheng until 1976. The re-settling of the lowland Lao on the Plain took close to three years as people painstakingly cleared the land of unexploded bombs and rebuilt the towns and villages. During this period government-supplied food ensured their survival, and today they are self-sufficient. The problems of transport and supply to the Hmong in the hills around the Plain were even more difficult. By 1980 Lao Information Minister Sisana Sisane admitted that only 3,000 families had been re-settled from their mountaintop abodes.[8] This hardly counts as mass forced re-settlement, and throws into question claims made by many writers that the Hmong have been leaving Laos because the government is forcing them *en masse* to give up their traditional way of life. The truth is that the Lao Government could not force them to do so even if it tried.

For the displaced people left in the strip stretching from West to East, from Ban Son through to Muong Ao, Muong Cha, and Muong Om, including the area around Phu Bia previously graced with Air America airstrips, the Pathet Lao attempted to consolidate the settlements already established for the Hmong by USAID. However, they were unable to provide unlimited supplies of food to sustain the settlements at their previous level and therefore Hmong spread out from these points to try to form villages and establish gardens in which they could plant their subsistence crops.

Much of the land around these USAID supply points had already been overworked and villagers had to move off into wild mountain forest to find new suitable areas. However, only those Hmong with sufficient stocks of rice for both food and planting were in a position to split off completely from these areas. Many of the displaced Hmong were destitute, while others were only able to establish themselves semi-independently, relying on some food and other inputs from the government.* The Hmong economy at the best of times is fragile and the cultivation of already overtaxed land made it even more precarious. Economic failure in either the lowlands or the highlands would spell disaster for the former refugees.

The ability of the new government to sustain the re-orientation of the mountain economy depended on the capacity of the lowland economy to produce food surpluses not only for the displaced Hmong, but also for the re-settled Lao around the Plain of Jars. As we have seen, the lowland Lao economy had reached a critical, in fact desperate, stage by late 1978. Already the shortages had sent people flooding across the Mekong, and the government obviously lacked the surpluses required to cover shortages in the mountains until the next harvest the following year. Floods had affected some of the mountain valley settlements that year as well, and hence even in normal conditions would require lowland sustenance to tide them over. Thus by 1979 the economic situation in the mountains was as serious as in the lowlands.

*It is worth recalling that the shortage of animals had been exacerbated by the slaughtering of them during the initial panic as Hmong tried to flee following the fall of Long Cheng in May 1975.

By this time other economic factors had come into play in the relatively over-populated area south of Phu Bia. Falling soil fertility cut heavily into yields, and swidden fields for many of the tribesmen were now at such a distance that thoughts of relocating the village, clan or family to a new area was under consideration by many Hmong. Food shortages had also made the population more prone to sickness, which in turn affected labour productivity in an essentially labour intensive economy, making the food situation worse. In the blaze of publicity surrounding the 'gassings' the fact that the vast majority of Hmong were saying that they had left because they had run out of food was ignored.

Because of the overcrowding in the area short-range migration was not realistic and hence many decided to head for Thailand where, because of the exodus of 1975, they now had relatives. Resistance groups, couriers from relatives in Thailand, and the rumour network informed them that conditions were much better in Thailand, and that they would be catered for in the camps there as the Americans had ensured prior to 1975.

Thus strong push-and-pull factors were present in 1979 to trigger what Jacques Lemoine calls the 'migratory fever' that periodically grips Hmong communities.[9] The movement in 1979 became something of a stampede because these broad economic factors combined to produce a general atmosphere of insecurity and panic amongst the Hmong in the southern environs of Phu Bia. The latent fear of persecution by the Pathet Lao or the Vietnamese re-surfaced, and the few stories of chemical warfare were now given a new and frightening relevance.

The movement of Hmong plummetted once again after 1979 as population pressure in the mountains eased. Moreover, economic conditions in Laos improved dramatically with an excellent harvest in 1980–81. By this time as well Thai attitudes to refugees had become tougher and re-settlement opportunities fewer.

The Fear

To understand the dynamic of the fear that spread among the Hmong in 1979, it is instructive to look at a similar event in another country with poor mass communications, rural parochialism, mass illiteracy, and social turmoil. The historian George Lefebvre has called it *The Great Fear of 1789: Rural Panic in Revolutionary France*. This Great Fear he said was 'one gigantic rumour'; yet he adds 'the danger was far from imaginary'.[10]

The panics in rural France also took place in an insecure economic and social environment in which rumours were allied to political upheaval. High prices and threats of famine were ascribed to hoarding by the government, its agents, the tithe collectors and the nobility. As the political and social conflict of the revolution deepened, it did not take long to discover that there was an élite conspiracy to halt change by famine. The widespread dislocation of the normal order fuelled the belief that retribution was in the air – and it was because this was always a *possibility* that Lefebvre says the Great Fear was not strictly imaginary.

There were many local panics that preceded the Great Fear where it was believed that bands of brigands were about to fall on villages and destroy them. Lefebvre cites the following example of how rumour and panic ran through the French countryside:

'On 4 July at about eight o'clock in the morning, between Burcy and Vire, an old woman was walking to her field when she was alarmed to see two rather strange men at the roadside; one was lying down apparently exhausted and distressed, the other was walking up and down with a desperate expression on his face. The son of a local bailiff came by on horseback: she told him what she had seen; she said they looked frightening, like brigands; he agreed, flew into a panic, clapped spurs to his horse and rode like the wind to Vire, shouting as he went that the brigands were coming: everyone who saw the two men pass along the road was convinced that they were dangerous. The rumour spread and grew with great speed; in Burcy, they said there were two brigands; in Presles, there were ten, three hundred in Vassy, six hundred in Vire; by the time the news got to Saint-Lo, Bayeux and Caën, there were supposed to be three thousand brigands gathered in the woods around Vire, looting, burning and killing. The local mayors who believed the rumours instantly called for help from every side: "The national guard of

Tinchebray", wrote the mayor to his colleague in Domfront, "with only five hundred guns, cannot hold out against the considerable forces poised to attack us and apparently increased hourly by every ruffian in the country. It is of the greatest urgency that the Domfront national guard arrive here with all speed by forced marches and with plenty of ammunition". Less than seven hours later, the tocsin sounded for twenty-five leagues around. In Caën, the authorities delayed no longer. General Ordener, at the head of the local garrison and the national guard, set out for the attack, whilst more than thirty thousand men rushed to join him. As soon as they realized it was a false alert, they hastened to reassure the rest of Normandy which stood on the brink of mobilization.'[11]

Lefebvre comments that when a population or an army expects the arrival of some enemy it would be unusual if this enemy were not sighted at some time or other. 'A suspicious character, a cloud of dust, less than this even; a sound, a light, a shadow is enough to start an alarm. Auto-suggestion plays an even greater part and they imagine that they see or hear something. This is how whole armies fly into panics. . . .'[12] The difference between the hundreds of local panics, which were a sort of prelude, and the Great Fear itself was the psychological shift from a lurking premonition of catastrophe to total certainty – the brigands were there in the flesh, they could be seen and heard. 'Mass hysteria would break out amongst the peasant women: in their imagination, it was already too late – they were raped, then murdered, their children slaughtered, their homes burnt to the ground; weeping and wailing, they fled into the woods and fields, a few provisions and bits of clothing clutched to their bosoms.'[13] Sometimes this happened simply because a sentry or someone accidentally discharged their rifle. A number of Hmong refugees I spoke with said they fled their villages after they had heard guns, or what they thought were guns, firing off in the distance. They had seen no one but assumed it was the 'Vietnamese'. As we have already seen, many Hmong interpreted the most everyday and ordinary actions by Pathet Lao soldiers, or an aircraft, as sinister omens and often acted upon them by fleeing.

The Great Fear spread across France by word of mouth and on

horseback. Private mail full of hearsay was read out publicly in the streets and found its way to the market place, that vital relay point for rumour. 'The vast majority of French people depended entirely on oral tradition for the dissemination of news. What would most of them have done with a newspaper in any case? They could not read and between five and six million of them could not even speak French. But for the government and the aristocracy, this means of transmission was a great deal more dangerous than freedom of the press. It goes without saying that it favoured the spread of false reports, the distortion and exaggeration of fact, the growth of legends. Even the most level-headed could not help believing what they heard because they had no way of finding out the truth. In the empty silence of the provinces, every word had the most extraordinary resonance and was taken as gospel. In due course, the rumour would reach the ear of a journalist who would imbue it with new strength by putting it into print.'[14] Much the same thing happened in the 'empty silence' south of Phu Bia. Against the background of economic and social insecurity, small skirmishes with any remnants of the Secret Army would quickly turn into 'major campaigns'; people fleeing because they had heard shots spread the fear to other villages who packed up and followed; and fears of Pathet Lao retribution against Hmong who had had anything to do with USAID were re-ignited. For the Hmong inside Laos the rumours of fighting and the use of gas did not get into print but were broadcast over Thai radio and Voice of America, and then travelled along the mountain rumour network. In late 1978 and throughout 1979 the airwaves were also filled with accounts of atrocities in Kampuchea, a Vietnamese invasion of Kampuchea, a Chinese invasion of Vietnam and potentially of Laos. Absorbed in a disjointed way these too fuelled the panic.

The Great Fear in France, however, was not a conspiracy, even though the revolutionaries believed it was being spread by the aristocrats, who for their part believed the rumours were the work of the revolutionaries. As Lefebvre remarks: 'There is no need to assume that the revolutionaries had deliberately planned to spread the rumours, but one must accept that the orators in the towns who encouraged the arming of local populations for political reasons did much to propagate them. They genuinely believed in the brigands. At the same time, however, the news operated to their advantage. . . .'[15] Similarly, the CIA-trained Hmong had every reason to promote or exaggerate stories of repression and chemical warfare, while genuinely believing them. General anxiety among the Hmong allowed the panic to spread unhindered because in the climate of the time everyone was expecting the worst.

The fear had already begun before 1975. A former official in the Pathet Lao government, Amphay Dore, when describing the fall of the old regime and the defeat of Vang Pao in his book *Le Partage du Mékong*, recounts the following tale which from our perspective is a fascinating insight into the origin of one rumour among the Hmong:

'It had begun with a goat and was first told to me by a friend in 1973 who had returned from Sayaboury province. "One day", he recounted to me, "a Hmong from the village of Nam Pouy was preparing himself to return home with his goats when one of them made a sound like human words. He cocked his ear and discovered that he was not imagining things when he heard repeated, distinctly this time:
After the war, death of the Hmong!
After the war, death of the Hmong!"
In order to ward off its foreboding prediction he instantly killed the animal. But he was extremely troubled by it: on the one hand, it was not customary to hear a goat speak; on the other, how could one imagine that the Hmong who had survived so remarkably in times of war could die in times of peace? The saying was, at the very least, puzzling. Yet from this extraordinary beginning the story swept like wild-fire through the mountains of north Laos.'[16]

Clearly the ground for fear among the Hmong had long been fertile.

A similar logic applies to American politicians, officials, and many journalists and aid workers, all of whom expected the worst after the Communist regimes took power in Indochina. For years many of them had predicted a massive bloodbath in South Vietnam, and although it never happened there were always right-wing fringe groups claiming it had, and waiting in the wings for retrospective vindication. Similarly, there had always been a core of

Westerners who before 1975 were quick to denounce either the Southern Vietnamese lowland regime, or the lowland Lao regime, for their treatment of the Montagnards. Just why Western societies have always produced groups who romanticize primitive societies need not detain us here, nor should the fact that they were often drawing attention to real injustices. The point is that these defenders of the Montagnards were all too ready to denounce the policies of lowland governments as 'genocide'. This peculiar brand of paranoia was supercharged after 1975 with traditional anti-communism and many were expecting that the worst would come to the Hmong after the Communist takeover, and many began instantly predicting their disappearance. At the first whiff of 'gas', these people felt vindicated.

When a bloodbath did occur in Kampuchea (although romantics had said it was impossible in such a 'gentle land'), it came as a surrogate justification for the long-held fears about what would happen in Vietnam and Laos. Then, with the region awash with horror stories from late 1978 onwards, chemical warfare stories leapt into the headlines and were easily believed. The flood of Hmong across the Mekong over 1979 only reinforced belief in them, hence setting up a continuous feed-back process which is still going on today as Hmong in Laos tune in to Voice of America or Thai radio, or even Vientiane radio broadcasting denials, to hear stories about gas that fuel rumours and speculation.

Conspiracy theories will not help us to explain the dissemination of the gassing allegations. A central argument of this book is that the allegations are almost certainly like the Great Fear, one giant rumour. It has no single point of origin, nor any single broadcaster. There is no question that it has been in the interests of certain groups, governments, and individuals to push the story – the remnants of the Secret Army, the CIA, the US Government, the Khmers Rouges – and it is extremely important to probe who is relaying the story and how. This is not the same as saying that any one of these groups hatched a plot to launch the allegations of chemical-weapons use. Nor is it to suggest that these stories are not genuinely believed when they are relayed. Rumours can begin and grow into 'truth' in the most random and anarchic ways, and need have no factual foundation whatsoever. All they require is an appropriate environment.

Gas Rumours Before 1975

At any time, isolating the original author of a rumour is well-nigh impossible. The origin of the gas story would appear to be western aid workers interpreting what were probably smoke bombs, rockets, maybe napalm, or indeed tear gas, as poison gas or other lethal chemicals. The potential for such a story to mushroom was clearly recognized by the Americans in the mid-1960s when they first began extensive use of CS gas in Vietnam. They instructed their troops never to use the word 'gas' and always to qualify it as 'tear gas'. In the Hmong camps there has never been such discrimination. Once the Lao story began, and the Hmong leadership observed what a tremendous impact mention of the word 'gas' had on aid workers, government officials and journalists, they soon began to solicit and promote such stories. Once the rumour process reaches this stage, it naturally has a life of its own.

There are a number of striking instances of just this occurring in South Vietnam before 1975. Writing in the mid-1960s when the US first started using gas in Vietnam, Kuno Knoebel observed:

> 'Non-lethal gases – such as tear gas – were also used. I have seen unconscious women and children dragged out of tunnels and bunkers into which tear gas bombs had been thrown. The effect on the peasants was frightful. Several times peasants who had been brought under control this way tried to flee, screaming. They believed the troops wanted to gas them to death. Communist agit-prop teams had an easy job convincing them that the Americans intended 'to exterminate the entire Vietnamese people in a horrible way with gas'. . . . Prince Sihanouk's minister of information in Cambodia told me he was convinced the Americans wanted to gas the South Vietnamese people to death in enormous concentration camps. Laotian General Ma knew "for a fact" that the Americans in Vietnam had already gassed close to a million peasants. None of this is true, but when relatively educated Asians believe such rumours, how difficult it is to explain to a peasant the difference between chemical spray, tear gas, and lethal gas.'[17]

We might add that these latter remarks apply not only to ignorant peasants, but to many Western journalists as well.

Another journalist writing around the same time about *The New Face of War*, Malcolm W. Browne, reported on the many rumours about US atrocities: disembowelling women, violating children, eating the livers of peasants, and 'most of all' stories about poison. Indeed, in 1964 Cambodia was complaining to the United Nations that the Americans were 'dropping deadly yellow powder over border villages'. Commenting on the defoliation programme that the US had initiated in the early sixties Browne wrote:

'Dropping such things from the sky generally seems unnatural to the Vietnamese peasant, even when he has been told by government leaflets what to expect and that he should not worry. Viet Cong agents had little difficulty convincing much of the population that America had launched a diabolical new kind of chemical warfare. Outbreaks of food poisoning and epidemics, which are common in the Vietnamese countryside, were blamed on the American spray. . . . The American poison myth grew. In one community, an old woman sat moaning on a curb one day. Passers-by asking what was wrong were told that an American military adviser had touched her basket of vegetables with a special poison stick, thereby destroying her market stock.'[18]

(It should be noted that Browne argued that the defoliants were harmless to humans, the opinion most widely held amongst journalists in Vietnam in the mid-1960s.)

In the early 1970s the US National Academy of Sciences conducted surveys into the effects of herbicides on the Vietnamese population. The surveys' findings said: 'A difficult area of inquiry concerned possible deaths due to the herbicides. Sickness and death are common occurrences in Highland villages, and infant mortality is particularly high. In addition, NLF/DRVN propaganda about the harmful effects of the sprayed chemicals, which began in 1962, stressed the fact that human beings – especially children – might fall ill and die if exposed; and both the RVN and the NLF/DRVN charged that water and food supplies were being poisoned by the opposing side in order to kill the inhabitants.'[19] The survey found that the Montagnards tended to report many more deaths than Lowland Vietnamese peasants. One participant in the survey, biochemist M. Meselson, commented before a Committee on Foreign Affairs enquiry in April 1980: 'The Montagnards said lots of people died of "medicine from the sky". I do not think the herbicide or CS gas we sprayed would kill people. I cannot understand it. Yet you have people who seem to be innocent, simple people, who are telling you these stories. So I am puzzled by this. . . .'[20] After our survey of primitive notions of health in the last chapter, the findings of the US report should not be so puzzling, and they do tend to confirm the idea that such notions provide a fertile base for the spontaneous propagation of rumours about poison and the causes of death.

Rumours of poison were particularly potent. They persisted despite South Vietnamese government efforts to check them, apparently by sending around teams which would, for example, stand up and drink glasses of defoliant! The peasants reacted to this, however, as some magician's trick. (We do not know what happened to the people who drank these concoctions.) The rumours about poison had an attraction greater than any attempt by the government to provide what it saw as a rational explanation. It was not, as they learned, a question of rationality. Moreover these stories were being encouraged and promoted by the NLF.

More relevant for us are the reports of poisoning that came from the Plain of Jars in the late 1960s and early 1970s. These were gathered by aid worker Walter N. Haney at the time.[21] It is worth quoting a number of Haney's interviews from this time because their tone helps us to understand the reports from the refugees since 1975.

Many of the refugees Haney spoke to talked about poison paper: 'The planes had dropped the gold and silver paper. Sao Si had gone out to the ricefield with her mother. She picked up some of it and smelled it. She became very drunk and threw up and died the next day. Usually we were very careful because the Pathet Lao had told us that it was poison. But Sao Si picked it up and smelled it before her mother could keep her from picking it up. The planes dropped the poison three times. (Later the village chief told me that the poison was dropped many times.)'[22]

Or another discussion with five refugees in 1970: 'The "poison" was sent down by the airplanes. We called it *Ya Phit* (poison medicine) or *Ya Beua* (exploding medicine). The planes dropped a bomb which broke open and sent out the paper, silver and gold paper. . . . They dropped it many times in 1967, 1968 and 1969. They dropped it all over. . . . If animals ate the grass on which the poison had dropped they would die. Pigs, chickens, ducks, buffalo, cows, even dogs died from the poison. We couldn't touch it, so we had to take sticks and puch it into holes and bury it.'[23]

There was also a report of a 'smoke bomb' that burst near a foxhole sheltering children: 'A smoke bomb fell near the hole. The kind which they shoot. Nan Boudi ate some vegetables near where the bomb had fallen. She got sick and died three days later. We think the bomb had poisoned the vegetables.'[24]

Or: 'The children had gone to care for the buffalo. They stopped to eat some sour leaves, the kind they regularly ate. But this time after eating the leaves, they started to throw up. Three days later they all died. The planes dropped the poison two days before. . . . The poison was like sheets of paper.'[25] Some described the paper as coming in various sizes and sometimes 'both green and white in colour. It would burn your feet if you stepped on it.' And there was 'another kind of poison which looked like salt. After buffalo ate grass on which it was dropped they died.'[26]

One district official, a refugee, gave a more careful account: 'Yes, there were many kinds of things which the villagers called poison. . . . No, I never saw any poison. In Xieng Khouang all I saw was the bombs that exploded sending out many white particles. If the chickens ate it they would die. It was small and white like salt.' Others cut in at this point to discuss the poison and they explained that the 'Vietnamese' had told them not to touch or pick up the poison paper, 'sometimes they called it *Ya Mao* (literally drunk medicine).'[27] And, indeed, many of the refugees described the effects as becoming 'like a drunk person', or simply: 'Died while fleeing on account of drunkenness.'

What are we to make of these reports? There were certainly enough descriptions of 'poison' paper, 'white salt' or *Ya Phit* for a gullible or politically motivated reporter or aid worker to conclude that the US was really carpetting the Plain of Jars with some kind of chemical poison. Haney, however, unlike the Americans who years later interviewed Hmong from the same region about 'gas', was hesitant about jumping to conclusions. (And unlike his compatriots later, Haney described carefully how he evaluated his refugee stories.) The most commonly described form of poison was the strips of paper that Haney surmised was radar chaff dropped to jam radar-controlled anti-aircraft installations in the area. 'For obvious political reasons', he writes, 'the Pathet Lao might have identified such radar chaff as poison. I suggested this explanation to one refugee. He replied that, yes, the planes sometimes did drop the "radar paper". He said that the poison paper looked almost exactly like the radar paper but could be distinguished from it in four ways: 1. If the paper poison was touched it would feel hot or at least warm. 2. If the paper poison was immersed in water it would bubble (reportedly making it toxic). 3. If the paper poison was hit or moved roughly it would give off a fine dust. 4. The poison paper was toxic to both plants and animals.'

Similar detail has impressed investigators into the chemical warfare stories, but Haney in this earlier situation observed that these distinctions made by his informant were tenuous (without saying why), and concluded that 'I think it is safe to assume that at least *some* [my emphasis] of the reports of the poison silver paper were merely reports of radar chaff.'[28] Curiously Haney did not feel confident enough to ascribe all the stories about poisoning to radar chaff, but nor did he speculate further. An analogous situation in the late 1970s would have sent the US State Department into a frenzy about Soviet poison paper. Some of the detail given to Haney, however, would seem to point in the direction of phosphorous bombs or rockets. Descriptions of the substance as hot or warm are one indication, and it is true that phosphorous smoke markers, often used by the US during bombing strikes, give off a toxic smoke. There is, of course, not enough information for us to draw definite conclusions about what the refugees were describing as poison. Their descriptions of poison paper do not correspond to any known weapon in the US arsenal in Indochina.

The testimony is intriguing because of the ease with which the refugees were prepared to associate the presence of this paper with the poisoning or death of loved ones or animals. That they were in a traumatic situation surrounded by death and destruction from bombs as well as disease is undeniable, and I would argue that it led to the acceptance of the stories about poison paper among the refugees.

The second type of poison described to Haney was of a granular or powdery texture, and refugees often said it looked like salt. They also made a striking reference to a poison looking like yellow flour. They compared the colour to the yellow of a khaki uniform. They reported that on one occasion it was dropped on a field and after grazing there thirty cows died. They said that if pigs or chickens foraged in an area where it had been dropped they would die with their flesh turning yellow and their intestines green . . . it would kill plants as well.'[29] Yellow rain, no doubt. . . .

This description corresponds to the effects of defoliation. Presumably Haney did not draw this conclusion because at that time use of defoliants by the US in Laos was still a secret. Only in early 1982 was it confirmed that the Americans had made extensive use of it in the south of Laos from 1965 onwards, though this tells us little about the use of herbicides in the north and around the Plain of Jars.[30] We do know that herbicides were used against hilltribe opium crops from 1971–73, but that was after Haney's refugee reports had appeared. To date there is no confirmation that the US used herbicides against peasants on the Plain of Jars before 1971. Nevertheless the refugee reports would indicate that they were in fact used in this region from 1967 onwards. Whatever we choose to believe, it is clear that the saga of the 'yellow rain' begins well before 1975.

Haney also collected a 'wide variety' of reports about poisonous devices, but he did not discuss them because they were often reported second hand or only by a single individual. Again, later American researchers working with the Hmong were less judicious.

At the presentation of Haney's report to a Senate subcommittee on refugees in Indochina in 1971 William H. Sullivan, the Deputy Assistant Secretary for East Asian and Pacific Affairs, was disturbed enough by the frequency of the reports of poison to issue an official disclaimer: 'United States forces, of course, do not employ any poisons or poisonous weapons in Southeast Asia or elsewhere.' The poison paper, he concurred, was probably radar chaff. 'The granular yellow powder remains unidentified, but the Defense Department notes that a wide variety of United States or communist equipment such as batteries, smoke canisters, parachute flares, and the like could produce a residue resembling a powder, some of which could be toxic to plants, animals, and maybe humans.'[31] He did not mention herbicides.

Leaving aside the obvious duplicity about the US claim not to be employing *any* poisons in Southeast Asia – what Sullivan imagined defoliants or CS gas to be we cannot say – it is possible to imagine the howl of incredulity if the Lao, the Vietnamese, or the Soviet governments offered a similar explanation for today's reports of 'yellow rain'.

The reports of the use of poison on or around the Plain of Jars were collected not only by Haney, but also by a USAID worker, Fred Branfmann, who interviewed hundreds of people from that region over 1970–71. Here are two examples of reports he collected.

A forty-two-year-old woman told him: 'In 1968 planes of many kinds came and killed people. In the war in Xieng Khouang I saw poison in packets like candy. We didn't know if the candy could be eaten. But after some people did eat it, they became drunk and threw up blood and died. Everyone just waited for the day of their deaths, as day and night the airplanes never stopped bombing. They dropped poison and napalm on the villages and in the forest, wherever the villagers stayed.'[32]

According to a thirty-eight-year-old man: '. . . we had to go live in the hills and forests so that we never saw the sun and our children turned yellow. The most difficult time for me occurred when I was living in one big hole with many other villagers and one day airplanes dropped smoke bombs on our hole, causing us to become dizzy and throw up blood so that we couldn't run away.'[33]

From these refugee descriptions of similar symptoms to those of the Hmong since 1975, should we conclude that the US was using lethal gas, or because they report haemorrhaging from the mouth should we conclude that the USAF was dropping mycotoxins? No.

Neither Haney nor Branfmann was specifically looking for poison stories as they were more concerned with the total condition of the refugees. In one sense this should make the stories more credible, and Haney says that when he did stumble across them he began by making very discreet enquiries about poison so that he would not put words or ideas into peoples' heads. He says: 'When I first heard the account of the children's deaths due to "poison" I did not quite believe it. I thought that the refugees were simply using the word "poison" to describe napalm which had not ignited. Only after I had returned to get details of the "poison" did I really comprehend that they were describing something quite distinct from napalm. After this first story I began making gentle inquiries about it in other refugee camps.'[34]

The story was picked up at that time and broadcast – unsurprisingly – not by the western media but by Communist media and propaganda teams who told peasants that anything dropped from US planes was poisonous. In many cases they were not entirely wrong. Indeed, Browne, who was not sympathetic to the Communists, admitted that 'the Viet Cong issued helpful pamphlets, explaining how to avoid the bad effects of spray.'[35] While a great deal of propaganda mileage was made out of the fact that the US was using poisonous sprays in Indochina, there was a basic common sense in the Viet Cong advice over and above that. Because they were not in a position to instruct the peasants on the differences between various war devices, they therefore advised them that everything that was dropped was dangerous and poisonous and should be avoided. Some people still ignored this advice and were killed, just as children on the Plain of Jars today, who have been told over and over not to play with unexploded bombs, still do so – with fatal consequences.

But once the Communists had encouraged stories about 'poison medicine', 'exploding medicine' or 'drunk medicine', they were not in a position to suddenly switch them off once they had taken power. Perhaps they are discovering the truth of this as they listen with bewilderment to the stories about 'medicine from the sky' coming from the Hmong refugees in Thailand.

These early reports from the Plain of Jars can, I think, help us understand the nature of the gassing stories told by the Hmong in a number of ways. First, once the story had spread that poison paper was a cause of death, then the mere presence of this radar chaff was obviously enough to establish a causal link between it and the death of a loved one from unknown causes. The vaguer notion of gas obviously performs the same function even more effectively. Second, if we believe the US government's claim that they did not use defoliants on or around the Plain of Jars prior to 1971, how can we explain the story of yellow powder except to say that refugees simply invented it as one means of explaining the carnage that had engulfed them? Thirdly, these people had lived through a massive and horrible bombing campaign and it is not surprising that bizarre stories about death, such as the accounts of mass gassing in South Vietnam, should take root and acquire wide credibility. Why such rumours are adopted by others, such as Western aid personnel, journalists or politicians is, of course, an entirely different matter. Finally, we must observe that these stories came primarily from lowland Lao and not Montagnards, who – if the US Academy of Science's observations were true also for Laos – would be more inclined to exaggerate the story.

While we cannot be certain that the refugees from the Plain of Jars were subject to defoliants, we do know for a fact that the Hmong and other hilltribes were subject to them from 1971–73.

In 1971, under pressure from the US government, the RLG declared opium illegal. Suddenly the Hmong poppy growers who had been assisted in their trade by Air America and had helped line the pockets of the corrupt lowland Lao elite, found themselves on the other side of the law. The *National Geographic* reported in January 1974: 'Brutal enforcement of the new law last year left the Hmong bitter. In Teu La, farmer Tsia Schoong told me with tears in his eyes, "Both my wives were working in the poppy field, with our babies over their backs. A cloud fell out of an airplane. They became like they were drunk. The poppy crop withered and died; so did all the vegetables and banana trees, and all of the dogs and many of the pigs. Little Eu Schoong, one month old, refused his mother's milk and died four days later. Two other babies who were in the fields also perished." Hmong in four nearby villages told similar stories and reported twelve more deaths from lethal spray. . . . no one would admit authorizing the spraying. One report claimed a mould killed the poppies. An American official said it might have been frost. "Who was responsible for this?" I asked General Vang Pao. "Your ambassador sat where you are", Vang

Pao replied. "He told me the Americans didn't do it. . . . All I know is the Hmong blame me." '[36]

This experience seems to have caused a deep revulsion among the hill-tribes and was an important element in the growing Hmong disaffection with Vang Pao. As we have already seen, one of the first revolts following the 1973 ceasefire was among the Secret Army in Ban Houei Sai when the rebels demanded that the ban on growing opium be lifted. This issue came up when I was interviewing the ex-CIA Hmong in Xieng Khouang about 'chemical warfare' both before and after 1975.

At Ban Nok I had already asked the Hmong whether they had heard anything about the use of gas around Phu Bia since 1975 (there was considerable confusion about what the term gas meant). They said they had not heard anything. So I asked about before 1975, upon which they answered that 'in 1970–71 the US and Vang Pao said we could no longer grow opium in the Phu Bia area where there were many gardens, and so they then dropped gas on the gardens'. I queried them about the difference between gas and defoliant. They replied that it was like powder – an intriguing description that fits gas more than a sprayed defoliant. It killed the opium, the banana trees, and grasses, though it did not kill the strong trees. People affected by it acted as though they were drunk, vomited and some died over the following year. The leaves on the bushes and on the opium plants looked like they had hot water poured over them.

At Ban Kuu the reaction was similar. They first said gas was used against fruit trees and opium around Phu Bia, but when queried about what exactly it was there was a great deal of confusion about how to describe it: *Ya Phit* (poison medicine), *Ya Phit Chimie* (poison chemicals) and *Ya Phit Raburt* (poison medicine bombs) were used interchangeably. They finally decided that there were two kinds: one was similar to DDT, the other was a chemical sprayed by an aeroplane that killed the trees and the opium – a distinction which escaped me. Moreover, they said that if you smoked opium gathered from the area where the plane had dropped the 'gas', you died.

They added that before Vang Pao became a general and very rich, he allowed the Hmong to grow opium because he understood their need for cash. The spraying of the opium showed that he no longer understood the Hmong's needs. Indeed, it may have been the spraying of the opium that finally lost Vang Pao the allegiance of this particular group of Hmong. The Communist government repealed the offending law early in 1976.

The significant feature of these interviews, however, is the confusion over how to describe what we know to have been defoliation among a group of Hmong not experienced at answering such questions.

The importance of this general experience, greatly resented by the Hmong, is that it could have provided the raw material out of which a potent rumour could be spun after 1975 which would be immediately acceptable to most Hmong who had never seen 'gas'. Indeed, perhaps it is this which led the State Department to claim in the *Hearing* of December 1979: 'Beginning in 1974, and gradually increasing in frequency in 1976 and 1977, there were reports of poison gas use by Lao and Vietnamese troops against insurgent Hmong tribes.'[37] As we noted in Chapter Three, the dating of the chemical warfare allegations from 1974 was changed subsequently, without any explanation, to 1976. It would appear that the State Department in its investigations came across references by refugees to clouds falling out of the back of planes in 1974 and jumped to the conclusion that it was Communist use of gas. However, they must have become aware that this referred to their own, not widely publicized, defoliation campaign. Thus references to 1974 were quietly dropped. Whatever lies behind this, it is easy to see how defoliation could provide the basis for the subsequent rumours of gas. An insight into how this process operates was gleaned by two aid workers in early 1981 when they asked a Hmong in Ban Vinai about the thousands of unexploded US bombs that are littered about the Plain of Jars and kill people from time to time. He answered that the Vietnamese had put them there.*

---

*Or take the story told to Haney: 'They only dropped poison in Tasseng Seng. And they dropped belts and pens. Very pretty pens. If you opened them they would explode. This was in 1969. I never saw them. I only heard about them. Many pens and watches. But you could not pick them up. If you wound the watches they would explode. But I never saw them: I only heard the news.' Still today, stories like this circulate on the Plain of Jars – of radios that are really bombs and if you turn them on, they explode. We know the US sowed the Ho Chi Minh trail area with thousands of sensors looking like leaves and natural objects, but as far as I know not bombs like those described above. Nevertheless the stories are fervently believed.

That many of the gassing stories represent a form of syncretism is suggested by some of the evidence gathered by the US. One refugee told a Foreign Service officer in mid-1979: 'Source saw one MIG drop the agent from a level of 10,000 feet in what looked similar to rice sacks. These sacks burst at an elevation of about 300 metres releasing a brown gas.'[38] This story by a former Secret Army lieutenant looks very peculiar until one remembers that for years USAID supplied rice to the Hmong in the mountains by flying over in C-46 planes and kicking sacks out of them to the soldiers and refugees below. It would appear that this soldier has dressed up an old story for a new occasion.

We have seen that rumours in northeastern Thailand of strange genital diseases had active and latent cycles. In this chapter we have argued that rumours are at their most potent during periods of social dislocation – and presumably the Hmong refugees' increasing uneasiness about Thai policy towards them in 1981 forms a vital part of the backdrop to the vaccination panic in Ban Vinai in early 1982. It was economic and social insecurity among the Hmong in the post-1975 period that made them so receptive to rumours and caused them to leave the country in panic, particularly when the economic crisis peaked in the highlands in 1979. Improved economic conditions since then have helped to slow the Hmong outflow to a trickle and there is an atmosphere of increased security and stability among the Hmong inside Laos.

7
Inside Laos

One reason why the chemical warfare allegations from Laos appear superficially plausible is that they fit into an all too familiar pattern of persecution of an ethnic minority by an aggressive and chauvinistic ethnic majority. Indeed, writers like Jane Hamilton-Merritt and Jean Larteguy have drawn a parallel between the Jewish holocaust under the Nazis and the fate of the Hmong today. Such comparisons, however, are wild and inaccurate.

There is no single ethnic majority in Laos capable of enforcing its will on an ethnic minority or minorities.* We noted at the beginning of this book that there are perhaps sixty-five identifiable ethnic groups in Laos. It is also the case that upwards of 200,000 Hmong continue to live in Laos without persecution, and tribal minorities are represented at all levels of government. Under the regime that came to power in December 1975 Faydang Lobliayao became vice-president of the People's Supreme Assembly alongside two other minority leaders, Sisomphone Lovonsay (Thai Dam) and Sithon Kommandam (Lao Theung). Nivau Lobliayao became chairman of the Committee of Nationalities, while Maysouk (Thai Lu) became minister of industry and commerce.

---

*Some people may wish to argue that this overlooks so-called Vietnamese domination of Laos. The Vietnamese, they argue, are extremely chauvinistic toward their own minorities and hence would be no better in Laos. It is true that the old Southern regime was chauvinistic towards the Montagnards, but the Vietnamese communists have a fairly good record in this regard. See, for example, the 1976 Preface in George Condominas, *We have Eaten the Forest: The Story of a Montagnard Village in the Central Highlands of Vietnam*, New York 1977. Also Martial Dasse, *Montagnards Revoltés et Guerres Révolutionnaires en Asie du Sud-Est Continentale*, Bangkok 1976, Chapter 3.

Below them were Hmong and Thai Dam, provincial governors and officials. At the very least, the conflict with the Hmong rebels was not a straightforward ethnic cleavage or antagonism.

It was precisely the old RLG's lack of power in the mountains and among the tribal minorities in Laos that contributed to its undoing. It was a government staffed by lowland Lao for lowland Lao, ultimately unable to enforce its will in the mountainous two-thirds of the country. Consequently it never really achieved the creation of a truly national state. By contrast the Communists have spent most of their thirty-three-year existence in the mountains. The leadership is still predominantly ethnic Lao, though its mass following has always been drawn from the highland minorities. Had this movement not developed a successful minorities or nationalities policy, it would never have survived. At the height of the war in 1969, for example, a Pathet Lao broadcast stated: 'In fighting the enemy everyone must try to make progress, foster love and cooperation among the masses and pay equal attention to the people of all nationalities. . . . We must eradicate the idea that the Lao Theung and the Meo tribesmen are a lower class.'[1] The Pathet Lao minorities policy was a precondition of its success as a nationalist movement and makes it the first Lao Government that can legitimately claim jurisdiction over the whole country. To do this, it required the active participation of all ethnic groups in the running of the country. Any ethnic vendettas would have unravelled this fragile new national fabric. And, ultimately, only a successful nationalities policy can redress the ethnic imbalance at the pinnacle of government through mass education.

The new Communist government is acutely aware of the everyday ethnic animosities in their multi-cultural nation. The government has attempted to combat these feelings by discouraging the use of derogatory terms for the various ethnic groups. Also, as an important means of national integration the Lao alphabet, rather than the English one used by missionaries, is encouraged for writing minority languages. In Xieng Khouang most of the music I heard over the public address system was that of the haunting Hmong *khene* (flute). But when I interviewed some Lao and Hmong refugees in Chiang Khong camp, they bristled with indignation about the fact that under the Communists some members of a small and previously oppressed ethinc group in Laos, the Khmu, had taken up important administrative posts in their areas. To them the Khmu were naturally inferior. It will be years before Laos is free from tribal and other ethnic tensions, but there is no doubt that the government is doing all it can to hasten the demise of these sentiments.

An unspoken assumption of many writers who present the remnants of the Secret Army as a threat to the viability of the new government has been a stark contrast between the lifestyles and culture of the lowlanders and the highlanders. They argue that the Communists were forced into taking drastic measures, like using chemical weapons, to bring them under control. They have assumed that the Hmong are much better mountain fighters than the Pathet Lao or the Vietnamese. This argument is weak on all counts. First, we have seen that the remnants of the Secret Army were not a viable long-term threat to government authority. Second, the majority of the Pathet Lao Army was made up of hill-tribe minorities whose battle experience was precisely in mountain combat in which they were a match for the CIA Hmong prior to 1975. After the Communist victory, when the Secret Army had lost its support system and its command structure, the PLA was more than able to tackle the rebels with conventional military means. This applies equally to the Vietnamese troops who operated alongside the PLA: they were also made up largely of tribal minorities from the ethnically similar Vietnamese side of the mountainous border. (For example, the 316th Division of the Vietnamese People's Army.) Possibly one reason why the gassing allegations appear so immediately plausible in the United States is because they accord so neatly with American military thinking as it applied in Vietnam. That is, massive application of superior technology against guerrilla forces. Yet it is well-known – certainly outside the Pentagon – that the most effective weapon in guerrilla fighting is a well-trained soldier who, by not killing indiscriminately, is best placed to win the all-important political struggle for 'hearts and minds'.

The allegations about chemical atrocities have also drawn on a reservoir of anti-communist belief in the West, predisposed to accept as truth any stories of abuses in Communist countries. These sentiments were reinforced by the revelations from Pol

Pot's Kampuchea. The horror of life under the Khmers Rouges tended to blacken all the regimes in Indochina, including Vietnam which overthrew Pol Pot. The fact that the latter now relies on Western diplomatic and material support for his survival is unlikely to affect such irrational anti-communist logic, incapable of distinguishing real crimes under Communist rule from US propaganda and speculation.

In fact, in contrast to the Khmers Rouges takeover, the revolution in Laos was characterized by a minimal level of violence and comparatively little retribution against members of the old regime. To be sure, high officials and members of the officer corps were sent off to 're-education' camps in the mountains, and thus one outcome of the revolution was a swapping of geographical positions by the two competing élites, with the losers despatched to the mountains to experience the hardships the revolutionaries had endured.

Estimates of the numbers sent to the mountains vary widely – a product of refugee exaggeration and government secretiveness about this matter. However, it would seem that it was between 15,000 and 20,000 people. For many of them life in the mountains was extremely hard. The areas they were sent to – particularly Houa Phan and Xieng Khouang – were among those most heavily bombed during the war. They had to begin rebuilding these areas, first by constructing their own quarters and clearing land – often of bombs – to grow food. In between, they were given lectures on communism and the Lao revolution and had to conduct criticism and self-criticism sessions.

Conditions were harsh and medicines in short supply, as in the rest of the country. Consequently, after 1976 a number of the older members of the RLG died from illness – such as Touby Ly Fong. Others have been shot while allegedly trying to escape – such as Ly Tek. Since 1979 most have effectively lived in internal exile, working in jobs concomitant with their skills with movement outside their province restricted. Many wives have joined their husbands in the mountains; other men have married in these areas and settled down. Others have been allowed to return to Vientiane over the past three years and though most of these soon leave for Thailand, many also decide to stay on and work for the regime.

While the wisdom of this policy is questionable, both economically and politically it has, as revolutions go, not been severe. Historically, successful revolutions and counter-revolutions (like the Suharto coup of 1965 in Indonesia) have involved the outright elimination of the losing élite. This did not happen in Laos, and a wave of terror was not unleashed on the country.

As a Communist government, the Lao People's Democratic Republic is no different in any fundamental way from most other Communist regimes. It is a one-party 'mass-democracy' in which individual liberties are subordinated to the 'will of the majority'. In practice in Laos – which lacks the most basic prerequisites for a functioning democracy such as mass literacy and a functioning national communication system – this means centralized authoritarian control by the Communist Party.

In the early stages of consolidation revolutionary governments are at their most unyielding and authoritarian. In 1976 and 1977 Laos endured a wave of nationalist and socialist dogmatism, frowning on 'capitalist' habits and western culture, initiating seemingly endless political seminars through the country which, while spouting optimistic forecasts about socialist transformation, seriously upset production and administrative efficiency and alienated many people. By 1979, following three years of poor economic performance, a hangover had set in, and a government sobered by the realities of power and feeling more confident of keeping it, began liberalizing all spheres of life. Nightlife in Vientiane soon became an endless round of *bouns* (dances, usually held in the grounds of the temples), people openly read Thai magazines and listened to Thai radio. Thai colour TV is there for all to see in the restaurants and cafés of Vientiane – despite official censorship. This is not the face of a police state. Indeed, the atmosphere compares favourably with the neighbouring one-party State, non-communist Burma. Even if it wanted to, the Lao Government does not have the capacity to crack down on the flow of information from outside the country. All of this facilitated my investigations into the charges of 'yellow rain' while inside Laos.

One of the most intriguing things about the issue of chemical weapons in Laos is that it is not a subject of rumour or even much discussion among the Lao population. This is not a result of censorship. People have heard the allegations of gassings on both Thai radio and TV and *Voice of America*, and the Government itself has publicized the issue by issuing denials through its daily paper *Sieng Pasason*. If gassing and the rest of it was occuring on a massive scale, then one would expect it to be a lively topic of conversation in the rumour networks of the country, especially as most news travels by word of mouth. Yet among the lowland Lao and other ethnic groups, apart from the Hmong, one finds no trace of it. All these groups mix in the various local and regional markets, yet it appears that only some kinds of rumours overlap, while others are ethnically and religiously specific. Gossip about gassing among the Hmong is geographically specific, and confined to those on or near the Vientiane Plain. Why certain rumours become cordoned off like this is an interesting sociological problem in itself. We have seen that at other times and places in Indochina tales associated with gassing or poisoning were relayed by all ethnic groups at all social levels. Why is this not the case in Laos today?

Perhaps what we are seeing is a spontaneous cultural scepticism along the lines of 'Oh, that's just a story the Hmong will tell you'. But the fact that the story only has credibility within one ethnic group inside Laos indicates a number of things. First, we find a cultural trait among Hmong whether they are refugees or not: that is, what a Hmong tells another Hmong should be accepted at face value. Second, the tale has a sort of spontaneous credibility because of persistent Hmong fears – historical and cultural – of lowland intentions towards them (though interestingly we do not find the same cultural paranoia among the other Lao Sung group, the Yao). Third, it would indicate that the notion of apocalyptic 'gas' warfare is particularly appropriate to the Hmong cosmological imagination. There are also a number of other subsidiary points. One of the major military problems with gas has always been its relative imprecision. That is, it does not always kill the people it is intended for. Wind changes can suddenly blow the gas back over the troops employing it, or indeed innocent groups, such as the Yao or the many other tribal groups which share the mountains with the Hmong. Yet we have no reports from these other groups, some of whom fought in the Secret Army and have also been resettled south of Phu Bia. Finally we have no stories of gassing from loose-talking soldiers, either to family or friends, and the Americans have found no ex-PLA refugees who have had any training in chemical warfare techniques. This absence of gassing stories from the many other cultural groups in Laos weakens still more the credibility of the whole story.

Some of these issues were highlighted in my first interview – apart from informal enquiries – on the gassing question inside Laos. It was with a middle-level Hmong Communist official in Vientiane, and was conducted without any government cooperation or knowledge. I used a lowland Lao interpreter who had worked for the US in bygone days and did not like the present government. We arrived unannounced at the official's house, woke him from an afternoon nap, and he agreed to talk.

After chatting generally about why he thought Hmong people had gone to Thailand, and why some were now returning, I asked if he had heard about gas. To my surprise he said 'Yes, it happened in Vientiane province.' How did he know? He said he was a well respected leader among the Hmong and when they had problems they came to tell him about them. He said he was told that the plane dropped yellow drops like medicine (this description almost sent my lowland interpreter into a fit of incredulous laughter). He said the people fell ill, got stomach aches from it, and that it also killed rice and vegetable crops. It had happened last August at Pha Mai and he had gone out to investigate its effects. He said he did not know who had done it, but he had been given a sample of the 'gas'. No, he did not have it now. I asked if he knew anything about reports from around Phu Bia – to which he replied categorically that there was no gassing around Phu Bia because his younger brother worked in the hospital at Muong Cha and if it was happening there he would have told him. He then spontaneously told a story about Hmong returnees who had told him that their food in Ban Vinai had been poisoned. They knew it was happening because they got a stomach ache, so they stopped eating. After that they decided to return to Laos.

When we were driving back after the interview my Lao interpreter, who referred to the Hmong by the more derogatory lowland term 'Meo', said that he had never heard anything about gassing before this interview, and, moreover, he would 'never trust anything a Meo said or told him'. This racist comment, one of the few

I heard, drives home the point about the cultural insularity of stories about 'medicine from the sky' in Laos. Yet, within a few hours I was able to crosscheck with a Western aid official who had been at Pha Mai at the same time in August; he said there had been no evidence of 'medicine from the sky' having been dropped there. Moreover fifty Hmong had returned to Pha Mai in 1981, which would indeed be strange if gassing was occurring.* It is also worth noting here that the Pathet Lao garrison at Pha Mai is almost entirely Hmong.

Another aid official said that he had been told by a Hmong near the Nam Ngum dam that a plane had dropped yellow powder there (he did not enquire when), which killed plants and rice and caused bloody diarrhoea. The Hmong said he had a canister in which it was dropped, but then added he did not have it with him, it was up in the hills. Then he said he had a sample, but could not find it. At which point the aid-worker decided that the story had been fabricated and probably picked up over foreign broadcasts.

Before my surprising interview with the Hmong official I had contacted the Foreign Ministry about going to Xieng Khouang province. Meanwhile they had arranged an interview that I had requested with the Hmong head of the National Minorities Commission, Niavu Lobliayao, brother of Faydang the vice-president of Laos. I asked Niavu to comment on the gassing allegations. He said it was not true that the Vietnamese or the Soviets were committing 'genocide' against the Hmong. 'People outside', and he singled out China, 'are trying to drive a wedge between the Lao government and the national minorities.' He said that the reality was that planes were flying from Thailand and dropping 'the bags of gas' (again, shades of pre-1975 USAID) on the Hmong. Where? In Muong Om and Muong Saysomboune subdistricts near Phu Bia. He knew because some Hmong people had told him.

Naivu's response was hardly one I had been expecting, but now that what I was hearing was 'official', as it were, I took up what I had already heard about gassing with the Lao Foreign Ministry. By doing this I knew I could be jeopardizing my trip to Xieng

*Some thirty to forty Hmong also returned to Ban Done over 1981; as we have seen, this was also the site of a number of alleged attacks.

Khouang and any further tolerance from the government. It was a risk that had to be taken. The Foreign Ministry officials were visibly shaken by what I had picked up, indeed bewildered by it. They denied flatly that any gassing was happening anywhere, by anyone, including so-called Thai planes flying into Laos to drop 'bags of gas'. As lowland Western-educated intellectuals, these people did not inhabit the cultural and intellectual universe of the Hmong. When I asked them to explain why this story was circulating among both Communist and non-communist Hmong and nobody else, they were puzzled, and they seemed to realize that it was not enough simply to attribute the story to the CIA and Vang Pao.

My trip to Xieng Khouang went ahead and the only advice given to me by the Foreign Ministry was to see if people raised the question of gas themselves without prompting, and only if they did not should I ask. There was still no attempt to closely monitor my movements in either Xieng Khouang or Vientiane in order to prevent me from stumbling upon any more accidental information.

As we have seen, the people in the Hmong villages around the Plain of Jars had heard nothing about gas. One may explain this simply in terms of their isolation. But in Phonsavane, the provincial centre, Hmong and other ethnic groups from various areas pass through continuously and hence it should function as a meeting point and relay point for rumours. I asked a number of independent sources, some of them officials in the old regime sent to the province for re-education, if gassing was a subject of rumour in Phonsavane, or in the market. The reply was negative. One of them had heard about it on *Voice of America*, but that was all – and this in a region supposedly subject to chemical attacks. Only by insistent probing did I get a third-hand report of a Hmong barefoot doctor, who himself had only heard that fighting had occurred around Muong Om and in which gas had been used.

The provincial governor of Xieng Khouang, Yong Yia, is a Hmong. He is a veteran Communist who joined the Lao liberation movement in 1946, and a native of the province. An intelligent and cheerful man, he talked freely and at length about the history of the Pathet Lao and about the political schisms that had occurred between and within Hmong clans as a result of the civil war. He pointed out that just as the lowland Lao aristocratic families were split into different factions so had the Hmong élite been split, Vice-President Faydang having been related to Touby Lyfoung through the marriage of his younger sister. Asked about the Hmong leaving Laos he replied that many had already begun to leave before 1975 because they had no gardens. After that they left because they had no food, while many who worked for Vang Pao also left. Keeping in mind the fact that the large concentration of Hmong south of Phu Bia is now re-zoned as part of Vientiane province, Yong Yia said the present composition of Xieng Khouang was 35,000 Hmong, 16,000 Lao Theung, and 49,000 lowland Lao. These figures, he emphasized, were rough estimates.

Government policy, he said, was to draw the Lao Sung into settled farming. But, because the government is poor, and Xieng Khouang is difficult terrain this will take many years. At present 70% of the Hmong in the province still live in their traditional way. As far as he was concerned, food was the key to attracting the Hmong to a more settled life-style. If they can be given security and shown how to increase their yields then government policy will work. Re-settlement, he added, does not involve collectivization. He dismissed the idea that there was large-scale Hmong resistance after 1975, saying that there had only been small bands and they had been mopped up between 1977 and 1979.

Yong Yia denies the charge about gassing, saying that it is an 'intrigue' of Vang Pao and the US, but he also said he thought that the refugees were probably attributing their earlier experiences with US 'poison', that is prior to 1975, to the Soviets and Vietnamese. He said he did not know the exact nature of the poison that the Americans dropped, but one sort killed you if you touched it. Another killed you immediately if you smelled the smoke. The survivors would be left with an extremely sore throat, he said.

After my return from Xieng Khouang to Vientiane I went to the re-settlement villages first established by Ly Tek in 1970 at Kilometre 52. In these villages there were 3,196 people, of whom 72% were Hmong. Some had briefly been at Long Cheng, but most had moved here to escape the fighting or Vang Pao's recruiters. I asked the Hmong leader there, Yong Pao Li, why he thought the Hmong were leaving Laos. He ascribed it to their lack of education and their narrow-minded parochial fears. In the new situation they felt scared if their relatives left for Thailand and this would set off a chain-reaction of migrations. He added that when Vang Pao and the Americans were in Laos they looked after the Hmong by dropping them food, and they felt that if they went to Thailand this would continue to happen.

It was at Kilometre 52 that I interviewed some Hmong returnees from Ban Vinai. One was a man in his fifties, Song Lee, who had gone to Thailand from Muong Om in late 1980 and had returned to Laos in November 1981. He claimed that some Thais came across to their village and told them that if they went to Thailand they would get money and a good life. But, he said, it was not true. They paid the Thais 5,000 *kip* ($100) to take them across the river to Thailand, but once they were across they were abandoned and were finally taken to Ban Vinai by police. He had crossed with his younger wife and his son. While in Ban Vinai he had quarrelled bitterly with his younger wife (it had something to do with his age but this was unclear and the details obviously embarrassing) and so he and his son returned to Laos to find his older wife whom they located living near Nong Het and brought her back to Kilometre 52. He said he had more relatives in Laos than in Thailand, and that is why he came back.

I also spoke with an old woman, Mee Va, who had gone to Ban Vinai in 1979 from Muang Ga Sai, in Vientiane province, and had returned to Laos at the same time as Song Lee. She had left Laos because other people around her were leaving. Her husband had died long ago and she had gone to Ban Vinai with only her daughter. While in Ban Vinai her daughter married, which committed her to her husband's family and the mother felt this weakened her ties with her daughter. Moreover she did not like the camp. There was enough food but one could not live normally; she could not leave the camp or 'the Thais would hit you on the head'. So she decided to come back to Laos to live with her son, whom she felt would care for her.

I asked them both if they had heard any stories about gas while in Ban Vinai and whether that made them scared of returning to Laos. Extraordinarily, they said they had heard nothing about gas, but had been told that if they returned they would be split up from their relatives. This was their main fear. Alongside the blaze of publicity about Hmong fleeing Laos because of poison gas attacks, these movements in search of relatives or a more secure life, on the part of a people described by Lemoine as 'economic nomads', appear as unusual rather than normal cultural habits.

I also asked Yong Pao Li if he had heard about poison gas and he replied that he had heard some rumours and that people at Kilometre 52 would sometimes discuss whether it was true or not on their half-day walk to the fields. He said there had been quite a bit of talk about it in late 1981 because in a village 17 kilometres from Kilometre 52 it was said that five people were out in a field when a fog came down. They had been unable to move. There was no vomiting and they looked quite normal otherwise. They had been sent to Vientiane hospital where one had died. He had heard that soldiers were called in immediately after it happened to look for the 'gas' but they could not find anything. He was personally very puzzled by this.

Yong Pao Li told me, in front of a Lao Government interpreter, that he had listened to radio broadcasts claiming that the Lao government is controlled by the Soviets and that they are using chemical weapons. But, because he had not personally seen any evidence of it, he did not know. He had heard stories from what he called 'the Chao Fa area' in 1976–1978. One person from this area whom he respected had told him about gas, and he was inclined to believe him. He said that many people at Kilometre 52 had talked about all this and he felt one had to believe some of it. He said even if there was not a lot of gas there must have been a little dropped somewhere for people to be talking about it. He concluded in a remarkably frank way by saying that he did not know if it was 'the enemy' who were dropping gas or the Lao government, but he was very puzzled by the whole story and would like to hear a clear explanation.

There is, clearly, a considerable amount of discussion about this issue among Hmong on the Vientiane Plain, although all the stories are second-hand. Yong Pao Li's logic, which is that where there is smoke there must be some fire, is shared by many people in the West, and obviously helps keep the story alive in Laos. However, among the Hmong at Kilometre 52 who are economically and socially secure it has the status of idle rumour; a social base of fear and panic is not present.

Leaving aside the intrinsic interest of Yong Pao Li's story, the context in which it was told was equally interesting. I had travelled to Kilometre 52 with an Australian Embassy official and two Western aid workers, all of whom sat in on the interview. I think it is fair to assume that since the Lao government knew of the nature of my enquiries, they would not have allowed an embassy official in particular to attend such an interview if they were out to cover up the use of chemical weapons in Laos. For me this was a fairly convincing demonstration that they feel they have nothing to cover up.

The Lao government has never denied that they had trouble with the remnants of Vang Pao's troops after 1975. For example, Vice-President Faydang said of the Hmong, in his Hmong New Year message in November 1978, that reactionaries had caused 'confusion and rifts among them in certain areas, for example in the Phu Bia area. As a result, due to their ignorance of the situation and the enemy's deception, a number of our Hmong compatriots have become stubborn and rebelled against the Government. . . . However, a large number of those compatriots finally realized the truth and returned to the Government side, and are now carrying out socialist construction. . . .' There was a much tougher statement by Chanpheng Sihaphom, director of the Information Department of the Lao Foreign Ministry, who in the same month said that only small groups of rebels were scattered in the areas of Phu Ma Thao and Phou Kiu. He said the government was trying to persuade the rebels to leave their redoubts and join the government side. 'However, those who refuse to heed the government's warning will be severely suppressed,'* he said.[3] These rebels never seriously threatened the government. What they were threatening were

---

*Similar remarks have been made by Thai politicians. For example, in March 1982 the Thai National Security Council Secretary General, Squadron-Leader Prasong Soonsiri, announced a plan to bring 500,000 hill-tribespeople within the government's legal control. He said 'violent measures may have to be employed against the armed hill-tribesmen who resist the change'. *The Nation* (Bangkok), 4 March 1982. Since what was called the 'Red Meo War' in the mid-1960s, the Thais have been grappling with Hmong and other hill-tribes' resistance to the Thai administration, and many have joined the CPT.

attempts by the government and aid agencies to bring health, schooling and agricultural extension programmes to the Hmong forced to settle south of Phu Bia because of the war.

The problems of re-settlement are formidable enough without rebels, as Sebanh Srithirath, chef du cabinet of the Ministry of Foreign Affairs, acknowledged in early 1979: 'It is not easy to re-settle the Hmong. They are superstitious and don't want to live in the lowland. But in the mountains we can't take civilization to them. There is no transportation or communication. They do slash and burn and so they don't have enough food. But in the lowlands they could get better crops and the government could supply them with needed materials. Sometimes disease is a problem when they first come down, but they have been re-settled.'[4]

The UNHCR has been active in helping re-settle people displaced by the war. In this respect they work closely with the UNDP, which provides capital and infrastructure for such projects. Since early 1979 they have had projects in the Muong Saysomboune area south of Phu Bia. A UNDP document in early 1979 summarized its activites in this area: 'Close to 80% of the population in the project areas are of the Hmong tribe. . . . The government is anxious, while re-settling this population in new community villages, to [create] . . . modern agricultural and livestock production. It is also the intention of the Government through improvement of the living conditions of the people, to stop the outflux of the Meos to Thailand. . . .'[5] In April 1979 representatives from the Mennonites, Quakers, UNDP, UN Drug Control, WFP, WHO, UNICEF, and FAO all toured villages south of Phu Bia from which many claims about gassing had come, and were in fact being made at that very time in camps in Thailand. They visited Ban Son, a former Vang Pao stronghold where there was now an agricultural cooperative for re-settled Hmong who were growing rice, maize and wheat on a farm of about 286 hectares. Very few Hmong in fact are in cooperatives (indeed very few Lao are); where they exist they have been found primarily as a last resort rather than from any ideological preference for this form of agricultural modernization. The severe shortages of capital equipment and draught animals made minimal economic cooperation an absolute necessity. The group also visited the village of Phong Sai (population 3,000) and

Muong Cha (population 6,000). They also visited Muong Ao, where 'we stopped at another Air America landing strip with a surviving American 108 mm (sic) howitzer. We had lunch (on Air France trays from our Soviet helicopter piloted by a Lao trained by the CIA). After lunch we visited the former military hospital which is now used as a dispensary. The dispensary was supplied with basic medicine, many from UNICEF.' They also visited Muong Om which had a population of 7,000 (80% Hmong, 5% lowland Lao, and 15% other ethnic groups). 60% were displaced persons who had only recently come to the area to burn fields in order to plant rice. 'However they need food to last until the first harvest; they also need tools to clear land. An irrigation system is being planned; 9,500 hectares of arable land can be irrigated which would take 6,000 persons off government food handouts.'[6]

The total population of Muong Saysomboune is 50,000 (40,000 Hmong) and this area was established as a district in January 1979 following the complete defeat of the rebels the year before. Lao officials claimed at the time to have re-settled about 12,000 people in the area and wished to bring the other Hmong who were still practising slash-and-burn subsistence agriculture into settled farming. However, this would have to wait until a basic irrigation infrastructure had been installed. The officials claimed that the Hmong who had already begun to work wet rice fields were very happy because of the higher yields, and more scientific animal husbandry allowed them to grow more pigs and buffaloes. For this reason they said the spontaneous reaction of the Hmong to re-settlement was good.

Thus this delegation had passed through nearly all the villages which many refugees in Thailand were claiming had been, and were still being, drenched with poison gas. Indeed a Vang Pao soldier I interviewed at the end of 1979 claimed to have been in a battle at Muong Om at almost the same time as the delegation and that chemical weapons had killed 2,000 people in the encounter. One cannot easily conceal these sorts of casualties, nor the aftermath of such a battle from which many people would still be reeling. Moreover it is impossible to imagine that the Lao government would take these organizations anywhere near an area where they were allegedly carrying out mass chemical warfare attacks, let alone set up aid projects in them.

No doubt a lot of Hmong were resistant to the idea of re-settlement, and the rudimentary forms of cooperation that it required. Indeed, their conception of some of the re-settlement villages may have been that they were like prison – which is in fact the feeling of many hill-tribespeople about the camps in Thailand. The more sensationalist journalists operating from Thailand have, of course, been quick to report that they are in fact 'labour camps'. After the Government had crushed the resistance and initiated a UN-assisted programme of re-settlement, rumours of forced reset-tlement obviously gained currency among many Hmong, adding to the insecurity and fears that fed the refugee outflow in 1979. However, as we know, very few Hmong have been re-settled in Laos, and even fewer in cooperatives.

The sociologist Yang Dao observed that in the late 1950s the Hmong around the Plain of Jars were spontaneously beginning to move down from the mountain peaks to take up more settled farming. Indeed, some had settled in Xieng Khouang township. After the devastating interlude of the war this is beginning again today and there are a number of Hmong who have set up small shops in Phonesavane, and are a permanent feature of the local market. Maintenance of peace around the Plain will no doubt accelerate this trend.

One final comment about the situation in Laos. Since the Chin-ese invasion of Vietnam, relations between Vientiane and Beijing have been very strained, and there are reports of occasional clashes on the Lao–Chinese border. The Lao government has accused the Chinese of stirring up trouble among the hilltribes in the far north of the country and of organizing a so-called 'Lanna Division' of Lao refugees that will be used to launch attacks on Laos. Haig's *Report* and some more imaginative journalists have claimed that considerable fighting is going on in the north. How-ever, little evidence has been produced to substantiate any of these claims. It should be noted that if fighting were going on, and use of gas was standard practice by the Pathet Lao or the Vietnamese, then one would have expected charges to come from any refugees streaming across into China from Phong Saly or Nam Tha provinces. Yet there are no reports from this region.

Talk about gassing can be found among Communist and non-communist Hmong inside Laos, but it appears to be idle rumour and speculation. On the Vientiane Plain, where there is a considerable flow of information back and forth from Thailand, people talk about it but because they feel economically, politically and socially secure it remains nothing more than chatter. In the event of sudden illness people will speculate about whether it is a result of the 'gas' that they have heard about. Yet the most striking fact was how little interest there was in the subject among the Lao generally, given the scale on which chemical warfare attacks are alleged to be occurring.

Enquiries among Hmong in January 1983, however, revealed increased concern among Hmong as a result of reports they had heard over *Radio Free Asia* and *Voice of America* concerning what they understood to be UN condemnation of the use of 'yellow rain' in Laos. Of course the UN had done nothing of the kind, but these Hmong felt that something must be occurring if such an important organization had thrown its weight behind the allegations. No doubt some variation of this interpretation is now being circulated through various Hmong communities inside Laos.

The Lao government has been content simply to dismiss the allegations as a 'big lie' spread by the CIA and Vang Pao supporters – which in one sense is true, but is hardly an adequate explanation. Nevertheless they placed no obstacles in the way of my broader sociological investigation – if one discounts a fairly slow-moving bureaucracy. The Lao government allows aid workers to travel extensively and to establish projects in areas allegedly being drenched with chemical weapons. Neither of these conditions would exist if 'genocide' was in process using top-secret and internationally banned biochemical weapons. They clearly feel they have nothing to hide in this regard.[7]

Evil Propaganda and Honest Delusion

We have seen that neither the refugee evidence nor the scientific evidence is sufficient to conclude, as the Americans have done, that Vietnam or the Soviet Union are using lethal chemical weapons in Southeast Asia. Nevertheless a barrage of propaganda and a dearth of rational discussion has led to a general popular belief that the Soviet Union is engaged in one capacity or another in this kind of warfare. However, untangling the skein of propaganda from honest delusion in the whole affair is extremely difficult. Propaganda and delusion are often inextricable in certain political and social situations and this would appear to be the case in Southeast Asia.

It is difficult not to interpret the dissemination of the poison-gassing story by the ex-CIA Hmong leadership as some kind of conspiracy by them, in league with their former paymasters, to mislead world opinion. The evidence pointing in this direction is the continuing liaison between this Hmong leadership and the Americans. The semi-secret status of Ban Vinai until 1978, the use of the Hmong for intelligence missions inside Laos by both the Thais and the Americans, and the instances of fabricated evidence, will always leave a pall of doubt over the origin of the gassing story.

One is also wary of the fact that the US has not seriously investigated whether the Hmong could be describing attacks by riot-control gases or defoliants. Haig's *Report* dismissed the possibility of the use of riot-control gases on what we have seen to be spurious grounds, and an Appendix to the 1980 *Compendium* stated: 'The United States does not believe that herbicides have been used on any scale in either of these countries [Laos or Kampuchea] in the past few years. If they had been widely used for military purposes (clearing large areas), we believe this would have been apparent.'[1] That is, the US could detect their use by satellite scanning. One cannot help but suspect that both of these lines of investigation were not pursued thoroughly because of America's extensive use of these weapons in Indochina before 1975. If something was happening in Laos, or Kampuchea, it was politically imperative for the US that it be worse than anything they had done before 1975. In other words a logic of escalation was built into the charges because the US could not credibly condemn others for what it had itself done only a few years earlier.

A fully conscious conspiracy is not required to explain why the gassing charges took hold among the Hmong or US officials, and aid workers and journalists. Each in their own way were predisposed to believe Communist atrocity stories, of which gassing has come to be the most prominent.

Returning for a moment to the issues explored in Chapter Six, and considering the sociological function of rumour in primitive societies, we can grasp how and why such a story could grip the imagination of the Hmong people.

The anthropologist Raymond Firth observed that rumour 'becomes an organizational mechanism or social instrument in the hands of individuals, seeking to remedy or improve a status position for themselves and for the groups they represent. It may tend to maintain rather than destroy social structure. . . . But it is a dangerous instrument. Whether its use be conscious or unconscious, rumour in a primitive as in a civilized society is rarely neutral.'[2] This comment is particularly pertinent in relation to the Hmong leadership of the refugees in Thailand. These leaders had suffered a blow to their prestige by their defeat at the hands of the Communists, and they had therefore lost command of many of the resources that were available to this military leadership – weapons, helicopters, food and money. Their prestige had also been challenged by the Chao Fa movement.

If these people wished to rally support for a return to Laos that many of them hoped to see, and in which a number of them still hope, then they needed some agency to powerfully re-assert their status position. They also needed something that would rationalize their defeat. The 'yellow rain' story has certainly functioned in this way for them.

Rumours, as we have seen, have their greatest impact in times of social turmoil when people feel themselves under threat. To be in *command* of a rumour that *explains* the chaos, the death and destruction gives those who 'control' the rumour a claim to special knowledge, and therefore a claim to power and prestige among those who they represent. It was in the interests of the Hmong ex-CIA leadership, most of whom had come to Thailand in 1975 before any claims of chemical warfare emerged, to believe in and promote stories of 'gassing', especially when they saw the *power* of these stories. As 'controllers' of the story this leadership became the spokesmen for the rumour to the world press and politicians, thus enhancing their authority. Indeed, the beauty of the allegation from their point of view has been its unverifiability; for as long as it remains unverifiable, and as long as it attracts the attention of the world press and politicians, the prestige and power of this leadership can only be enhanced.

Another dimension of rumour is that those who have relayed the story feel that their pride is damaged if they are not believed and hence are very likely to spread alarming gossip about those who refuse to take them seriously. To accuse sceptics of being Communist sympathizers is a very effective form of social coercion – not exclusive to the Hmong – and ensures that it is difficult to criticize the evidence.

The chemical weapon story also performs the function of providing the Hmong with another element of social cohesion. 'Gas' is a vague notion for the Hmong and therefore any number of fears, anxieties, and inexplicable events can be projected onto it. Indeed, it would now appear to occupy the same functional role in their culture as that played by spirits. This 'great fear' binds the Hmong together in their common situation as displaced refugees, in which social disintegration is a constant danger.

Rumours circulate in all societies, but are generally of small importance. Relative social stability and the capacity to check their veracity determine whether idle rumours become wild rumours on which people are prepared to act. A population ravaged by war, starvation and disease, like that of the Hmong, is primed to produce and believe the most hysterical rumours, and these have material force inasmuch as they are fashioned out of the elements of that experience and express or 'explain' it. In a discourse that mixes fantasy and fact only the most careful analysis will discover the reality it expresses.

The 'great fear' that gripped sections of the Hmong in Laos after 1975, particularly in 1979, is broadly explained by a conjunction of economic and political crises. Despite the impression given by most Western writers, the 'fear' was of much more than gas. Indeed, most ordinary Hmong who fled across the Mekong said nothing at all about gas, but spoke in a general way of fear of 'the Vietnamese' and poverty. Gas, along with many other bizarre stories about medical experiments, was just one element of the general fear. But it was the element which for very specific reasons most gripped the imagination of westerners. Originally produced in the complex interaction between ex-CIA Hmong refugees, aid and intelligence officials, the notion of gas developed into the most important piece of political capital in the hands of the old Hmong CIA leadership. As we have already insisted, they did not necessarily hatch it cynically, but they ran with it, nurtured and propagated it because it was in their interests to do so. They had every reason to welcome such a story, none to question it, and because of this they probably believe what they are saying. We do have some evidence of what we would see as straightforward fabrication of evidence on the part of this group, but in a mental universe where fact and fiction blend so easily it is obvious that fabrication does not require a sense of duplicity – in much the same way that a shaman produces a stone from a sick person's head with no consciousness of trickery.

As the main organized force among the Hmong refugees, the ex-CIA leadership fed the story through its own organization, and back into Laos, spontaneously sowing a crop of gas stories. This organization in turn provided the gas 'victims' for American government interviewers and journalists. Inevitably the allegations spread beyond this group to ordinary Hmong, first by word of mouth and later by radio and other media, and it is these versions that bring out most clearly their character of rumour by the very naivety of their descriptions. The detail they describe seems to show that they are ascribing natural calamities to an ill-defined idea of 'gas'; as we have noted this fits neatly in an animistic cosmology.

A similar argument applies to Kampuchea, with the proviso that there is much clearer evidence of cynical manipulation of the story on the part of the Khmers Rouges leadership.

This rumour-mill has been fuelled by many western journalists, aid workers and politicians. Some of them have done this in a straightforwardly cynical fashion. For example, a Congressional Sub-committee in February 1980 asked two CIA agents, Edward M. Collin and Bruce B. Clarke, whether their information on chemical warfare was more than mere hearsay. Collin replied that there was no confirmation. When Republican Congressman Robert J. Lagomarsino commented that repeated news reports on this issue led people to believe it was actually happening, Clarke replied: 'I see nothing wrong in circulating such reports.'[3]

Few are as cynical as this. Most aid workers, who are an important source of information for journalists, have no specialist knowledge or experience of the region, and the environment of the camps is not conducive to calm questioning of the refugee stories. Interestingly, those with the most experience tend to be the most cautious about the chemical warfare stories. For journalists, gassing is a sensational story and few of them have had the time, or spared the energy, to check it carefully. The general political environment of Southeast Asia has encouraged propagation rather than prudence. As a result, there is now a feedback mechanism producing these stories anew – aid workers who may have relayed or procured stories, and Hmong who may have told them, have them legitimized in print. 'The Truth' stares back at them in black and white in the pages of the *Bangkok Post* whose banner headlines scream about the 'Holocaust in the Hills' of Laos.

We remarked in Chapter Three that there are some parallels between the current charges of biochemical warfare in Southeast Asia and the germ warfare charges made against the Americans during the Korean War. In February 1952 Chou En Lai accused the Americans of committing 'the heinous crime of employing bacteriological weapons'. These charges were vigorously denied by the Americans who said it was all Communist propaganda. But despite this denial, many felt that it had turned out to be a propaganda triumph for the Communists, even though researchers have subsequently concluded that the US did not appear to be guilty. Nevertheless China and North Korea continue to believe the story some thirty years afterwards, and a recent Japanese magazine uncritically reported the claims of a North Korean paper *Tong-il Shin-bo* that a recent outbreak of Manchurian fever (epidemic haemorrhagic fever) was caused by US Army experimentation with biological and chemical weapons.[4]

No concrete evidence has been produced to support these charges. However, a recent upsurge of haemorrhagic fever in China appears to be a side-effect of the new agricultural policies there. According to the *Far Eastern Economic Review*: 'The increase in single-family farming has meant that more families are storing their own surplus grain without adequate protection against rodents. The disease is carried by rats and is easily communicable to human beings.'[5]

One of the few rational contemporary comments on the Korean allegations was that of a distinguished Australian expert on viral diseases, Sir Macfarlane Burnett. Because so much of his statement parallels the argument of this book it is worth quoting at length – though we might in the present context replace his references to 'Communist' by 'American':

'Memorandum by Sir MACFARLANE BURNETT, FRS, Director of the Walter and Eliza Hall Institute, Melbourne, Australia. Special Adviser to the Australian Delegation to the Seventh Session of the United Nations General Assembly.

During the first half of 1952, there has been extensive distribution throughout the world of propagandist literature of communist origin accusing the United Nations forces in Korea of using bacteriological warfare methods ('germ warfare') against the North Korean people. In some publications technical evidence in support of the charges has been presented.

Most of the evidence is presented more or less in the following form: A named individual, soldier or farmer, states that he saw an American plane flying low. It appeared to drop something that did not explode. Then either he found on reaching the spot that there were accumulations of insects on the ground which he assumed had been dropped by the aircraft he had seen, or an outbreak of disease took place in some village in the vicinity.

Subsequently a laboratory investigation was made of the insects discovered on the ground or of the patients suffering from the outbreak of disease.

Pictures of the insects and detailed accounts of the investigations of insects and of human patients in bacteriological laboratories have been published. The accounts are of the same type as one would expect from any laboratory, working under difficulties and with rather inexperienced personnel which had been called on to undertake such work. I should say at once that I find no reasons to question the good faith of the findings of most of the laboratory workers. I am not referring to either the political leaders or the scientists under Communist direction.

From the pictures published and the descriptions given, the insects were correctly identified as *Muscid* and *Tipulid* flies, stone flies, and *Callembola* (spring tails). None of these with the possible exception of Muscid flies has ever been shown to be concerned with the transmission of disease. They are, however, of types liable to be found in groups on the surface of the ground or snow after a sudden cold change. There is no reason to doubt that accumulations of such insects were actually found.

It is stated that bacteria of Salmonella and Shigella types were obtained in cultures from the flies. This would not be an unexpected finding from any type of filth-feeding fly in any part of eastern Asia. The claims that a Rickettsia was isolated from Collembola and an encephalitic virus from a Tipulid fly ("daddy-long-legs" or "crane fly") are not credible to anyone conversant with modern work on these organisms, but they represent a very common type of occurrence in laboratories where inexperienced workers are dealing with viruses on Rickettsiae. The claims are presumably based on mis-interpretations of symptoms produced when insect emulsions are injected into experimental animals. They may well have been advanced by low-level workers in good faith.

The two points to be stressed in regard to this aspect of the evidence are:—

1. There is no evidential connection whatever between the American plane's low flight and the appearance of insects on the ground. Such accumulations of insects of these types can be seen occasionally as purely natural occurrences which would be of no interest whatever and would therefore be unnoticed and undiscussed in ordinary times. It is inconceivable (a) that if any Western entomologist or bacteriologist should wish to liberate disease germs over enemy country, he would

dream of using harmless insects and spiders of the types reported – and (b) that having collected and infected such insects, he should find means of releasing them from aircraft to be distributed in groups of this type on the ground.

2. The laboratory facts given as evidence are within the technical competence of the workers concerned, true. But as they stand, they have no evidential value whatever in regard to the claim that insects deliberately infected with agents of human disease were dropped from American planes.

Apart from the discovery of insects on the ground, the other evidence provided is in regard to a number of small epidemics of infectious disease, an isolated case of cholera, a small outbreak of what appears to have been pneumonic plague, the occurrence of a group of cases of anthrax, and a prevalence of intestinal disease amongst the human population – noted in villages or on farms some time after the passage of a UN plane. Now these are occurrences which may be expected at any time in Korea and Manchuria; there is no reason to doubt that they occurred as reported in the communist propaganda. Bacteriological studies gave the findings to be expected and again we can accept the findings as essentially true.

Here again the communists have seized on what were obviously natural occurrences and connected them quite unconvincingly with the appearance of UN planes in the vicinity. As in the example of the insects previously discussed, what is presented as evidence may quite possibly be factually true. But it simply has no bearing on the question of whether or not the responsible organisms were dropped from United Nations planes.

It might be interesting to consider what would be the adequate evidence which a competent and honest North Korean scientist would need to convince himself that outbreaks of disease in certain villages were due to enemy action. He would know that in pre-war days similar outbreaks occurred and he would also know that with the disorganization of wartime they would be expected to be more frequent. Obviously he would have to show that the number of cases of disease was sharply increased in those villages over which UN planes had flown low as against those not so visited. Further the cases would have to be shown to occur at a time consistent with the incubation period of the disease in question. There are adequate statistical methods available to analyse data of such a sort and, if honestly collected and tabulated facts of this sort were available, a logical decision could be made. It is, of course, highly improbable that such data, if they existed, would be provided to an enemy or neutral organization. It is also certain that any intelligent group of statisticians and public health workers could, if they so wished, produce faked statistics of this sort to support charges of germ warfare.

I have come to the conclusion that the significance of the scientific evidence quoted has been grossly and viciously distorted. Evidence showing disease prevalence may well be genuine – it probably always has been – but it does not establish that germ warfare has been prosecuted.

To understand the situation and to attempt to remedy it, we shall have to call on the psychologist and psychiatrist rather than the bacteriologist. I am quite certain that bacteriological warfare methods were never used by the UN forces in Korea. The communists' own evidence alone is enough to convince me of that. I am almost equally confident that a great number of those providing the evidence, peasants, soldiers, entomologists, and bacteriologists, were stating what they believed to be the truth and that their statements are reasonably accurately reported. And yet there has been released over the world as a result, a flood of vicious hysterical propaganda pushed with the utmost intensity by all communist organisations.

At one level, it is simple deliberate propaganda designed to produce and increase hate and fear of the opposing group. It may have been specially fostered as a means of destroying the tradition in China that the United States had a special generosity and effectiveness in improving the health of the Chinese people. Communism has been responsible for some good and much evil, but there has probably been nothing quite so mean and evil as the attempt by its propagandists to destroy the effect of American efforts in the past to bring the benefits of modern medicine to China. It is a subtle and perhaps effective way of making people forget the work of the mission hospitals, of the great Peking Medical School built by the Rockefeller Foundation, and the great numbers of Chinese students trained in western science and medicine by the United States. The bringers of health are now branded as disseminators of disease.

We of the west, however, pride ourselves on the effectiveness of our application of science to human affairs and it is of the essence of the scientific approach that we cannot deal with unwelcome happenings, whether physical catastrophes, epidemics of disease or outbreaks of human hatred and violence, by feelings of indignation, and resentment. We have to try to understand the situation dispassionately and on that basis of understanding look for remedies.

All through history there have been outbreaks of mass hysteria – in the sense of large numbers of people being driven to behave in unusual antisocial fashion. In the Middle Ages in Europe there were outbreaks of dancing mania. There was the strange phenomenon of the Children's Crusade. In pioneer America there were the religious manifestations of the "Shakers" and the "Holy Rollers". As a less spectacular manifestation of the same phenomena, we have the more recent episodes in which an epidemic of delusions sweeps a countryside and people of unchallengeable honesty report seeing the Loch Ness monster or a flight of flying saucers. Perhaps in many ways the flying saucer phenomenon has analogies with what has happened in Korea and Manchuria. For a time any strange visual effect in the sky was a flying saucer to someone in southern United States, just as any biological happening that seemed unusual to the observer in northern Korea was likely to be brought forward as evidence of germ warfare. The similarity could have been complete if the United States government had adopted and disseminated the view that the saucers were Russian vehicles of espionage and sabotage and ascribed every unexplained fire, explosion, or epidemic to their action.

There are no easy answers to mass hysteria stimulated and intensified by government-sponsored propaganda. But we can hope that the delusion we are discussing will in the course of time fade away like the Loch Ness monster and the flying saucers. The Soviets, too, have their pride in science. There may be as many biologists in the countries behind the iron curtain as in the British Commonwealth. Every one of these biologists knows in his heart that the propaganda on germ warfare is a lie based on a delusion and from each there must be spreading consciously or unconsciously a ripple of disbelief.

It is our place in the United Nations to try to counter what we believe to be a mixture of evil propaganda and honest delusion, not by counter charges but by an attempt to understand and explain the situation to the world – including, we might hope, Russia and its satellites. Truth may not be easy to accept when countered by threats and incessant denial, but in the end, it will always prevail.'[6]

For obvious reasons the State Department would be very reluctant to accept a similar assessment concerning current US allegations. However, it does appear that many people in the US and elsewhere have been willingly deluded, while others have manipulated the chemical warfare allegations to suit their own purposes.

The Politics of Re-armament

Chemical and biological warfare is outlawed by the Geneva Protocol of 1925, signed by all the major powers. Its full title is *Protocol for the Prohibition of the Use in War of Asphyxiating, Poisonous or other Gases, and of Bacteriological Methods of Warfare*. The US subsequently failed to ratify this agreement largely because of effective agitation against it by the already powerful US Chemical Warfare Service. Only in 1970 was this agreement put before the Senate again for ratification, which took another five years. Japan was the only other major power not bound by the agreement until 1970. Most major signatories to the agreement only renounced the right to first use of chemical and bacteriological weapons, and the agreement did not outlaw stockpiling of these weapons.

When the Americans finally consented to the Geneva Protocol, they said that their 'understanding' of it was that it did not proscribe the use of either tear-gases or defoliants.* This interpretation of the agreement was backed by Portugal, and by Australia who as America's ally in Vietnam was using CS gas there.[1] Almost all the other signatories, including the USSR, considered tear-gases and defoliants outlawed as weapons of war. The US stuck to its interpretation for obvious reasons. Even though it did not ratify the Protocol until 1975, Washington said it acknowledged the agreement's status as customary international law. It would have stood self-condemned for its previous use of chemical agents in

---

* However, the US did not register this 'understanding' as a formal reservation when it ratified the Protocol.

Indochina, had it accepted the majority interpretation. Part of the reasoning behind the majority interpretation was that the use of tear gases in war could quickly provoke an escalation to more lethal gases, and lower the threshold of constraint on chemical warfare. It would appear that this did not happen in Indochina because the Vietnamese did not retaliate in kind; one of the critical ingredients of escalation was absent. Nevertheless, with respect to the majority interpretation, the US flouted the Geneva Protocol by its actions in Indochina.

In contrast, there is no serious proof that the Soviets have ever broken the 1925 agreement. Some allegations were made in the mid-1960s that the Soviets could have supplied Egypt with gas to use against rebels in the Yemen. These charges have since been revived by a number of people, in the context of the charges now emanating from Southeast Asia and Afghanistan. Serious commentators are inclined to believe that Egypt did deploy gas in Yemen, but can find no evidence of Soviet involvement, although some have suggested that left-over supplies of British mustard or phosgene gases were used.[2]

A serious aspect of the mycotoxin charge is that the possession of toxins for offensive purposes was specifically barred by the most recent major agreement between the powers covering this area of weaponry – the 1972 'Convention on the prohibition of the development, production and stockpiling of bacteriological (biological) and toxin weapons and on their destruction', which came into force in March 1975. Article One of this convention states that the signatories will 'never in any circumstances develop, stockpile or otherwise acquire or retain: 1. microbiological or other biological agents, or toxins whatever their origin or method of production, of types and in quantities that have no justification for prophylactic, protective or other peaceful purposes; 2. weapons, equipment or means of delivery designed to use such agents for hostile purposes or in armed conflict.'[3] The convention enjoined the parties to destroy whatever stocks they possessed within nine months. The signatories were also proscribed from

---

*The same reasoning applied more strongly to Australia, which had ratified the Protocol in 1930.

supplying any such weapons to other states. Thus if the charges emanating from Southeast Asia were true, the Soviets could be violating not only the 1925 Protocol, but also its sister Convention of 1972 by both developing toxin weapons *and* supplying them to the Lao and Vietnamese governments.

The 1972 Convention grew out of the backlash against American use of chemical weapons in Indochina. In November 1969 President Nixon announced that the 'United States shall renounce the use of lethal biological weapons, and all other methods of biological warfare.' He also 'reaffirmed' US renunciation of the first use of 'lethal and incapacitating chemical weapons'.[4] In late 1970 America began to phase out its herbicide programme in Indochina. The Soviet Union and its allies had in 1969 already launched a diplomatic offensive on the issue by proposing a comprehensive chemical and biological weapons agreement spanning irritant gases and defoliants, and nerve gases and toxins. During negotiation of the 1972 Convention, Soviet demands for a comprehensive agreement were dropped because of US resistance to the inclusion of defoliants and riot-gases in such an agreement and differences over verification provisions. Yet both sides could agree on the outlawing of biological weapons and decided to formalize an agreement in two stages. The 1972 Convention stated that it was 'a first possible step towards the achievement of agreement on effective measures also for prohibition of the development, production and stockpiling of chemical weapons,' and that both sides were 'determined to continue negotiations to that end'. Today the Soviet Union still claims that the 1972 Convention 'is one of the most important disarmament agreements . . . it was one of the first steps toward actual disarmament in the whole history of international relations'.[5]

However, we should not be mesmerized by government statements. States enter into agreements because they perceive them to be in their interests, not because of some higher morality. President Kennedy noted many years ago: 'Even the most hostile nations can be relied upon to accept and keep those treaty obligations, and only those treaty obligations, which are in their own interests.'[6] In April 1980 Rear Admiral Davies explained during a Congressional Hearing on chemical warfare that: 'US adherence to the (1972) Convention . . . was not based on trust of the Soviets. A US study, in which all interested agencies participated, concluded that biological weapons were impractical instruments of warfare. . . . Thus the US did not give up biological weapons due to reliance on the Convention. Rather, having rejected them, we wanted treaty restraints on others. It is in our interest to try to hold the Soviets to the Convention, and to encourage adherence by other nations.'[7] There is no high-minded morality here; clearly both the Soviets and the Americans had concluded that there was no military advantage to be gained from the use of biological or toxin weapons, and that it was in their mutual interests to outlaw them.

With respect to the current allegations, the question really boils down to this: has it been in the Soviet Union's interests to break the 1972 Convention and the 1925 Protocol? The answer to this must be based on both factual and strategic considerations. If the answer is no, then we need to ask whether it has been in the interests of the United States to make it appear that the USSR has flouted these important international agreements.

Protagonists of the 'yellow rain' theory in Southeast Asia have tried to prove their case by pointing to Soviet preparedness for chemical warfare, and argue from this that it is standard Soviet practice to use chemical weapons. Sterling Seagrave, for example, in *Yellow Rain** assumes that *every* allegation ever made against the Soviet Union concerning chemical warfare is correct. Not one example he cites is proven. Indeed, this sort of argument can easily be reversed. We can point to the equally formidable chemical weapons stockpile in the USA, and deduce from it that chemical warfare is standard American practice as well. Indeed, according to Seagrave's logic, all allegations made against the US should look more plausible because of American tardiness over ratifying the Geneva Protocol and its proven extensive use of chemical weapons in Indochina. The facts are that chemical weapons occupy roughly the same place in both Soviet and US strategic thinking and we cannot be asked to accept allegations about their use on the strength of references to preparedness alone.

To date the USSR has always indicated changes in its strategic

---

* *Yellow Rain: A Journey Through the Terror of Chemical Warfare*, London 1982.

thinking or its dissatisfaction with agreements through official pronouncements, in much the same way as the Reagan administration signalled its dissatisfaction with SALT-II. Neither the American Government, nor the other proponents of 'yellow rain', have produced any evidence of a change in the Soviet attitude on this question. In fact the Soviets have stated complete satisfaction with earlier agreements and have urged the US to continue negotiations for the banning of chemical weapons. The Haig *Report* indicates that the Soviets have changed their mind by quoting a 1977 East German *Textbook of Military Chemistry* which simply defines toxins and indicates the way they could be used in combat.* It hardly qualifies as a statement of preparedness, let alone one of policy or intention. In 1977 the US and the USSR began bilateral talks aimed at reaching an agreement banning chemical weapons in accordance with the 1972 Convention. By mid-1979 they had reached broad agreement on the scope of the convention and on a system of on-site inspection as the means of verification by challenge. However, in the wake of the Afghanistan invasion and the

---

* The quote reads: 'Toxins are designated as toxic agents which are produced by biological organisms such as micro-organisms, plants, and animals, and cannot themselves reproduce. By the middle of 1960 the toxins selected for military purposes were included among the biological warfare agents. In principle this was understood to mean only the bacterial toxins. Today it is possible to produce various toxins synthetically. Toxins with ten to twenty amino acids can currently be synthesized in the laboratory. Toxins are not living substances and in this sense are chemicals. They thus differ fundamentally from the biological organisms so that they can be included among chemical warfare agents. As a result of their peculiarities they are designated simply as "toxin warfare agents". They would be used in combat according to the same principles and with the same methods used for chemical warfare agents. When they are used in combat the atmosphere can be contaminated over relatively large areas – we can expect expansion depths up to 6 kilometres before the toxin concentration drops below lethal concentration fifty . . . the toxin warfare agents can be aerosolized. They can be used primarily in micro-bombs which are launched from the air or in tactical rockets. Toxin warfare agents concentrates can be applied with aircraft spray equipment and similar dispersion systems.' *Report*, pp. 17–18. In response to this the Soviet *Critique* drew attention to 'a report of the Secretary-General of the United Nations entitled "Chemical and bacteriological (biological) weapons and the effects of their possible use" (1969), containing a description of the properties of *botilinis* toxin and of botulism, and a report of the World Health Organisation (WHO) entitled "Health aspects of chemical and biological weapons" (1970) describing the properties of *ricin* and *botulinus* toxin. The logic of the State Department report would imply that both the United Nations and WHO are engaged in preparations for a toxin war.' p. 12.

changing mood in Washington these talks were discontinued after July 1980 by the US, which said at first that it now wanted to 'revise' its position, and then argued that the USSR was 'unwilling' to provide for effective verification measures.

Problems of verification are real enough, but they have been used as a convenient means of sabotaging negotiations in the past.* Western statesmen have been able to claim that verification is a simple matter in the West, while it is impossible in the communist bloc. This ignores the harsh fact that military activity in both systems is a closely guarded secret. Why have a KGB or a CIA if this was not the case? Verification measures are contracted between sovereign states, and are not at present subject to democratic rules. The Soviets argue that their side 'is interested no less than anyone else in ensuring dependable verification of the observance of the adopted commitments. Verification, however, is not an abstract category; verification measures should strictly conform to the character and scope of the restrictions agreed upon, and should be worked out along with the latter.'[9] The Soviets appear to be insisting on specific measures rather than abstract and general principles.

There is no doubt that workable verification procedures are difficult to elaborate, given the desire of all military establishments to maintain secrecy, especially with respect to activities not covered by agreed bans. Soviet Lieutenant-General M. Mitranov has outlined some of the problems of verification in the field of chemical and biological weapons: 'Talking about control, one must bear in mind that modern achievements of biology and related sciences (biochemistry, biophysics, molecular biology, genetics) have resulted in higher effectiveness of biological substances as

* In 1955, when the Soviet Union, after years of resistance, accepted Western proposals for arms reductions and accepted in large part western proposals for verification, the US suddenly shifted ground and Eisenhow r proposed his 'dramatic' 'open skies' method of verification. As David Horowitz commented: 'Instead of an agreement which would have liquidated the nuclear threat, and the arms race, the US was asking the Soviet Union to exchange one of its most important military assets (secrecy) for information which it essentially had, and to do this without the prospect of a programme of disarmament which would remove the Strategic Air Command bases by which it was encircled.' *From Yalta to Vietnam*, London 1977, p. 275.

means of waging warfare and in the obliteration of the boundary between biological and chemical weapons. The possibility of effective international control over the banning of biological weapons is considerably handicapped by the fact that modern microbiological industries producing in peace-time antibiotics, vitamins, ferments, fodder protein, amino acids and biological means of plant production can be rapidly switched over to the production of any pathogenic organisms. Therefore, with regard to control over biological and chemical weapons a great deal should be based on the mutual confidence of the sides participating in the talks.'[10] From this perspective the massive chemical and biological industries in the West look frightening when viewed from Moscow, and the Soviets have a real interest in discouraging an arms race in this field. But given the practical problems involved, Mitranov argues, the only really effective means of ensuring adherence to agreements is a lowering of international tensions.

Yet over the past few years tension has increased between the two superpowers and a new Cold War atmosphere has been created in the United States. Not surprisingly this climate encouraged demands for an arms build-up within the United States itself and for a strengthening of NATO military capabilities. This enhanced the fortunes of all military lobbies, including the formerly powerful chemical weapons establishment. Alexander Haig made it immediately clear to Congress in May 1981 that chemical munitions were an 'important component of the Administration's overall defence programme.' He was followed by Secretary of Defence Caspar Weinberger, who, mirroring the Reaganite belief that US-Soviet parity equals Soviet superiority, declared: 'It is absolutely essential for the United States to begin promptly the process of redressing the chemical imbalance between ourselves and the USSR . . .'[11] In August 1981 tenders were called for the construction of a nerve gas munitions plant at the Pine Bluff arsenal in Arkansas and simultaneously a new school for nuclear, biological and chemical warfare training was opened at Fort McClellan, Alabama. A chemical trade publication termed this 'The Quiet Comeback of Chemical Warfare', which was reflected also in the funding figures. In 1969 the US CBW effort boasted a $350 million annual budget, the participation of sixty American and several foreign universities, and at least twenty private firms. Following Nixon's National Security decision this establishment was scaled down: there were only 2,000 people in the US Chemical Corps in the early 1970s. By 1981 this Corps stood at 6,000, President Reagan had allocated $483 million dollars for chemical weapons in his 1981–82 budget, and had requested a further $705 million over 1982–83, while the 1983–84 chemical warfare budget is expected to exceed one thousand million dollars.[12] There is no question but that the resurgence of the chemical weapons establishment in the US has been faciliated by the allegations from Southeast Asia.

The allegations have also been used by the US as a bargaining point with its NATO allies. US strategic aims in Europe include not only a modernization of NATO forces through deployment of Pershing and Cruise missiles, but also a reassertion of American control over its increasingly refractory allies. The US has been attempting to discard the old 'double key system' (nominal joint control) for a 'single key' command structure in Europe which would give the US direct control over unleashing these latest weapons against the Warsaw Pact. This attempt to tie its allies directly to Washington has been resisted by all NATO countries except Britain. It is in this context that one must view Alexander Haig's claim about Soviet use of chemical weapons in Southeast Asia while in Bonn in September 1981. He was there to negotiate the modernization of NATO forces, and was confronted by some reluctant allies as well as a large anti-nuclear movement. Hard-pressed to present anything but semantic evidence for Soviet non-compliance with SALT-I, or with the general understandings reached during the negotiations for SALT-II,[13] Haig attempted to use the mycotoxin allegations in an attempt to convince the Europeans that the Soviet bloc will not abide by agreements unless confronted by superior force. (Only this ulterior motive explains the unseemly haste with which Haig released what was subsequently shown to be extremely weak evidence.) The chemical weapons controversy here rejoins the contemporary debate over nuclear weapons.

The US has not eased the pressure on this issue since Haig's Bonn statement. He was followed in November by the director of the Bureau of Politico-Military Affairs, Richard Burt, who proclaimed: 'Ever since the US began to voice its concerns over reports of chemical weapons use, critics have demanded that we produce the smoking gun. . . . Physical proof. We now have the smoking gun.'[14] The smoking gun was a twig and leaf on which trichothecenes could, the US claimed, be detected. Burt's sample of 'yellow rain' did not stand up to scientific scrutiny. However, the main aim of his statement was to try and influence a group of UN experts who were then visiting Thailand to investigate the allegations made by the US.* In December 1981 the team reported that it 'found itself unable to reach a final conclusion on whether or not chemical warfare agents had been used' in Southeast Asia.[15] Undeterred, President Reagan set the stage in February 1982 for the manufacture of binary nerve gas weapons; in March Haig followed with his Report to Congress, and the Commander-in-Chief of US forces in the Pacific called for the deployment of chemical warfare weapons in the Asia-Pacific-Indian Ocean regions.[16] By any standards this was a major campaign in favour of chemical weapons. Moreover, the decision to produce binary weapons has important strategic implications. In this type of chemical weapon the two agents are packaged separately and only mix to become a nerve gas when operationalized. They are considered much safer to store and transport, overcoming one of the main objections of a number of US allies in Europe to these weapons. (They also raise problems of verification and proliferation.) This decision would appear to be integral to US plans for an arms build-up in Europe.

The Soviet Union has reacted cautiously to the abuse hurled from Washington and has continuously argued that issues of arms control can only be solved by negotiation rather than by threats. The Soviet Union, and its allies Vietnam and Laos, have consistently denied that they have used any chemical weapons, and the Soviets have specifically denied that they have ever produced mycotoxin weapons. It remains true that the US has not produced any proper evidence that the Soviets have developed mycotoxin

---

*The Lao and Vietnamese governments have refused to co-operate with these investigations on the basis that any investigation into chemical warfare in the region by the UN should look at the effects of American use of chemical warfare there before 1975.

weapons. The Soviet response to the American decision to go ahead with binary weapons has been more ominous. The Soviets do not as yet possess these weapons, but their production by the US would have a predictably escalating effect. Responding to Reagan's February announcement Soviet General Kutsevich said: 'The Soviet Armed Forces will undoubtedly have a counter-balance to any weapons, including binary weapons.'[17] In other words the US decision could trigger a chemical arms race.

It is obvious that Soviet strategic thinkers and planners do not want a renewed arms race in Europe in either nuclear or chemical weapons, a race that would clearly drive the European NATO coun-tries closer to the US. They have no conceivable interest in doing this. The idea that they have resorted to the use of bio-chemical weapons in Laos, Kampuchea or indeed Afghanistan in order to achieve tactical advantages against forces which can easily be con-trolled by conventional means, in exhange for major strategic los-ses in Europe and globally by their breaking of major arms control conventions, is only really sustainable if we assume that the Soviet leadership is incredibly shortsighted politically and not the wily schemers we are led to believe they are. Only one writer, Sterling Seagrave, has attempted to support the chemical warfare allega-tions in a strategic sense by asserting that mycotoxins are a new generation of weapons, which are much more powerful than nerve gas and would give the Soviets a strategic advantage in Europe. The fact that the Soviets are not trading on this supposed advan-tage would appear to belie Seagrave's speculation.

If war is really an extension of politics by other means, then it is also impossible to uncover a rationale for the use of bio-chemical weapons by either Laos or Vietnam. As we have shown, the Hmong resistance never represented a major threat to the Vien-tiane Government and could be coped with by conventional means. Vietnam has one of the best fighting armies in the world which has shown itself to be more than a match for the Pol Pot forces. Indeed, Pol Pot and the other Khmer resistance groups on the border only survive because Thailand provides them with sanc-tuary if they come under pressure from the Vietnamese army. To crush these groups would involve confronting the Thai army and so escalating the conflict. But this further underlines the political rather than military nature of the problem. The Vietnamese have concentrated their efforts on winning diplomatic recognition for the Heng Samrin government in Phnom Penh and an acceptance of a new balance of power in the Southeast Asian region by Thailand and its allies. Why should Hanoi jeopardize these diplomatic efforts by breaking international arms conventions?

A number of commentators seem to believe that the Soviets may be engaging in bio-chemical warfare in Laos, Kampuchea and Afghanistan for the purpose of testing new equipment. The 'testing' argument is probably the weakest of all those that have been furnished in an attempt to argue that the Soviets are engaged in bio-chemical warfare. Of course all military apparatuses wish to combat-test weapons, but unless political conditions permit it, they cannot do this just for the sake of it. After all nerve gases have never been combat-tested and this has not prevented their development and stockpiling.

While the Soviets, the Vietnamese and the Lao governments have until recently reacted fairly rationally to the accusations hurled at them, the aggressive rhetoric of the United States has begun to elicit a bellicose response. *Some* Soviet commentators have revived the Korean warfare charges against the US which have largely been ignored since the mid-1960s.[18] Indeed a Soviet Army manual on these issues produced in 1967 made no mention of the Korean charges, and this appears to reflect the majority view in the Soviet leadership.[19] The USSR, however, has been prepared to publicize Cuban charges that the US spread disease among its pig population. The Vietnamese for their part have made sporadic accusations that the Chinese used 'gas' during their invasion of Vietnam and that the Thai army has also used 'gas' on the Thai–Kampuchean border. They have produced no evidence for these charges.

Allegations about biochemical warfare play on volatile emotions and can quickly lead to irrational political rhetoric. In this respect the US Government has been the worst offender. Significant progress was made in the early 1970s towards an effective agreement on the banning of biochemical weapons. The allegations that have emerged from Southeast Asia have significantly retarded that process. As we have seen, the charges are so far based on shoddy evidence and indeed they appear to be founded on wild speculation. It will be a tragic irony if the achievements of modern science are set to work producing horrendous new weapons of war on the basis of village rumours and superstition.

Notes

Chapter One: The Allegations

[1] The *Wall Street Journal*, November 3, 6, 13, 1981.
[2] *The Guardian*, August 8, 1982.
[3] *Chemical Warfare in Southeast Asia and Afghanistan*, Report to the Congress from Secretary of State, Alexander M. Haig, Jr., March 22, 1982, p. 6.
[4] Press Release of the Embassy of the USSR, Canberra. March 15, 1982.
[5] Ibid. November 3, 1982.
[6] Richard S. D. Hawkins, 'Contours, Cultures and Conflict', in Nina S. Adams and Alfred W. McCoy (eds.), *Laos: War and Revolution*, New York 1970. p. 6.

Chapter Two: The Rise and Fall of the Secret Army

[1] Don A. Schanche, *Mister Pop*, New York 1970. p. 79.
[2] Jean Larteguy with the collaboration of Yang Dao, *La Fabuleuse Aventure du Peuple de l'Opium*. Paris 1979, p. 216.
[3] Schanche, pp. 88–89.
[4] ibid. p. 245.
[5] Quoted in W. E. Garret, 'No Place to Run', *National Geographic*, January 1974, p. 111.
[6] In Alfred W. McCoy with Cathleen B. Read and Leonard P. Adams II, *The Politics of Heroin in Southeast Asia*, New York 1972, p. 274.
[7] *The Asia Magazine*, August 19, 1973.
[8] In Garret, op. cit. p. 107.
[9] Catherine Lamour and Michel R. Lamberti, *The Second Opium War*, London 1974, p. 126.
[10] See D. E. Ronk, *FEER*, December 26, 1970. Emphasis added.
[11] *Keesing's Contemporary Archives*, Nov. 27–Dec 4, 1971. p. 24959.
[12] Christopher Robbins, *The Invisible Airforce: The True Story of the CIA's Secret Airlines*, London 1979, pp. 217–226.
[13] *KCA*, August 18–24, 1975, p. 27278.
[14] *New York Times*, June 16, 1975.
[15] *KCA*, August 18–24, 1975, p. 27278.

[16]Robbins, p. 135.
[17]Larteguy, p. 244.
[18]ibid. p. 245.
[19]*Bangkok Post*, May 31, 1975.
[20]*Far Eastern Economic Review (FEER)*, August 29, 1975.
[21]*Bangkok Post*, July 15, 1975.
[22]*Bangkok Post*, July 15 and 16, 1975.
[23]*FEER*, August 1, 1975.
[24]*KCA*, January 30, 1976. p. 27541.
[25]United Nations High Commission for Refugees, *Thailand: Refugees and Displaced Persons from Indochina as of December 31, 1981*. Table 11a.
[27]*FEER*, March 28, 1968.
[28]Bernard B. Fall, *Street Without Joy*, New York 1975, p. 276.
[29]*Bangkok Post*, January 7, 1976.
[30]*Bangkok Post*, January 21, 1976.
[31]*Bangkok Post*, January 24, 1976.
[32]*FEER*, February 13, 1976.
[33]June 28, 1976.
[34]*Bangkok Post*, July 23, 1976.
[35]See also Ga Ya Lee, 'The Hmong: An End to the Running?', a research paper presented by the Hmong-Australia Society, August 1981; and Jacques Lemoine, 'Les Ecritures du Hmong', *Bulletin des Amis du Royaume Lao*, Nos. 7–8, 1972.
[36]Tito V. Carballo, *Bangkok Post*, October 24, 1976.
[37]*Bangkok Post*, December 4, 1977.
[38]*The Australian*, December 31, 1977.
[39]*Bangkok Post*, December 7, 1977.
[40]*Bangkok Post*, December 1, 1977.
[41]*Bangkok Post*, November 28, 1977.
[42]*Bangkok Post*, December 7, 1977.
[43]*Bangkok Post*, December 1, 1977.
[44]*Baltimore Sun*, October 31, 1978.
[45]ibid. Also Neil Kelly, *The Herald* (Melbourne), October 2, 1978.

Chapter Three: The Refugee Evidence

[1]*Cambodia: Year Zero*, Harmondsworth 1978, p. 13.
[2]ibid. p. 15.
[3]Nick Cumming-Bruce, *The Guardian Weekly*, September 27, 1982.
[4]Cameron Forbes. *The Age*, August 16, 1980.
[5]*Hearing*, p. 19.
[6]John Hail, *Focus* (Bangkok), December, 1980.
[7]*Compendium*, p. 56.
[8]*Hearing*, p. 19.
[9]ibid. p. 21.
[10]ibid. p. 27.
[11]ibid. p. 29.
[12]*Compendium*, pp. 46–47.

[13]ibid. p. 90.
[14]ibid. p. 53.
[15]ibid. p. 94.
[16]*Update*, pp. 21–25.
[17]ibid. p. 33.
[18]*Hearing*, pp. 24–25.
[19]ibid. p. 31.
[20]*Bangkok Post*, March 7, 1982.
[21]*Report of the Group of Experts to Investigate Reports on the Alleged Use of Chemical Weapons*, United Nations General Assembly, 36th Session, November 20, 1981. p. 34.
[22]ibid. p. 48.
[23] For example, the *Wall Street Journal* editorials mentioned in Chapter One make much of these 'gas masks'.
[24]Nick Cumming-Bruce, op cit.
[25]*FEER*, January 15, 1982.
[26]*Compendium*, p. 33.
[27]*Report*, p. 18.
[28]*Update*, pp. 26–27.
[29]*Report*, p. 6.
[30]*Compendium*, p. 60.
[31]*Report*, p. 19.
[32]Quoted in Jaap Van Ginneken, 'Bacteriological Warfare', *Journal of Contemporary Asia*, Vol. 7, No. 2, 1977, p. 147.
[33]*Report*, p. 7.
[34]*The Age*, September 17, 1981.
[35]*Compendium*, pp. 120–122.
[36]*Christian Science Monitor*, July 14, 1981.
[37]International Rescue Committee, Bangkok, 'Report No. 1 on CW Use in Kampuchea/Laos by PAVN. Poisonous Chemical Substances and Their Dangerous Effects', Panat Nikom, July 12, 1982, p. 4. Also, International Rescue Committee, Bangkok, 'Answers to Questions About Toxic Chemicals, Capt. Nguyen Quan, Report No. 2', Panat Nikom, September 10, 1982.
[38]Communication from Nguyen Quan, Panat Nikom Camp, to Dr. Townsend, IRC, September 11, 1982.
[39]Communication from Amos R. Townsend, October 8, 1982.
[40]May 24, 1982.
[41]*The Age*, November 10, 1981.
[42]*Report of the Group of Experts*, p. 22.
[43]Elizabeth F. Loftus, *Eyewitness Testimony*, Cambridge (Mass.) 1979, p. 87.

Chapter Four: Mycotoxins and Missing Evidence

[1]*Science*, Vol. 217, July 2, 1982.
[2]*Report*, p. 6.
[3]ibid. pp. 7–8.
[4]*The Age*, September 16, 1981.
[5]*Report*, p. 6.

[6]ibid. p. 27.

[7]ibid. p. 29.

[8]For a good overview see J. Fred Swarzendruber ' "Yellow Rain": Unanswered Questions', *Indochina Issues*, 23 January, 1982.

[9]*Science*, Vol. 214, October 2, 1981.

[10]'Study of the Possible Use of Chemical Warfare Agents in Southeast Asia, A Report to the Department of External Affairs, Canada', by H. B. Shiefer, Toxicology Group, University of Saskatchewan, 1982. p. 34.

[11]J. P. Robinson, 'Haig's Mycotoxins: A Commentary on the New American Charges of Chemical/Biological Warfare in Cambodia, Laos and Afghanistan', Discussion Paper, University of Sussex, October 26, 1981. There is an excellent earlier background piece by this author as well: 'Chemical and Biological Warfare: Analysis of Recent Reports Concerning the Soviet Union and Vietnam', *ADIU Occasional Paper No. 1*, March 1980.

[12]Prepared statement by Dr. Daniel Cullen, Research Associate, University of Wisconsin before the Subcommittee on Asian and Pacific Affairs, Committee on Foreign Affairs, US House of Representatives, Washington DC, March 30, 1982.

[13]*Report*, p. 17.

[14]ibid. p. 30.

[15]ibid. p. 17.

[16]John Cookson and Julie Nottingham, *A Survey of Chemical and Biological Warfare*, New York and London 1969, pp. 295–6.

[17]ibid. p. 24.

[18]'Chemical and Bacteriological (Biological) Weapons', Letter dated May 20, 1982 from the permanent representative of the USSR to the UN addressed to the Secretary General, UN General Assembly, 37th Session, May 21, 1982, pp. 3–4.

[19]See *Science*, July 2, 1982.

[20]*Reader's Digest*, October, 1980.

[21]International Rescue Committee memorandum by Amos R. Townsend, MD, Bangkok, May 12, 1982.

[22]Watson, Mirocha, Hayes, 'Occurrence of Trichothecenes in Samples from South-East Asia Associated with "Yellow Rain",' unpublished MS 1982; Watson and Mirocha, 'Analysis of Trichothecenes in Samples from South-East Asia Associated with "Yellow Rain",' unpublished MS 1982.

[23]Schultz, *Update*, op cit. p. 11.

[24]An interesting background paper is A. Wallace-Hayes, 'Mycotoxins: A Review of Their Biological Effects and Their Role in Human Disease', *Clinical Toxicology*, 17(1), 1980.

[25]*An Epidemiological Investigation of Alleged CW/BW Incidents in SE Asia*, Prepared by Directorate of Preventive Medicine, Surgeon General Branch, National Defence Headquarters, Ottawa, Canada, 1982.

[26]See the letter by Daniel Cullen and R. W. Caldwell in *Science*, August 27, 1982. Also, Dave Denison, 'Add One Cup of Yellow Rain . . .', *The Progressive*, September 1982.

[27]'The Examination of "Yellow Rain" Specimens Received at MRL in April 1982', by Dr. H. D. Crone, Department of Defence, Defence Science and Technology Organisation, Materials Research Laboratories, Melbourne, Victoria. Organic Chemistry Division, Technical Report. (No. 82/14) August 16, 1982.

[28]Alan Dawson, *Bangkok Post*, April 17, 1982.

[29]*International Herald Tribune*, March 9, 1982.

[30]*Bangkok Post*, February 22, 1982.

[31]*The Age*, April 17, 1982.

[32]Schultz, *Update*, p. 7.

[33]'Chemical and Bacteriological Weapons', Report of the Secretary-General, UN General Assembly, 37th Session, December 1, 1982, p. 17.

Chapter Five: Disease, Danger and Medicine from the Sky

[1]Nguyen-Ngoc-Thien, *Contribution à L'etude medicale sur les Méos*, Hanoi 1952, pp. 90–92.

[2]*Bangkok Post*, February 15, 1981.

[3]*Bangkok Post*, January 28, 1982.

[4]*Bangkok Post*, January 12, 1982.

[5]*Los Angeles Times*, November 22, 1979.

[6]Garret, *National Geographic*, op. cit.

[7]*Compendium*. p. 44.

[8]ibid. p. 54.

[9]ibid. p. 54.

[10]ibid. p. 54.

[11]ibid. pp. 85–86.

[12]UN Investigation, op. cit. p. 34.

[13]Jane Hamilton-Merritt, *Bangkok Post*, February 15, 1981.

[14]Cited in Joel M. Halpern, *Laotian Health Problems*, Laos Project Paper No. 19 (c. 1962). Department of Anthropology, California University. p. 2. See also: Gail F. Breakey and Emmanuel Voulagaropolos, *Laos Health Survey: Mekong Valley 1968–1969*, Hawaii 1976.

[15]*New York Times*, April 25, 1977.

[16]*Compendium*, p. 84. Also *Hearing*, p. 86.

[17]Dr. F. C. Maddox, March 28, 1982. Private communication with author.

[18]Both Haruff's and Amayun's statements are in *Foreign Policy and Arms Control. Implications of Chemical Weapons*, Hearings before the Subcommittees on International Security and Scientific Affairs and on Asian Pacific Affairs, of the Committee on Foreign Affairs, House of Representatives, 97th Congress, March 30 and July 13, 1982. US Government Printing Office, Washington, 1982.

[19]Nguyen-Ngoc-Thien, op. cit. pp. 76–79.

[20]*Psychology Today*, August, 1981.

[21]*The Globe Mail*, February 7, 1981.

[22]Communication with the author, November 2, 1981.

[23]*Singapore Straits Times*, March 7, 1982.

[24]*Bangkok Post*, March 20, 1982.

[25]*Psychology Today*, op. cit.

[26]ibid.

[27]*Bangkok Post*, March 7, 1982.

[28]Halpern, p. 17.

[29]*Report*, p. 22.

[30]*The Age*, November 8, 1982. See also the Canadian *Epidemiological Investigation*, op. cit., Annex B-10, for further evidence on malaria problems in the Kampuchean border region.

[31]*Epidemiological Investigation*, op. cit. Annexes D and E.

Chapter Six: Flight and Fear

[1]Garret, op. cit. p. 97.

[2]Yang Dao, *Les Difficultés du développement économique et social des populations hmong du Laos*, University of Paris, April 1972, p. 167.

[3]ibid. p. 44.

[4]Guy Morechand quoted in Yang Dao, ibid. p. 55. See also George L. Barney, 'The Meo of Xieng Khouang Province', Laos Project Paper No. 3. Department of Anthropology, California University.

[5]W. R. Geddes, *Migrants of the Mountains: The Cultural Ecology of the Blue Miao (Hmong Njua) of Thailand*, Oxford, 1976, p. 29. See also R. G. Cooper, 'Resource Scarcity and the Hmong Response: A Study of Settlement and Economy in Northern Thailand', Ph.D. Dissertation, University of Hull, 1976.

[6]Geddes, pp. 41–42.

[7]Jacqui Chagnon and Roger Rumpf, 'Report on a Visit to Sayaboury Province', May 9, 1979. American Friends Service Committee, Vientiane.

[8]*Christian Science Monitor*, February 1, 1980.

[9]Jacques Lemoine, *Un Village Hmong Vert du Haut Laos*, Paris 1972, p. 45.

[10]London 1973, pp. 65 and 74.

[11]ibid. pp. 54–55.

[12]ibid. p. 50.

[13]ibid. p. 156.

[14]ibid. pp. 73–74.

[15]ibid. 131.

[16]Amphay Dore, *Le Partage du Mékong*, Paris 1980, p. 71.

[17]Kuno Knoebl, *Victor Charlie: The Face of War in Vietnam*, 1967, pp. 257–8.

[18]Malcolm W. Browne, *The New Face of War*, London 1965, pp. 36–37.

[19]*The Effects of Herbicides in South Vietnam*, Part A, Summary and Conclusions, National Academy of Sciences, Washington, DC, 1974. pp. vii–64.

[20]Hearing Before the Subcommittee on International Security and Scientific Affairs and on Asian and Pacific Affairs of the Committee on Foreign Affairs, 96th Congress, April 24, 1980, Washington 1980, p. 33.

[21]Walter M. Haney, 'A Survey of Civilian Casualties Among Refugees from the Plain of Jars, Laos', in *World Refugee and Humanitarian Problems*. Hearing Before the Subcommittee to Investigate Problems Connected with Refugees and Escapees of the Committee on the Judiciary United States Senate, 92nd Congress, July 22, 1971. First Session. Also Appendix II of the Second Session, May 9, 1972. In the following references I shall simply refer to 'First Session' or 'Second Session' and give the page reference.

[22]First Session, p. 81.

[23]ibid. p. 82.

[24]ibid. p. 86.

[25]ibid. pp. 86–87.

[26]ibid. p. 93.

[27]ibid. pp. 93–94.

[28]ibid. pp. 98–99.

[29]ibid. p. 99.

[30]*New York Times*, January 25, 1982. A recent American study offers some additional, but contradictory, information about the use of defoliants in Laos.

During a Hearing in 1970 Admiral McCain, when speaking in support of crop destruction, 'cited several incidents, including one in Laos where he attributed a significant role in Vang Pao's capture of the Plain of Jars to crop destruction missions which had taken place in August 1969.' *Operation Ranch Hand: The Airforce and Herbicides in Southeast Asia, 1961–1971*, William A. Buckingham Jr., Office of Airforce History United States Airforce, Washington DC, 1982, p. 171. However, the table on p. 201 in the same study lists no herbicide operations between February and September 1969.

[31] First Session, p. 66.

[32] *Voices From the Plain of Jars*, compiled with an introduction and a preface by Fred Branfman, New York 1972, p. 108.

[33] ibid. p. 114.

[34] First Session, p. 98.

[35] Browne, op. cit.

[36] Garret, op. cit.

[37] *Hearing*, p. 46.

[38] *Compendium*, p. 55.

Chapter Seven: Inside Laos

[1] Asian Notes, No. 136, May 7, 1969.

[2] *SWB*, November 30, 1978.

[3] *SWB*, November 22, 1978.

[4] Report by J. Yoder, Mennonite Central Committee, Laos, March 14, 1979.

[5] 'Agricultural Development Poles in the LPDR', UNDP, April 1979.

[6] 'Report of Visit to Resettled Persons in Xieng Khouang', John and Beulah Hess-Yoder and Roger Rumpf and Jacqui Chagnon, respectively, Mennonite Central Committee, Laos, and American Friends Service Committee, Laos. July 27, 1979.

[7] Chagnon and Rumpf did further investigations into this issue in Laos during January and February 1983. Their findings bolster much of the preceding argument. (Verbal communication to the author, Laos, January–February 1983.)

Chapter Eight: 'Evil Propaganda and Honest Delusion'

[1] *Compendium*, Appendix, p. 7.

[2] Raymond Firth, 'Rumour in a Primitive Society with A Note on the Theory of "Cargo" Cults', in *Tikopia Ritual and Belief*, London 1967, p. 157.

[3] *Der Spiegel*, No. 36, February 22, 1982.

[4] *AMPO*, March 8, 1976, pp. 52–57.

[5] *FEER*, July 9, 1982.

[6] *Current Notes on International Affairs*, Vol. 24, No. 3, March 1953.

Chapter Nine: The Politics of Re-armament

[1]Stockholm Peace Research Institute (SIPRI), *The Problem of Chemical and Biological Warfare*, Vol. III, 'CBW and the Law of War', London 1973.

[2]Cookson and Nottingham, op. cit.

[3]SIPRI, Vol. III, op. cit., p. 173.

[4]Harris and Paxman, pp. 171–2.

[5]*Soviet News Bulletin*, USSR Embassy, Canberra. April 19, 1982.

[6]Quoted in David Horowitz, *From Yalta to Vietnam*, London, 1967, p. 278.

[7]'Strategic Implication of Chemical and Biological Warfare', op. cit. p. 52.

[8]On these and related issues see: J. P. Robinson, 'Chemical Arms Control and the Assimilation of Chemical Weapons', and John Lamb and Brian Mandell, 'How Arms Control Begins at Home: the American and Soviet Cases', *International Journal*, Vol. XXXVI, No. 3, 1981. Roy and Zhores Medvedev, 'The USSR and the Arms Race', *New Left Review* 130, November–December, 1981. G. K. Vachon, 'Le Contrôle des Armements et les Armes Chimiques', *Revue d'Etudes internationales*, Vol. XIII, No. 1, March 1982.

[9]*Pravda*, January 22, 1982 (TASS translation). See also 'Basic Provisions of a Convention on the Prohibition of the Development, Production and Stockpiling of Chemical Weapons and on Their Destruction', USSR Proposal to the Second Special Session of the United Nations General Assembly on Disarmament, June 21, 1982.

[10]'Myths and Realities of a Chemical Threat', Novosti Press Agency, 1982. (No specific date given.)

[11]*The Age*, August 28, 1981.

[12]Jamie Kitman, 'A Nerve Gas We Can Love', *The Nation*, July 5, 1980. A. O. Sulzberger, *New York Times*, September 28, 1980. *The Age*, August 28, 1981. The *Age*, February 10, 1982. *New Scientist*, February 25, 1982.

[13]See Robert J. Einborn, 'Treaty Compliance', *Foreign Policy*, No. 45, Winter 1981–82.

[14]Testimony before Senate Subcommittee on Arms Control, November 10, 1981.

[15]UN Investigation, op. cit. p. 34.

[16]*The Age*, March 26, 1982.

[17]*Soviet News Bulletin*, Embassy of the USSR, Canberra, March 15, 1982.

[18]Made by the Head of the Press Department, USSR Ministry of Foreign Affairs, Yuri Chernyakov. Press Release, op. cit.

[19]Arkhangelskii et al., *Bacteriological Weapons and How to Defend Against Them*, Moscow 1967.